EUNICE GARDNER

The World at Our Feet

The story of two women who adventured
halfway across the globe

W. H. ALLEN
LONDON
1957

AUTHOR'S NOTE

Although I have been as careful as possible, I ask the reader to forgive any mistakes in the spelling of foreign words and names. On a hitch-hike it is impossible to keep detailed records, and languages were never my strong point in any case!

Made and printed in Great Britain by
John Gardner (Printers) Ltd., Hawthorne Road, Liverpool, 20
for the publishers, W. H. Allen & Co., Ltd., Essex Street, London, W.C.2.

CONTENTS

ILLUSTRATIONS

1

Australia on a Shoe-string

WINTER had come again, and I stood at the window looking out onto a darkening, and wet evening.

"One day I shall travel round the world, see l the things one reads about and always—always I shall follow the sun," I muttered fervently.

My mother, who had heard that wish a hundred times, glanced up from the pile of mending and gently remarked, "It all sounds very nice, dear, but what will you use for money—buttons? You'll need a fortune to travel even half-way round the world."

I was barely thirteen then and, needless to say without a fortune, but by the time I was old enough to take advantage of it, the British and Australian Governments introduced a new scheme. They were offering passages to Australia for £10.

To me, who had only had to date a few flips to Paris, Scotland and Ireland, Australia seemed a very far cry—half the world away, but at least I would see a few countries en route.

I could find no one in my home town affected with the wander bug, but felt there must surely be others: perhaps, once I had set off on my own, I would meet someone.

So one grey October morning I waved goodbye to family and friends and headed for the sun: for Sydney in Australia, with twelve pounds sterling in my purse, which had to last until I found a job.

We sailed into Sydney Harbour one glorious, sunny December morning, and as I beheld the Harbour Bridge and near skyscraper buildings of the clean looking, bright city I felt a slight rising panic for I had to get a room before nightfall and a job as soon as possible. I had only £6 0s. 0d. after five weeks aboard. But Australians are a big-hearted people and even though they may be returning home after many years' absence with family and friends eagerly awaiting them, they still find time to ensure that a stranger is welcomed and settled in.

So it was that immediately we had docked beneath the famous

bridge one Australian rang through to book a room for me at the great Y.W.C.A. building in the heart of the city, while another deposited me safely there and added yet another telephone number to my already half filled notebook and yet another invitation to "drop in any old time."

Although I had scarcely been a day in a strange city and a new continent I felt I was among friends. Standing that evening, high up on the open roof of the Y.W.C.A. building with a couple of Australian girls, looking over the city, I experienced a thrill of excitement; the neon lights of the city winked a welcome below, couples strolled beneath the trees and palms in Hyde Park across from the building. The shores all round the Harbour were bright with light and warmth. The Harbour Bridge flung a curved span of brilliant lights from the city across to the North Shore and, over the still Harbour, the Manly Ferry skimmed merrily.

Next morning the *Sydney Morning Herald* displayed a fantastic array of vacant jobs. I think a hairdresser can go almost anywhere in the world and find a good job.

With a small family of hairdressers in the city, but over-looking the greenness of Hyde Park, I was soon receiving £14 14s. 0d. for a 40-hour week, of which I gave back, quite cheerfully, only 27s. for income tax. Furnished flats were quite expensive, ranging from 5 to 10 guineas a week, but there were many rooms for single girls, and small flatlets, if one didn't mind spending a few evenings hunting for them—all at a reasonable price.

However, I soon dicovered it was much more fun to live in a large Salvation Army Hostel, five minutes from the city and ten from Bondi Beach. It was worth putting up with a small room more like a cubicle, and having to be in by eleven thirty each night, for the joy of plenty of company. Here I paid £3 15s. 0d. a week for full board. Regularly each week £5 went into my bank book, and even then I had more to spend than I ever had in England.

It was wonderful to realize that each week-end the sun would be shining. It wasn't a matter of chance—we could make arrangements weeks ahead to go sailing in the Harbour or surfing at Bondi or any one of the many Pacific beaches around Sydney.

Five months later I had my first experience of a temperature of 108° with a 98% humidity, I knew how a rubber surf board felt as it rode before a crashing "dumper," the terror when the Shark Bell rang at Bondi and everyone fled from the water in a matter of seconds. I was no longer amazed when people told me "they shot through like a Bondi tram" (meaning they vanished quickly), that they were "crook in the guts" (not well), that a thing was "Ridgy Didge" (the truth), or I was to "pull my woolly skull in and give my feet a chance" (which told me merely to "shut up!").

Although I could never quite get used to the way even the nicest girls frequently and cheerfully used the word bloody, I was no longer shocked when the Australians explained with a lyrical pleasantness that "the bloody thing was unbloody thinkable." By now I liked the Australians a lot. I liked their open-hearted warmth. I liked their open-air life and I wanted to see more of their great country. So far, though, I had met no one who wanted to "go outback."

One weekend I lay on the sandy beach of Coogee with Audrey, one of the English girls from the hostel. Audrey had been two years in New Zealand before landing in Australia six months previously. She was due for a holiday.

"I'd like to come with you," she said, unusually serious for uproarious Audrey. "But when I took this job I promised I'd stay at least a year, and I can't break a promise. I could take my fortnight's holiday—and perhaps another week and come with you as far as time allowed."

"I thought I'd head North to Queensland. They say the winters in Townsville and Cairns are sunnier than Sydney's best summer," I thought aloud. "I know Sydney only gets four months' winter—and not as we know winter—but I think now is the time to move. We could reach Cairns, have a look at the Barrier Reef, and you could return in three weeks. Maybe I could stay on and get a job—or come back with you if I didn't like it."

"Cairns is 2,500 miles away," Audrey said, snuggling deeper into the sand as a cool breeze wafted in off the surf. "To fly or go by train—there and back—is going to take a chunk out of my return fare to England. I don't know that I can afford it yet. I've not been saving very hard. Only £80 in six months!"

"Only £80!" I laughed. "Imagine typists at home buying all the things you have and still being able to say that. I've saved £90 towards my return fare, but if we both use some of our fares we can make it up quickly enough by saving hard for a few weeks once we're working."

Audrey lay silent for a while, her eyes closed, her short, dark hair fluffed by the breeze. The tanned bodies on the beach were thinning out, the faint strains of music from surrounding portable radio sets no longer intermingled with the sounds of crashing surf. It was getting cool. As I shivered suddenly, Audrey opened one eye:

"How about hitch-hiking to Cairns and coming back by train?" she asked, suddenly very thrilled with herself. "Think of all the people we'd meet—that's the way to know a country!"

"Hitch-hike?" I was dubious. I hadn't thought of that, although I had once hitched from Paris to Marseilles, but then I'd had very little money and it had had to go a long way.

"They do it a lot in Australia," Audrey went on with her usual bouncing enthusiasm. "Several of the girls at the hostel have packs."

And so it was arranged, but the day before we were due to leave, a cyclone hit the Queensland coast for the length of a hundred miles.

Audrey sat on the foot of my bed, discussing this unexpected turn of events.

"Well, they say the roads are closed because of fallen trees— we could work in to some of the outback cattle stations instead."

"The radio said the trains are still running up the coast," I said. "Let's go by train to Brisbane and see what they say further North. Sometimes the nearer one is to calamity the less awful it seems. Anyway, the roads may be cleared in a couple of days. We can catch the night train tomorrow."

At 6.30 the following evening we hitched our packs onto our backs, waved to the girls peering from the hostel windows, clambered into a rattling "toast rack train" and headed for Wynyard Station.

The crowds were amused at our slacks, windcheaters and packs. When they noticed the small Union Jacks stitched to our ski jackets their smiles broadened. The conductor eyed us saucily as we rattled down Elizabeth Street and called out cheerfully, "How much of Australia have you seen?"

We laughed. "We've just started. We're heading for Cairns."

"My word, you'll love it!" the conductor said enthusiastically. "Queensland's a great place. My ma lives in Gympie, a hundred miles from Brisbane. Here, I'll give you my address. Call in and give her my love."

He wrote the address down leisurely on a slip of paper and handed it over to us.

"She'll make you stay a week—that's Queensland hospitality. I think I'll buy a pack and join you." He sounded envious, a trifle homesick.

We laughed, feeling suddenly as free and lighthearted as the air: if this was a forerunner of Queensland friendliness we were in for a good trip.

Through rich pastures and banana plantations spreading over the hills as far as one could see we came next day to Brisbane, capital of Queensland. The air was warmer already, the wide, clean streets were thronged with brightly dressed women and tanned men in shirt sleeves. There were many wooden houses standing on piles. Some say these piles are for better circulation of air when the temperature reaches over 100°, others that they are to keep away the destructive white ants who can literally eat into a house until it crumbles to dust. The space beneath the houses was surrounded by lattice on which grew brightly flowering creepers. In the gardens banana trees gently waved their fronds, paw paws hung green and oblong from their straight tree trunks and blossom scented the warm sunny streets.

The people looked more relaxed and moved at a slower, more casual pace than they had in the much larger and busier Sydney. Gladly they directed us to a small hotel and, after a few enquiries, we were soon making plans to head North next morning for we hoped the roads would have been cleared by the time we reached Gin Gin, where the heart of the cyclone had struck.

By 9.30 next morning we were walking merrily along the wide, main road that headed North from Chermside, a suburb of Brisbane. Here we were, with not a care in the world and three whole weeks to explore the coast of Queensland and the people. Our objective was Cairns but, if we didn't get there, no matter— there were plenty of small townships within a hundred miles or so of each other where we could laze in the sea and dally if we wished.

Audrey and I had always found each other good company, and now, with the feeling of excitement and complete enjoyment of a wonderful carefree day, we laughed and joked gaily as we swung steadily along.

"Once a year, just to get this exhilarating, carefree feeling, everyone ought to set out on a hitch-hike in Queensland," I remarked happily to Audrey as we paused to peel off our ski jackets, stuff them into our packs and roll up the legs of our slacks. We had previously decided not to hitch any traffic, but see how far we could get by relying on the friendliness of the Queenslanders.

Funnily enough it was a young German who was the first to pull up his battered little ancient car and, with a friendly smile and a very slight accent, to offer us a lift to Petrie, ten miles further on. Kurt Grieger had emigrated to Australia with his young German wife eighteen months ago. By both working for a year they had saved enough money to buy a small plot of land at Petrie and for Kurt to begin to build a modern bungalow. Each week-end they travelled the ten miles in their small, shaky car to put a little more work into the building.

Kurt smiled shyly as he told us with pride, "In a few months we will move into the house. My wife works to-day, so I finish the roof alone. Do you not think Queensland is a lovely state? We are very happy now." He paused. "Sometimes, the time after the War in Germany is like a bad dream to us, but we forget. I shall perhaps raise some chickens or later buy a small cane farm. Who knows? There are many things a man can do here."

At length we reached Petrie and Kurt insisted on showing us over the small, one storey house.

We reached Gympie, 106 miles North of Brisbane, by mid-afternoon, after another two unasked lifts. Now the centre of a rich dairying district, Gympie was once the scene of a spectacular gold rush, so we learnt from our last "lift," who was a resident of the picturesque country town. Altogether over £14,000,000 worth of gold was mined in the Gympie area and here the famous "Curtis Nugget" was found—975 ounces of pure gold.

Here, too, we found jolly little Mrs. O'Harren, the Sydney tram conductor's mother, who plied us with food, large cups of tea and many questions about the "old country." Although she had been barely three when she arrived with her parents in Brisbane, she still clung tightly to the far-off land as her real home. In her open-hearted Queensland way, she would have had us stay a month or more but, as the afternoon was still only half through, we thanked her and, with another lift, reached Maryborough a few hours later.

Maryborough is a pleasant, prosperous but flat town situated on the banks of a wide river. It conforms to the usual Australian country township with its wooden and brick buildings, many with iron roofs and iron awnings jutting over the wide pavements to shade shoppers and shop windows from the all-day sun, a few green public gardens, rows of modern buildings a few storeys high, where the glint of new glass, chrome and plastic vies self-consciously with the older wooden houses and pubs—or hotels, as Australians call them.

We slept with the wooden shuttered doors to our bedroom

opening out on to the wide, peeling, wooden verandah, for the nights were already growing warmer.

Early next morning after a breakfast of huge but rather burnt steaks, we headed out of town. A young commercial traveller, John Trent, soon stopped to pick us up and as we sped along, pointed out the great trunks of felled trees that now lay along the sides of the lonely road.

"You should have seen this road four days ago," John told us with a grimace. "From Maryborough to Rockhampton that cyclone ripped up trees, and playfully laid 'em down again—all over the road. There's one spot—you'll see it soon—not a single gum left standing where there had been hundreds."

This sounded rather fantastic but later we could see that most of the trees still dotted over the landscape were old and dried, easy prey for a raging cyclone.

Suddenly, as we topped a rise, the valley below resembled a patchwork quilt of variegated greens from a tender yellowy green to a deep, vivid green which extended as far as the eye could see.

"What a huge banana plantation," Audrey exclaimed.

I wasn't so sure.

"Look's more like maize or barley to me," I said.

John Trent chuckled humorously. "I guess you wouldn't recognise it if you've never seen it before. It's sugar cane. That's the stuff I work with."

Our commercial traveller turned out to be a travelling analytical chemist.

"I told you I was going to Isis," he explained. "There's a fairly large sugar mill there. When the cane's ripe, it's cut and taken to the mill in lorries where it's processed into sugar. Brown sugar—not the white refined sugar you know. The refining's done later at a large central refinery or at the port it's shipped from. Mostly the cane's taken to the mills on small cane trains— we passed over one of the tracks a while back, remember? The track comes shooting across the road out of the cane each side."

Audrey laughed ironically.

"They don't bother with gates, do they? Only a few warnings before one gets to the track."

I had to agree that I thought the tracks obsolete.

"Oh no," John said definitely. "That's the main way of getting the heavy cane to the mills. Mind you, those trains can be pretty dangerous if you're silly enough to forget to stop before a crossing. When the cane's high and ripe each side of the road and track, it's easy enough for one of those trains to knock any car well out of their path. There've been a lot of accidents where people just won't stop before a track to listen for the train whistle. They take a chance and often don't know what hit them."

He lit a cigarette and threw the almost full packet into my lap with a generous "Keep those, I've plenty more."

Audrey didn't smoke but, to her joy, he retrieved a large slab of soft chocolate from beneath the bonnet of the car and bade her laughingly to eat it before it melted all over him.

"Where do you come in?" I asked, reverting to the subject of the sugar cane.

"Well, there are lots of little bugs that love sugar cane and it's my job to see that they don't eat it all before it reaches the mills or even later when it's on its way all over the world. You've heard of 'burning off the cane'?"

We shook our heads.

"Oh, I see, I'll have to start at the beginning," he laughed. "Cane takes many months to grow from setts to the height this stuff is all along here. About 10 feet, isn't it? When its feathery flower at the top has died, then small sections of the field are 'burnt off.' the fire sweeps through the dried old leaves and weeds, cleaning out any rats and snakes who've nested in it, and leaving only the blackened sugar cane which is then easier to cut and load. The cutters may look as though they've been up the chimney after an hour or so, but that way it's easier to cut and they don't get any snake bites. 'Burning off' is done a section at a time and against the wind, for if a cane field is fired care-lessly or the wind changes suddenly, then the fire can sweep through a whole plantation of hundreds of acres in less than an hour, and trap many cutters. The cane farmer's home is usually in the middle of the cane and anyone inside gets roasted alive before they can escape. A whole family a few hundred miles North were wiped out like that last year."

We gasped in horror.

"It doesn't often happen," John assured us. "That's the first tragedy for ten years."

"Anyway, after all that burning off the cane, there were still a few bugs who could survive and we've had quite a job fighting them to make the sugar keep for an indefinite period. Now, at last, we think we've done it. That's why I'm on this trip to check a few samples from the Isis Mill."

Presently over the high cane we saw smoke belching from the whitish corrugated Isis Mill, and the faint, sickly smell grew steadily stronger.

"How would you like to take a look over the mill?" John asked. "If you like, I'll get the foreman to take you round. It's a very interesting process, if you can stand the awful smell of molasses at close quarters."

Audrey and I expressed our delight and were soon deposited with the smiling foreman, while John went off to check his samples.

The tanned and leathery face of the foreman wrinkled kindly as he explained: "Don't get many people wanna see inside a sugar mill—they can't stand the smell for long."

"I'm not sure I can stand it for long," Audrey laughed, holding a handkerchief to her nose.

He led us into a covered shed where trucks and trains were emptying their loads of long cane into a cavity where a conveyer belt pushed them ever forward onto a loud, rotating wheel of glinting sharp knives, which slashed the lengths of hard cane into fine shreds. The foreman laughed merrily as we stepped back quickly from the cavity.

"Wouldn't it rock you to fall in there?" he drawled.

Into the stifling, throbbing belly of the mill we followed the long gully of crushed syrup which only recently had been long cane. We peered into great cauldrons high in the roof as the boiling mass bubbled sickeningly with loud plops. The heat was like a furnace near the huge boilers, and we were glad to clamber back down the rickety iron ladders, white with cane dust, and pick our way through to where the thick syrup was spun in long vats to dry and at last appear as glinting, brown sugar.

"How you goin' with the smell?" the foreman asked cheerfully, as at long last we watched the sugar being put into bags.

"I think I'd feel perpetually sick if I worked here," I said.

Audrey's horrible grimace expressed her feelings better than words.

"Aw, you'd get used to it. I don't smell a thing now. I've worked in it for twenty years. Anyway, you've seen the lot. From here it goes on to the Refinery."

He thrust his hand deep into a vat, pulled out a handful of brown crystals and poured some into each of our palms.

"You've never tasted sugar like this," he said proudly. "It's the sweetest and shiniest there is. Now you'd better both get some air, or you'll be passing out on me."

Still chuckling, he led us from the corrugated tin building. We thanked him and made our way across to John's car, very glad to be away from the cloying, nauseating odour.

"Sometimes the more I see of other people's work the luckier I think I am to be a hairdresser," I remarked to Audrey, who was inhaling large gulps of fresh air. Her dark eyes looked worried.

"If I ever wanted to go mad, I've just seen the job to make me. Remember the lad who was sewing the tops of the bags together? Imagine sitting, day after day, months into years, in that drenching hot smell, just slowly sewing down a never-ending stream of sugar bags—ugh!" She shuddered and was never afterwards to smell the distant sickliness of mills without recalling that lad.

2

New Companion

LATE in the afternoon just outside the tiny township of Gin Gin, Audrey and I sat by a billabong—the ground around had been made into a camping area. Shaded from the brilliant sun by tall gums, we ate the sandwiches we had bought and lazily watched an old swaggy arrive.

"Gosh! He's the real thing!" Audrey exclaimed softly, her eyes dancing. "He looks as though he's walked a long way. Look, he's got his swag all neatly rolled."

We watched delightedly as, taking no notice whatsoever of us, he unrolled his swag and spread it out on the green turf; soon he placed a blackened billy can over the wood he had collected which he lit, then, taking a packet of tea from the folds of his swag, he measured the tea in the palm of his hand and threw it into the bubbling water, after which went a couple of gum leaves. Suddenly he looked up and laughed as he saw us watching.

"That's how to make a real good brew of tea. Like a cup?" he invited us.

"Yes, thanks a lot. We'd love one," Audrey assured him merrily.

"Got any cups then?" he asked. "Come and fill 'em up."

It was a "real good" brew all right, although the faint taste of eucalyptus from the gum leaves was a taste we had not acquired, but it certainly gave the tea a refreshing difference.

"I didn't think we'd ever meet a real swagman," I said, sipping the scalding black tea. "I thought they were a thing of the past."

His eyes twinkled in his sunburnt face.

"My word! Lots like me, we like to wander, never in one place more than a few days."

"How do you live though?" Audrey asked.

"On what folks gives us," he said quietly. "I do a few odd jobs, and, mind, I never take a lift. A swaggy always walks where he's going. It's a great life." He nodded at our packs, saying with a touch of hauteur, "You're hitch-hiking, eh? How long you been waiting?"

Audrey wasn't going to let him get away with that.

"You're not the only one who walks, my good man," she admonished him. "We've walked for the last two hours and we don't ask for lifts. If someone offers a lift, of course we take it."

"Oh, oh, sorry, Ma'am—what you do's your own business anyway. Here, have another cup o' tea."

A little later George Curtis, a commercial traveller from Rockhampton, pulled up by the billabong, shared a can of black tea with us and our swagman and took us on with him. We reached Miriam Vale at 8 o'clock that evening. Miriam Vale consists of a length of railway track, a wooden railway shelter, one hotel, one café-cum-stores and a handful of houses. As he pulled up at the front of the wooden hotel, George told us :

"I'm too tired to drive any more to-day. I'm gonna stay here the night and go on early tomorrow to Rockhampton. It's only three hours away, but I've had it for to-day. Why don't you get a room as well?" he suggested kindly. "Then you can come on with me in the morning. I don't suppose you want to walk on now it's dark, do you?"

"No thanks," we said together. "What time will you be leaving in the morning? We'll be ready."

"6.30 O.K.? I'm just going to put the car away. By the way, if you want a meal, I doubt whether the hotel will give you one now. See that light down the road? You can get one there. See you in the morning then."

We watched as he swung the car round the corner of the hotel and then made our way through the tropical ferns and leaves covering the wooden verandah into the interior. There, propped against the stairs, sat two huge haversacks, one adorned with small flags of many countries, European countries we found on closer inspection, and I said to Audrey:

"It looks as though we've real competition here. Wonder who they are and where they are from?"

"I wonder if they're English?" Audrey said excitedly.

"Yep, that's what they are; don't tell me we've another two pommy hitch-hikers," laughed a tubby, jovial man who appeared suddenly from behind a doorway. He eyed our small Union Jacks.

"Four pommies in one evening. This place is waking up! I guess you'll be wanting a cheap room too."

Within a few minutes we were shown to our room.

"If you want a meal, there's a place down the road," the hotel-keeper said casually. "That's where the other two have gone, maybe they come from your home town. You'd better go and say hullo."

"We mean to, thanks," we told him. "We'll go and see what sort of competition we have."

He laughed with uninhibited loudness and thumped off down the wooden stairs. Five minutes later we were pushing open the shaky door of the rather bare looking café. The only occupants were two girls who sat at the far end. These must be our rivals, we thought. As we approached, they looked up and, seeing our Union Jacks, they smiled and eyed us with interest. Audrey quickly sat down next to them and excitedly began to fire questions.

Both girls were about twenty-four years old, I reckoned. Miriam Davis was dark and rather more reserved than her fairer friend, Diana Williams, who eyed us quizzically as she spoke, with the most candid blue eyes I had seen for a long time. By the time we had been served with a huge grill apiece and dug our hungry way through, we knew quite a lot about each other. We found we had all left Sydney on the same day, been in Brisbane at the same time and left there on the same day.

"It's a wonder we haven't seen you before," I exclaimed.

"We'd heard of you though," Diana laughed. "We must have been following you, for several people have asked whether we knew the two other English girls in red."

We found we were all heading for Cairns.

"We came this far with an elderly couple who've a sort of van-cum-caravan," they told us. "The husband's recently retired, so they're going right round Australia in easy stages. Think it'll take them about two years," Diana laughed. "They've a piano in the van; she's a wonderful pianist, so we've had wonderful sing-songs all the way along to-day. You should see people's faces as they hear the piano when we pass them!"

"Who's the one who's been all over Europe?" Audrey asked. "We've been looking at the flags."

"Oh, they're mine," Di said. "I did a five month's hike round Europe before I left to come out to Hobart where my parents had emigrated. I shall go back to Hobart and settle maybe after this trip, but Miriam is sailing home to England in three weeks, so we thought we'd see as much of Queensland as we could before she goes back."

Presently we ambled back to the hotel to take a shower and write letters.

"Maybe we'll all meet again in Cairns," I said rather half-heartedly.

I didn't really think we would, except to say 'hullo.'

"All the best if we don't," they wished us.

As I settled down to sleep I hadn't the faintest glimmer of an idea that I was destined to travel 26,000 miles with one of these strangers through three vast continents.

Next evening Audrey and I reached Marlborough, another tiny township, where we experienced our first primitive shower. You simply tipped a bucket of water over yourself by means of a long string. If you were quick enough the water found its mark, but more often than not the stream of water missed and continued away through a hole in the side of the wall, carrying away with it the stray cockroaches.

Early next morning a road worker, on his way out to a road grader, took us on thirty miles; the bitumen sealed roads were getting scarcer the further North we travelled. I eyed the great monster grader by the side of the lumpy uneven road as we unloaded our packs.

"My! That's a lonely sort of job!"

The man laughed.

"Too right, but I like it. Nothing but the sun, the birds and a few passing cars. Someone's gotta keep these roads level. If it weren't for we graders, there'd soon be no cars along this north road till it's sealed."

"It'll take a good many years before the road's sealed all along in Queensland. What is it, about 2,000 miles?" Audrey asked.

He nodded. "It's gotta be done though, so they reckon, by the end of next year for the Olympic Games in Melbourne, you know. That torch is gonna be run from Cairns right down to Melbourne—3,500 miles."

"They'll have to get a move on then," we laughed and left him to climb into the high seat of the huge grader to begin his lonely day's work.

Half an hour later, at the top of a slight rise, we eyed the straight, narrow road ahead, on to the distant horizon, and, without a word, we both dropped our packs beneath the shade of a gum tree and spread ourselves on the sparse, dry grass. I chuckled.

"I don't mind walking when I don't know what's around the next corner, but this is different!"

It was 9.30 and a hot, breathless morning. We had entered the Tropic of Capricorn the day before on reaching Rockhampton. Lazily we sat propped against our packs, listening to the laughing chuckles of the kookaburras high in the tall branches of the gums. Large green grasshoppers buzzed drowsily in the hot sun. Later Audrey unrolled her partly dried washing and draped it over the surrounding bush.

"You'll have to move quickly if anything comes along," I chided her.

"Well, we've been here an hour already and nothing's come, so perhaps we'll be here all day."

"Perhaps," I said. "I don't mind. We've a flask of tea and sandwiches! I'll just lie here and roast. It's a wonderful way to spend a day."

Her hanging out completed, Audrey stretched out again.

"I know one thing," she remarked. "Tomorrow I'm sure we can put our slacks and jackets at the bottom of our packs, and start wearing shorts."

Two and a half hours drowsed past, then, away in the distance, came the faint sound of an engine.

"Quick!" I exclaimed. "The washing! We must be walking when it gets here."

It was a car, a large one. It had three occupants, two of whom waved merrily as they hurtled by in a flurry of dust.

"Blow them!" Audrey exclaimed, but as I playfully shook my fist after the girls' grinning faces, the car came to a halt a hundred yards on. Laughing thankfully, we greeted Diana and Miriam and clambered aboard as the driver drawled in a pleasant Queensland voice : "Your friends thought they'd play a trick on you, and asked me to drive on. Sorry to give you a scare!"

He was a pleasant character, highly amused at having found four pommies "doing" Queensland, and only too pleased to explain helpfully about the many things that caught our eyes and fancy in the next 160 miles to Mackay, where, at the wooden verandahed building of the Y.W.C.A., he dropped us all late that afternoon.

On the next five hundred miles to Cairns it seemed that Audrey and I were never to lose sight of Diana and Miriam for longer than a few hours. For each day, although we set out from towns at different times, somehow during the day, either their driver would pick us up, or our driver would squeeze them in. So eventually we all reached Cairns together a few days later, and finding that the only accommodation (and, incidentally, the cleanest and most reasonable) in the People's Palace was a large room for three with an extra bed on the balcony, we booked it and decided to stay together for our five days in Cairns before starting on the journey back as arranged. The People's Palace, by the way, is run by the Salvation Army.

Cairns, situated on Tropical Bay, is Australia's most northern city, an important port for the northern sugar area and Cairns hinterland. It is a modern, but small city with a population of nearly 17,000. From Cairns you can get to Green Island, one of the lovely tropical islands which form part of the great Barrier Reef, to the Atherton Tableland, a fertile plateau which rises inland, and even further north to Mossman and Cooktown, once a thriving pearling port of thousands but now with a population of a scant 600. We knew that from Mossman the road was barely a narrow track on to Cooktown but we had heard a lot about the famous Cook Highway which had been built along the rugged coast on the fringe of the South Pacific from Cairns to Mossman. It was only a little way out of Cairns that the elderly driver of a large Land Rover offered us a lift to Mossman. As soon as he found out we were English, George Bailey's delight knew no bounds.

"Well, would you believe it!" he exclaimed. "You're the right company for my Land Rover. I've just bought it. You'll never guess what's special about it! It's the one the Queen and the Duke used on their tour of Queensland!"

So, of course, from then on, how could we resist whenever we passed a car, cyclist, person or child, sitting upright and imitating the Royal wave.

George had business in Mossman, but except for a few black skinned aborigine fishermen, there seemed little to do or see there for us. But George knew better.

"If you like to wait a while, I'll take you back to Cairns in about two hours—and while you're here there's a famous collection of beautiful seashells you ought to see. Like to?"

We thanked him, so he dropped us off at a wooden café, and left us to browse around in the rather dark interior, exclaiming in awed wonder as the conchologist showed us his fabulous collection of rare shells.

The Great Barrier Reef—that unique coral formation which girds the coast of Queensland for a distance of 1,250 miles from southerly Moreton Bay up to the very northerly Cape York—is the greatest single tourist attraction Queensland, or indeed Australia, can boast. The Reef consists of innumerable bays, atolls and islets, with an unbelievably intricate system of individual reefs and shoals, together with six hundred islands, large enough to be named. With an ideal climate, tropical lagoons and the beauty of coral formations the famous palm-fringed, coral-girt islands are within twenty or thirty miles of the Queensland coast.

There is a regular launch service to Green Island from Cairns, and it was around this palm-sheltered island that we explored the coral, picking our way over the many-coloured jagged formation of the reef in old, borrowed sand shoes, peering through glass-bottomed boats as they glided slowly over the calm waters round the island and exclaiming fearfully at the sight of monster clams in their dangerous coral beds.

And the two grey looking sharks which followed the launch all the way back to Cairns Harbour!

For a week I had watched, waited and wondered, and so had Diana. By now, of course, she knew my idea of possibly staying on in the North and gradually working my way inland to Alice Springs and up to Darwin. So for seven days two complete strangers had weighed each other's actions and words and, perhaps because we were both English with the same delight in a strange continent, we found each other not lacking the essentials of close friendship. On a rainy evening which kept the four of us indoors, sewing or writing letters, Diana began to explain and I knew what she was going to say.

"Before Miriam knew the date of her ship's sailing, we had planned to go as far as Darwin at least. I've been wondering, Eunice. I know Audrey has to return to Sydney, but I can just as easily return to Hobart in a few months as in a few weeks. How about us two going on?"

"I'd like to," I replied with a pleased grin.

"I've been wondering whether you could put up with me."

It was as simple as that. Audrey, with a wicked gleam in her eye, began a lurid account of my failings as a fellow traveller, and then sighed longingly: "Oh, I wish I hadn't to go back, then the three of us could go. Why, why, did I make such a promise?"

We thought it out from every angle searching for a loophole of escape from that promise, but staunch Audrey's word was her bond, however much she would have liked to be released from it.

So we began to plan. As Diana wanted to see Miriam and several more friends off on the ship at Brisbane, it was arranged that she, Miriam and Audrey would hitch back to Brisbane and Audrey would travel on the last lap to Sydney by train alone. First, however, the four of us would hitch the 200 miles south to Townsville where I would wait and find a job until Diana returned some ten days later. Then from Townsville we would strike West to Mount Isa and Alice Springs.

Enthusiasm waxed strong and at one point it seemed almost as if Miriam might cancel her passage and join us, but as she had not been home for four years, she eventually decided to carry on with her original arrangements.

In the midst of the excitement there came a loud knock on the door. It was Jack Walters, an Englishman who, with a Canadian friend, Bob, was staying at the People's Palace. We had met them at breakfast one morning.

Jack held a battered pair of socks aloft in his hand as he sauntered into the room.

"Ha, hum! Sorry to intrude on you, girls, but I've run out of wool. Darning wool. Got a hole as big as a spud in this here sock. Can you take a peek in your dilly bags and help a poor fellow out?"

At out first meeting, I had noticed about him a complete casualness allied to an underlying natural reserve. It was a strange mixture. Even in his usual garb—a much washed pair of trousers and old shirt—he still had an air of distinction about him. It may have been the unusual sight of a moustache, which he clipped so evenly, or it may simply have been that he was English. By the time some darning wool had been found in Diana's kit and his sock was being mended, he had heard most of our plans and he eyed us with a new respect.

"You'll do O.K. to Alice and Darwin. I've been right across from Townsville to Wyndham and Broome in the Nor' West. There and back—done it twice. No reason why girls shouldn't do it too," he said easily.

"How about work?" I asked. "Can one find a job?—Doesn't matter what it is."

"Oh! for a man there's plenty. Droving, unloading the ships as they bring in stores, and there's always work in the meat works—they're at most of the ports. But for girls, I'm not so sure—but I guess there's always something—you could try your hand as barmaids." He laughed, amused at the thought.

"Well, we don't mind," Diana and I assured him, "as long as we get paid. It would make a change."

Diana handed him his finished sock and he contemplated the neat darn.

"By jingo, that's as good as my mother used to do," he exclaimed. Then, flippantly : "If I offer my services as guide for croc. shooting, pearl diving and char making, could I always have my socks darned like this?"

We laughed and thought no more of it.

Two mornings later, as the four of us headed out of sunny

Cairns, we met him on his way to Cairns Meat Works to find a job. We wished him luck, never realizing how much a part of our trip he also was to become.

Townsville, on the shores of Cleveland Bay and 832 miles north of Brisbane, is the third city of importance in the State, although still, to our minds, just a small coastal town. The principal tourist attraction is Magnetic Island which is an aquatic playground five miles offshore where pineapples are farmed.

Next day we boarded the launch which took us from Townsville to Magnetic Island and spent the day sunbathing and swimming in one of the crystal clear bays, eating ripe pineapples, cut straight from the stalk.

Next morning, the three girls hoisted their packs higher onto their sunburnt shoulders and, with a cheery wave, set off down the long road to Brisbane and for Audrey, Sydney.

As I turned my solitary steps back into town, having escorted them to the end of the palm-tree lined main street, I already missed Audrey's cheerful naiveté. Luckily there was too much to do and think of to feel lonely for long. What was ten days? It would soon go!

I bought a paper and chuckling to myself as I recalled Jack's words about future jobs, I decided to get some experience and thoroughly scanned the marked column for barmaids.

I had no idea when I was interviewed by Norwegian-born Jess Yorgensen that she was more commonly known as "the terror of the Queensland Coast."

She owned a hotel and wanted a barmaid, and when I explained to this large, masculine woman (not too vaguely I hoped) that I'd helped a friend with a hotel in England, she very charmingly took me on and I moved into "The National" to start work at six o'clock the following morning.

I hadn't realized how much cockroaches love beer until, at 6 a.m. when I staggered downstairs to my first task of polishing the bar counter and saw the teeming, writhing mass of cockroaches crawling over the length of it. There were long ones, short ones, grandpas and youngsters, all cavorting merrily before my astonished eyes. I wondered for a moment if I'd have to polish them as well as the bar top, but most of them scuttled swiftly over the sides of the bar and disappeared into thin air save two three-inch monsters who steadfastly regarded me and tried unblinkingly to outstare me for the next three minutes : they were wise enough to know I couldn't do a thing until they went. They knew I was an amateur, but as Jess Yorgensen bustled in, they disappeared like two brown streaks of lightning.

"You should have had the polish on by now," she exclaimed.

"Hm—cockroaches," I muttered feebly.

"Ah, they know a stranger to these parts," she laughed gleefully. "You'll have to get used to them. Squash 'em—they make a lovely pop. By the way, I suppose you know all the terms for beer? If not, you'd better learn 'em—schooners, ladies' waists. Schooners are the usual.

"They're a good crowd who come in but don't let me catch you flirtin' with 'em." She eyed me appraisingly. "You're a bit nervous for this sort of thing but you'll learn. Now after the bar, I want all this brass cleaned—O.K.? I'll be back at 9.30."

I contemplated the brass with a sinking heart. I hate cleaning brass and evidently the late Captain Yorgensen had bequeathed to his wife's hotel more brassware than anything else from his last ship.

All day I precariously balanced handfuls of schooners to the thirsty mob who frequented "The National." They were a casual, friendly crowd who laughingly bet me, when Jess Yorgensen was well out of hearing, a pound apiece if I could last a week working for the 'old girl.'

"No one stays long," a friendly linesman told me seriously. "We reckon she's saving on tax by swapping round."

"Well, wait and see," I told them. "I think she's all right."

"Hope you're right. We'd like you to stay. Nice to see a fresh face round these parts. But remember we warned you. I've seen her tempers. She's throwing bottles before you can whistle, so don't stop to argue if she's got the bottle look."

I laughed with more bravado than I was feeling.

"If she throws anything at me, she'll get it straight back, don't worry."

By mid-morning an elderly bookie sat on what was obviously his usual stool in the corner.

"My word, you'll do me," he informed me delightedly as I set his drink before him and then hastily retreated to safety behind the bar.

By lunch time he was pretty 'full' but managed to make his way clumsily out through the swing doors, still muttering thickly, "My word, you'll do me."

Two evenings later he became a trifle aggravated at my pointedly ignoring his remarks and, whether by accident or design I shall never know, he left his stick jutting out as I was gingerly negotiating a tray load of dirty glasses. Too late I saw the stick and the ensuing crash as the tray hit the wooden floor, scattering broken glass in all directions, made many inhabitants of Townsville lock themselves in, fearing the "terror" was once again on the warpath.

As I packed my things next morning I thought of Jess Yorgensen's last curt statement: "You're not really cut out for a barmaid, are you?" I felt bound to agree with her. After paying for two dozen broken glasses, I had £4 extra in my pocket. At least I could live for a few more days without drawing on my diminishing bank account.

Back in Townsville, I changed digs three times that day before finding a small, clean room where the cockroaches were an inch smaller than they'd been elsewhere. Meals could be cooked in the kitchen at the back and the bright-eyed little woman who owned the building soon allotted me a small ice box on the verandah where I could keep my food. Praying for Diana's early return and not being in the mood to dine alone in the deserted kitchen, I wandered into the main street to search for a cheap café-cum-milk bar.

Ten yards ahead of me a small car deposited a lone figure and pack on the pavement.

"Thanks a lot, mate," said a casual voice. The car pulled away and a sun-bronzed face and moustache turned towards me, grinning amiably.

"Well, fancy! And hullo. I'm starving. Let's go and have some tucker, eh?" said Jack Walters blithely scooping up his pack and leading the way into the nearby milk bar. We ate heartily and talked like old friends, for even a slightly known face can make all the difference to a strange town. He chuckled heartily at my shortcomings as a barmaid.

"I thought you were going after a job at the Cairns Meat Works?" I asked him. "What brought you down here?"

He pulled a wry face.

"There was only one job, shovelling slime into an incinerator. I was up to me knees in it—and the stench! I stuck it for two days to get some cash, then I reckoned there'd be more work in Townsville. Heigh-ho here I go—and here I am."

His eyes twinkled. "Did any one ever tell you you're a real honey blonde?"

"Well, not in England," I said in surprise. "But plenty of sun and salt water soon works wonders."

"Ah ha, good old England," he chuckled airily. "Maybe I'll

go back one day. Now, where'm I gonna stay to-night? It'll have to be cheap. Where are you living? Any room for me?"

"I don't know. I know there are two small buildings—one for men and one for women. Come back with me and see," I said eagerly, anxious to keep his easy humour within reach: he was the only link I had with the other three, surely now a thousand miles South.

Luckily there was room for him in the men's section. In the mornings the owner brought his breakfast for me to cook with mine and I grew to know him well in the laughter-filled days before Diana's return.

Nothing seemed to worry him. Casually, easily, he took things as they came, making them suit his purpose not he theirs. Perhaps life in the outback had taught him this knack. It was a refreshing change although often rather impracticable. For a few days I forgot there was such a thing as work and he would join me in the afternoons at the shark-proof swimming enclosure after he had done a morning's work, to swim and talk, and recite dreamily reams of poetry. He was the complete dreamer.

After wandering all round Canada for a couple of years, he told me, he had worked a ship to Australia and continued his wanderings. He was one of those restless spirits who must perpetually drift, wandering in search of they know not what.

One wet afternoon we retired to the public library where he unshelved heavy, dusty volumes of poems, and the dark gloomy afternoon outside was forgotten as I sat spellbound, transported to another world, listening to his favourite Kipling. It was Jack who could discover a rare evening for music lovers in this far-away northern town, Jack who could stroll casually into a chromium-plated milk bar with an improvised fishing line in one hand and smilingly suggest they might supply some scraps as bait for his line. It was Jack also who, at 11.30 a.m., could return to the milk bar with a large fresh catch and cajole the astounded owner into cooking it while we waited, insisting he join us later as we ate, and who, when I told him he had "the devil's own cheek," merely chuckled : "There's no harm in asking anyone for anything. It's a free country; they can just as easily reply yes as no."

The morning I was to start working for a hairdresser in the main street I found a letter from Audrey with other mail from home, awaiting me at the Post Office.

"*I am back safely and my holiday is over*." she wrote, giving a lively picture of their journey south. Then: "*I started work again yesterday. I have packed all your things and put them in the luggage room, so they will be safe until you return, whether it be weeks or months. All send their love and wish you a wonderful journey round their 'God's Own Country.' Give my love to Diana when she returns. She is a great companion. How lucky things turned out and how I wish I, too, was going with you both. God be with you both on the journey."*

Two days later, a fortnight since she had left and the day before my birthday, Diana returned. I came home from work to find her sitting on the wooden verandah steps. Joyfully we greeted each other.

"My goodness, you're brown!" she exclaimed enviously. "I bet you've been swimming, sunbathing and not working, you lazy dog."

Soon she was laughing heartily at my accounts of the last fortnight. Once more I realized how much alike we were: it was easy to explain to her—she caught on quickly to ideas and, more important, we laughed at the same things.

Our hilarity quickly brought Jack from his room next door to greet her with his usual quizzical expression. How merry the drab little kitchen became that evening as the three of us fell over each other in our cooking of the large meal, laughing, talking, planning.

"I brought back my old cooking equipment—the one I used round Europe," Diana told me. "So we're O.K. for camping out, and after seeing your nylon dress even when it had been crushed in a pack for days, I made one myself before Miriam's ship sailed."

"What about blankets for sleeping out?" Jack asked. "The days are hot but the nights can be damned cold further inland."

Diana had one small blanket, I had none for Audrey and I had never planned to camp out. Diana said thoughtfully :

"We really need sleeping bags. It's a bit of an expense but they're a necessity. How about getting one each tomorrow, if we can? It's really all we'll have to buy."

So we arranged to shop in the morning and spend the afternoon on the beach: Diana was determined to catch up on my sun tan.

"Then for a special treat," Jack said, a twinkle in his eye, "as it's Eunice's birthday, I'll splash you both to the pictures. But don't expect this sort of thing every week," he warned us. "Perhaps I'll even buy a bottle of plonk and we'll celebrate properly; after all, tomorrow is my last day with you."

He was suddenly rather subdued, then, looking from one to

the other with a slow, unpredictable grin on his face, he wailed suddenly: "Who's going to darn my socks when you've gone?"

"You'd better pack them and send them to us by kangaroo," I joked.

"Or boomerang might be more direct," Diana quipped.

"Well, I guess I *could* always saddle a kangaroo and bring 'em to you m'self," Jack said whimsically.

How good life was when we three were together! Now Diana was back, Jack treated her with the same easy, affectionate banter with which he always treated me. Only once one afternoon when he thought I was sleeping on the hot sand after a swim had he softly kissed my cheek. Later I was to wonder if I had dreamed it, for he was once more the brotherly banterer.

As we celebrated my birthday with Jack's promised bottle of "plonk," sitting on the steps at the front of our 'house' (for no drinks were ever allowed inside), I think we all knew that, not two, but three merry wanderers would be heading "outback" tomorrow although nothing had actually been said about Jack joining us.

It wasn't until Diana and I were nearly packed next morning that he breezed in through the open door of our room, his small bundle of belongings under one arm, the corners of his moustache lifted in a faint grin as he drawled lightly: "I reckon you need me with you, huh!"

Diana and I looked at each other and chuckled.

"Well, now we've settled that," Jack said, "come on. The day's awastin', the morning mist has flown. Step lively, we've gotta get to Charters Towers to-night."

"Get out," Di laughed as I aimed a loose, handy orange after his retreating figure.

Two miles out of Townsville Diana and I sat sunbathing in shirts and shorts on our packs by the side of the lonely road.

Eyeing us appraisingly, Jack said : "Well, I reckon I'm not needed here. I'll go and have a snooze behind that gum tree; don't forget to tell 'em you have a brother behind the tree and wake me up when something comes."

He made off towards the gum tree. Half an hour later the driver of an ancient Utility greeted us: "G'day, where you'se going?"

"We're heading for Mount Isa via Charter Towers. Is there room and for our brother, please?" we asked, putting our carefully laid plan into operation. "He's having a sleep."

He laughed amusedly. "Sure thing. I'll wake him."

A loud honk on the blower brought Jack quickly to join us, and we all clambered thankfully into the Ford. Twenty miles on, our minds lulled by the heat and amiable chatter, we answered our driver's question without a second thought, "Well, we're all quite a way from home, Tasmania for me and England for you three—but which part of the old country do you all come from?"

"I'm from Sussex," Diana said.

"And I'm from Kent next door," I explained.

"And I came from Buckinghamshire," Jack said breezily.

We all realized our mistake as quickly as the driver, but, luckily, he howled with laughter at our three sheepish faces and took no offence.

Diana laughed ruefully.

"Whew, it needs too much concentration even for white lies in this heat. I think we'll abandon that plan in future. From this moment you are disowned, Jack."

"Pity! And I was just beginning to like being a brother. Sorry I spoilt things for you," he remarked facetiously.

We reached Charters Towers at 6 o'clock. In the usual small, deserted camping area just outside the flat township we unrolled our sleeping bags, gathered sparse wood for the open brick fire and brewed the billy with water from the many laid-on taps and ate our rather burnt-up steaks seated on a covered log by the warmth of the leaping flames, for the night air now suddenly had a slight bite to it.

Charters Towers is built almost completely of wood.

"It used to be famous for the three Gs," Jack explained lightly, nonchalantly holding a large steak in his hands and chewing thoughtfully at the corners.

"What are the three Gs?" we asked innocently.

"Gold, girls and goats. The gold has all gone now, so have the girls, but the place is still alive with goats." He surveyed us merrily across the flickering firelight. "That's all I can tell you about Charters Towers—there's nothing more to tell, except this. If we leave here early enough in the morning we won't have to pay the two shillings each camping fee that an odd individual comes to collect every morning."

Next morning from beneath our new sleeping bags and a thick layer of ground frost, Diana and I were awakened rudely by a howl of rage. It evidently emanated from Jack who stood, dressed, glaring wrathfully at the two newly frayed corners of his blankets.

"Those wretched goats," he cried. "Look what they've done to my best blanket!"

As usual Diana and I saw the funny side (our own bag corners were quite sound) and Jack was soon laughing with us.

"Maybe that's to pay you back for wanting to clear out before paying your camping fee," Diana told him.

Poor Jack! But what a wonderful way to start a day. The early morning sky was clear and blue, the sun gave promise of another hot day, birds chorused blithely in the trees and we had awakened with laughter on our lips. Half-way through breakfast the figure of a large, tubby individual, riding a very small bicycle, appeared on the horizon and wobbled alarmingly towards us over the uneven ground. Jack suddenly disappeared. The camping fee collector was a friendly man who stayed to share a cup of tea before handing us our receipt for 4/- and wobbling on his way again. Jack reappeared.

"Some people could get away with murder," Diana told me darkly.

Jack chuckled and breezily began folding his chewed blankets.

"Fair's fair," he told us with a pained expression. "If I'd wanted me blankets chewed, I could have slept in the road. As they were chewed anyway—I shouldn't *have* to pay, but just in case he couldn't see me point, I decided against leaving the decision to him. Now—come on, give us a smile with those big blue eyes, Di," he cajoled.

What else *could* she do?

Later in the sun-drenched little township we bought stores, tins of food, butter, bread and fruit and, after a leisurely three hours' wait on the other side of town, were given a short lift by a local inhabitant going out to inspect his old gold claim. The car must have been almost as old as the claim: there were no windows, doors or roof, but at least it went, or rather it coughed and choked laboriously for the next fifteen miles when it suddenly blew off its water cap with the heat and sprayed us all with boiling water.

Luckily the contents was by then fairly low, or we might not have been able to fill up again so quickly from a spare tinful of water which the old miner carried, and rumble on. Having been told that this happened roughly every fifteen miles, we were very grateful to be set down ten miles further on where, luckily, our red dusty road on to Hughenden parted company with the old miner's road.

By a dried-up creek a little further on we ate our sandwiches, finished the tea in the flask and waited patiently for another lift.

"You ought to have brought a water bag, not a flask," Jack

32

told us. "You can always find wood for a fire to make tea, but you can't always find water."

By 3.30 in the hot, dry inland heat we were all very thirsty. Diana was too lazy to move, so Jack and I set off down the bed of the creek carrying the billy can to see if we could find a small pool. For twenty minutes we plodded along the loose, sandy creek bed. We were on the verge of deciding that it was completely dry when we saw ahead a small, black, wooden shack.

"Anyone at home?" Jack called loudly from behind the fencing which surrounded the deserted looking shack. The only answer was a loud, fierce barking from within.

"Looks as though they've gone to town for the day," Jack said slowly, "but there's a large water butt over there: they wouldn't like us to die of thirst, would they?"

With which he vaulted lightly over the fence and made towards the butt. The barking grew fiercer and I watched fearfully as Jack filled the blackened billy can and began to carry it back. Suddenly there came a mighty clatter from within the shack and two feet of bristling black fur hurled itself through an open window. There was foam round the dog's mouth, and it was quite obviously looking for trouble. Straight for Jack's slowly retreating figure it came.

"Jack! Quickly!" I shrieked. "The dog's out—run, run!"

With a quick backward glance he took to his heels and, clearing the fence in one mighty leap, dragged me to the shelter of some adjacent trees. Now, however, the dog seemed quite content to stay behind his fence and growl menacingly, but, alas, our billy can of water was once again quite empty. There was nothing for it but to return to Diana, who looked from a distance as though she was quietly burrowing herself into the creek bed. When she saw us, she waved triumphantly.

"Look, I've found some water! I remembered they always dig for it in these parts—don't they?"

Sure enough at the bottom of the hole was a small pool of sandy, muddy looking water. There were also a few bugs for good measure.

"We can't drink that!" I exclaimed in disgust. Jack eyed me scornfully.

"And why not? We'll leave it for a bit, till it's settled. If there are many bugs left then, they'll just get boiled, see!"

He laughed merrily enough but there was a hint of exasperation at our dubious faces.

"Look, one thing you gotta learn, gals. You're in the outback now and you take your water as it comes—and be thankful for it. Now come on, let's boil the billy. I'm too hot to wait for it to settle any longer."

It was 4.30 in the afternoon and the sun's heat, which had scorched us all day, was now tempered with a pleasant breeze. All day we had travelled barely forty miles. By a lonely creek we sipped our scalding tea, trying not to notice the small black bodies that floated regularly to the surface.

"I wish someone would hurry up and come along," I said, surveying the sandy, uneven track that led on to the horizon.

"I suppose we are on the right road, Jack?"

He lifted an eyebrow.

"There *is* only one road; this is it, straight on to Hughenden, 150 miles West."

Diana laughed sleepily.

"It looks as though we'll be sleeping out—right here. I'm too lazy to move, anyway. We're in no hurry, are we?"

"No," I admitted, "but I'd love a shower. We might get one at Hughenden."

"Go and stand in the puddle," she told me with a chuckle. Jack raised himself on one elbow.

"You just dare! We may need that for our morning brew up."

"Ah, whose turn to get up and make the tea in the morning?" Diana asked, adding wickedly, "Don't forget I like mine at 6.30 right here, milky but not too sweet."

"And I," Jack said with a chuckle, "like mine when the sun's two inches away from the horizon, and a kookaburra's laughed three times."

From where I was sitting I watched excitedly in the distance a sleek Utility which nosed quietly over the horizon and sped towards us.

"In that case," I chuckled, "you'd better fight it out between you—I'm going on to Hughenden with this fast approaching Utility!"

At 10.30 that evening, in record time for the state of the hundred and fifty miles of bumpy, unmade road, we reached Hughenden. The lights of the tiny township winked sparsely here and there, but spilled out in an orange warmth from the long, low, wooden hotel as we drew up before it.

"Thanks for the company," Nick Prescott, the young Australian driver, said as he helped pull our packs from the back of the Utility. "I get pretty fed up with that stretch when I'm on my own—my word, I do!"

Later, after a meal and a hot bath, Diana and I returned to our cheap room and sprung gleefully into bed (Jack had staked his claim to one of the line of beds on the open verandah). How soft the mattress felt after the dry hard earth of the previous night.

"How quickly one learns to appreciate the ordinary, small, luxurious things of life when one goes without for once," I sighed ecstatically to the top of Diana's head as she snuggled lower into the mattress.

For a moment she came up for air.

"There's another thing I'm learning. Instead of our going down on our hands and knees to thank people for lifts, they all make out we've done them a favour by having *our* company, *and* they seem to mean it. It's wonderful, isn't it? There's no feeling of obligation. I guess there'll be a lot more to learn before we've finished this trip," I said sleepily. "That's what's going to make it such fun."

"I wonder what Jack did with that steak we bought in Charters Towers?" Diana said as we dressed early next morning. "We ought to economise and use it for breakfast instead of buying breakfast."

I could not withhold a wry grimace.

"I can never get used to eating meat for breakfast. It's not civilized," I muttered as the smell of frying bacon wafted up the stairs.

"Well, I don't like meat for breakfast either, but as we've got the meat, we'll eat it."

"Okay, you win. I suppose it's good to have someone to look after the financial side," I admitted, admiring her ability to resist the delicious odour of the frying bacon.

Jack soon retrieved the steak from the hotel keeper's wife who had thoughtfully placed it in an ice box overnight. We hoisted our packs on to our shoulders and made our way out of town. By a dry, sandy creek a hundred yards wide, we stopped beneath a white-barked gum tree; in its shade we built a small fire and were soon all busily devouring our wood-scented steak, washing it down with sweet tea. Every few minutes we changed our positions as the sun rose higher and the shade crept inwards towards the tree.

"Boy, I'll defy anyone to tell me there's anything that tastes better than a barbecued steak," Jack said. Now he looked neither poet nor dreamer as he held the greasy steak by two hands and chewed hungrily. Sunbrowned, casual and unshaven, he looked a real down-to-earth outbacker. He pointed suddenly up the wide, dry creek to where—a hundred yards further up one side of the creek bed—a solitary figure had appeared from a low shelter of branches and leaves and was making his way towards us.

"Any steak left?" Jack asked, "We're gonna have a visitor for breakfast: I'll brew the billy again."

"G'day," the newcomer greeted us as he squatted himself down in the shade, pushing an aged, much-thumbed hat almost on to the back of his neck. His weather-beaten face hadn't seen a razor for a good many days, but his eyes held a twinkle. His trousers were rumpled but clean and his shirt stuck to his chest in long patches with sweat. Casually he accepted the steak and the mug of tea which Jack offered him.

"Found any gold lately?" Jack asked brightly, evidently recognising him for what he was—an old prospector.

"Yep, found a good 'un back in '36."

The old timer's eyes burned suddenly at the memory of the excitement of that claim.

"Fair dinkum, she was a real beaut. Worked her for a coupla years till she ran out. Nope! Never found one like that agin anywhere."

He finished his mug of scalding tea in one gulp.

"'Course, I found bits since: some opals, copper, some gold in the Kimberleys down near Hall's Creek. Ah, you been there, have you?" he exclaimed as Jack nodded at the mention of the once famous gold town in the West.

"I gotta a beaut lump of uranium back in m'humpy—picked that up near Mount Isa." His eyes glowed again. "That's where they found the 'Mary Kathleen.' My word, she was a beaut!"

The 'Mary Kathleen' was one of the richest strikes of uranium ever to be found in Australia: every Australian and New Australian has heard of the 'Mary Kathleen.' He pulled a grey rag from his trouser pocket and wiped the remains of steak from his sun-browned face and gnarled, sunburned hands. Then slowly he replaced it, and looked long and thoughtfully at us.

"Yep, that lump o' uranium should have given me a clue to the 'Mary Kathleen' but I didn't have a geiger counter. You just gotta have a geiger counter for that stuff. My word, by the time I'd had m' sample checked and realized what I was on, some other fella had made a claim. Fair dinkum, I might a bin a mighty rich fella to-day."

"I wonder how many prospectors have said the same?" Diana asked, not unkindly. "Why don't you give it up and get a good steady job? You might soon be rich that way."

The old prospector gave a soft chuckle.

36

"Rich! Who wants to be rich? I bin roaming this country since I can remember. It's my life. I'll go on roaming till I die. Thanks fer the beaut tucker," he said cheerfully as he rose to go. "By the way, I got something in m' humpy I'd like you all to have. Come on over!"

Thinking excitedly of opals and gold nuggets we followed him back to his primitive shelter where he proudly showed us his small collection which he kept in a battered old tin. All that was left of many years' prospecting. Then, after scrabbling for some minutes inside the humpy, he brought out three small, screwed up packets of paper and solemnly handed us one each. Back at our own "camp," we hastily unscrewed our small parcels to find not, as we expected, a gleaming opal or nugget of gold, but a small screw of loose tobacco and three cigarette papers!

3

Prospecting for Uranium

THREE weeks before we reached Hughenden, Ernie
Maddison, a young Australian of thirty two, had left
Mount Isa 500 miles West in his loaded 'Holden' and set
off for the Queensland coast on a month's holiday, leaving the
management of his small club in Mount Isa to an English
friend. It was the first real holiday he had taken since returning
to Australia after three years in a Japanese concentration camp,
to find that his wife had left him. Still lonely and with a deep
bitterness which two long years had done little to heal, he
meandered for three weeks up and down the Queensland coast
and then, because he was a gentle, serious Australian who made
friends slowly, he admitted to himself that he wasn't enjoying
his holiday and headed, a week earlier than intended, inland and
westward towards Mount Isa, his beloved club.

Of course we knew nothing of all this when, just outside
Hughenden, he pulled up late that afternoon to squeeze two
large packs and a swag on top of his luggage in the back, and
three extra bodies into the front seat. It certainly wasn't the
best or most comfortable way to travel for the next four
days over four hundred and fifty miles of uneven, unmade road
but it was certainly one of the happiest, most carefree weeks we
had ever spent. By the time we reached Richmond later that
evening, some of our infectious joy of life had instilled itself into
Ernie.

All next day we drove on singing lustily for him the songs we
had learnt at school. He loved them. Diana and I particularly
learnt a good deal more about each other's lives and thoughts as
we answered his many questions. Then, after much good-
natured chaffing, he suddenly lost the last of his reserve, his
unhappiness seemed to slip from him and he, too, laughed and
sang unembarrassedly the songs of Australia for us, the songs
the sheep shearers sang as they sat around their camp fires at
night, songs about their tucker boxes and, of course, the one and
only "Jolly Swagman," in which we could join with him singing

loudly and untunefully as he bumped and bounced the car over the lonely, sparse landscape. The creeks were all dry now. Creeks with fascinating outback names such as "Black Jin Creek," "Little Gum Creek," "Big Gum Creek." "Green Water Creek." Ernie laughed as Di read the last saying, in his slow drawl: "Whoever named that one had a mirage for even when there's water there, the only colour you can call it is just plain muddy."

We had reached the country where kangaroos in their numbers would retreat from our pathway for a few leaps, then half turn and regard us shyly with large eyes. The tiny "Joeys" sought the shelter of their mother's pouches against these unusual creatures who stared back at them with such delight. From the long yellow grass flocks of wide-winged turkeys, disturbed by our approaching car, would fly straight into the sun, always straight for the sun. When I remarked on this, Ernie chuckled.

"It's instinct—their only defence, try shooting one with that sun blinding your eyes. They're clever, those wild turkeys."

"What do they taste like? Have you ever shot one?" Diana asked for we had seen two guns in the back of the car.

"Oh, I've never shot one myself but they're beaut to eat—as long as you don't remember that they feed on the ticks off sheep and cattle."

Diana and I shuddered with disgust, and Jack, remembering what I had told him in Townsville, eyed me blithely as he said casually:

"Well, Eunie's got a few prizes for shooting. She can shoot us one and we'll roast it over the fire some evening. I'll make a spit like they used to have in the olden days."

"O.K., I'll have a try," I told him laughingly, "but don't rely on anything or you may go hungry—and don't expect me to eat it!"

Occasionally a long necked mother ostrich, small furry balls of fluff fluttering around her feet, would regard us quizzically from the shelter of nearby vegetation. I could never get used to the sight of trees which, at a distance, looked weighted with bright blue, green, pale pink and grey blossoms, only to shed those "blossoms" as we neared, in a sudden cloud as budgerigars or gallahs winged from their resting place and soared skywards.

When we reached Julia Creek that second evening, we exclaimed wonderingly to Ernie:

"What on earth do people find to work at out here?"

The World at Our Feet

It was a small wooden township scattered forlornly in the middle of a yellow-looking flat plain.

We had forgotten for the moment the long, straight line of railway track that for two days had crawled along beside our dusty road. Ernie grimaced wryly, his keen grey eyes searching for the camping area as he spoke, "I agree these Western townships all look pretty god-forsaken. Richmond, Julia Creek, Duchess, they're all there simply to keep the railways going. Most of the inhabitants work on the line, while the few remaining look after the stores and pubs. I grant you they're raw-looking townships, but this is a raw sort of country, I guess."

To the sausages and chops we bought in the township's one butcher's shop to barbecue back at the camping ground, we added two plump pigeons, which Ernie and I had shot during the day. They tasted delicious.

Later, at the only hotel there, Diana and I, towels and soap tucked under our arms, presented ourselves to ask for a hot bath, for we were coated with dust. The hotel-keeper looked a trifle dubious :

"Well, I don't want to use too much water—otherwise I'd say yes right away."

"Oh, we understand. You're short of water, are you?" we asked.

"Oh no, plenty of water," he assured us surprisingly. "It's just that we've no proper drainage here and the waste water, instead of flowing away, flows right back under the hotel: this place is built in a hollow and it's gonna fall clean down one day —all because of a soaking rotted foundation."

We had to commiserate with the poor fellow: this really was the raw side of Australia, but luckily we got our bath.

All next day we drove on westward through the bush. A few families of wild boar roamed the country but, though we had visions of succulent roast pig to eat at our camp fire that night, those tough, wily boars had other ideas and fled swiftly into the bush at our approach. About mid-day Ernie suddenly pointed ahead with a low exclamation:

"Look, dingos—two beauts!" he said, braking the car slowly to a standstill and reaching for a gun. Sure enough on a slight rise of ground ahead two great, yellow dogs sniffed the air tentatively. Dingos! It was the first time Diana and I had seen these wild outlawed killers at close range. Nobody is certain of the dingo's origin. Some say he and the Black Man crossed the Eastern land bridge together long before the ocean encroached to

40

make Australia a separate continent. Theories apart, dingo bones have been discovered in company that seems to prove an antiquity dating long before Man first came to this vast continent.

"There's a £2 reward on each of their scalps," Ernie said softly as he loaded the gun swiftly and slipped out of the car.

"Stay where you are and don't make a sound!" he warned, "I'm gonna see if I can get one."

Still the huge dingos stood poised gracefully on their hillock as Ernie darted swiftly towards them from bush to bush, in an effort to get near enough for a certain kill. Suddenly, as we watched excitedly from the car, the great yellow dogs bounded across the roadway ahead, making for the long grass on the other side. As the last one had almost reached the grass the loud report of Ernie's rifle cracked through the hot still air. The dingo gave a mighty leap into the air as the bullet struck.

"Got him!" Jack cried. "There's one that won't bother any more sheep."

But the dingo, with a weird moaning howl, could still run on three legs and dragged its way quickly after its mate into the low bush. As we scrambled from the car, Ernie shouted:

"Wait here—it can't get far—I'm going after it. Don't follow. Snakes!" With that urgent reminder he, too, disappeared into the bush.

A few minutes later we heard another sharp rifle report, then silence. Half an hour slipped by, then another and still, for all our calling and shouting, he didn't return.

"Come on, girls, we'll boil the billy—he'll need a brew up when he gets back," Jack said lightly enough, but his eyes anxiously scanned the shimmering bush.

"You think he's missed the track?" Di asked quietly. Jack nodded.

"Could be—that bloody bush all looks alike when you can't see the road. He shouldn't have followed the dingo."

I opened the car door and stepped out, then, with a gasp, quickly leapt back pulling the door to with a slam. At the noise, a long, brown snake roused, its small head swaying backwards and forwards three feet in front of the bonnet, then turned and glided swiftly for the grass at the side of the road. I let out a long breath, while Diana laughed hollowly.

"He looks as scared as we feel."

"He is," Jack told us with a chuckle. "Those don't attack unless they're trodden on. Now come on—the fire. We'll have to dampen the wood so that it smokes.

Twenty minutes after the huge fire we had built had belched

41

its smoke into the brilliant clear sky and we had but one small teacanful of drinking water left, a bedraggled, sweating Ernie found his way back from the bush: the dingo had got away, but we were all too glad to see each other to worry about the £2 for the dingo's scalp.

Late that afternoon we bagged our wild turkey, a fine fat bird easily weighing twenty pounds.

"We'll never roast that over a camp fire," Jack said. "We'll just have to wait to try it until we reach Mount Isa."

Only as we eventually stowed the turkey excitedly into the back of the car did Ernie tell us laughingly:

"By the way, don't spread this around Mount Isa. There's a £50 fine for anyone who kills a wild turkey."

At mid-day on the fourth day the poor, loaded car hiccupped alarmingly and refused to budge another inch. After tinkering with the engine for an hour in the blazing sun Jack and Ernie gave up.

"It's the battery that's dead," Ernie explained, "and we're only forty miles from Mount Isa. Wouldn't it rock you! We'll just have to wait. Someone'll be by in a day—maybe two. We've enough water for one can of tea, but no washing from now on," he warned. "You can shower all you want when we reach Mount Isa."

Pushing the car beneath a shady gum tree we settled down to while away the next twenty-eight hours, when luckily a small party of returning uranium prospectors appeared and cheerfully towed us into Mount Isa.

Ernie's small cool cabin stood on a slight hill at the rear of his modern, newly built club. The cabin consisted of two rooms and a minute kitchen. Insisting that the three of us should stay with him until we found work, Ernie gave up his bedroom to Diana and me, and from chairs and an old sofa made up beds for Jack and himself in the other. From the cabin one could see away to the boom mining township with its two dusty main streets. Corrugated iron and wooden awnings of Chinese and Australian owned stores shaded the sleepy looking town but the three large modern hotels were already doing a roaring trade. From across the dry wide river, which cut the township down the middle, rose the great steel chimneys and buildings of the copper works and mine. For here was the reason for Mount Isa's existence: its fabulous mineral wealth of copper, lead, zinc, gold and, even more recently, uranium. It was the great copper works, however, which dominated the southern side of the township. Although still only early evening, lights were beginning to wink on all over the works and the belching sulphur fumes from the tallest chimney trailed in the clear air away across the skyline of the furthest hills. Ernie stood with us at the door of the cabin and pointed across the river.

"If you can get a job over on the mines side, in the canteen or suchlike, you'll get good money—made up from the copper bonus, because it's not so good working where there are sulphur fumes. But don't tell them you're only staying a short while unless they ask."

He paused tentatively. "Of course the hospital here'd be only too glad to take you girls on, they're always short staffed. That's the most needy place if you feel like being Good Samaritans."

"Well, I'll try the mines," Jack said. "But see that dark patch of green right in between the township and the mine?" He pointed below. "That's the Mount Isa swimming pool, the most beautiful oasis this side of the black stump. I vote we spend the next two days doing nothing but lazing and swimming there, huh!"

"Lazy dog!" we all chaffed him good humouredly, but the vote was carried unanimously.

It was at the beautiful Olympic pool, built from the wealth of the mines, that we began to realize just how many different nationalities lived and worked together in the small Western mining township. There were Czechs, Germans, Italians, French, Swedes, Finns, Dutchmen. Almost every European nationality was represented. The swimming pool by day and evening was like a United Nations Assembly, with so many different tongues calling backwards and forwards across the wide pool. To the Aussies all these nationalities were just "New Australians." The greater number were men. The women in Mount Isa were outnumbered by them 10 to 1.

The local dances were a boost to any girl's morale. The surplus men stood in the centre of the dance floor, with the dancers circling them, and as every dance was an "Excuse Me" it was not surprising that most girls had changed partners at least five times before completing one circle of the smallish floor. Although great fun for a change, especially when one has been brought up in a country seemingly of surplus women, it could be rather maddening, for just as one was just getting used to a new partner's step he himself was excused and one had to start all over again, and so on throughout the evening. Most of the "New Australians," we found, reckoned to work for a couple of years at the mines (where they earned from £25 to £40 a week) and then, with a large bank roll, return to the coast and cities to find a wife and a small business. A lot, however, were saving hard to return to their native lands. Serious and terribly hard working, many hated the raw, easy-going continent and found it impossible to bridge the gap between themselves and casual Australians. Any single girl working in Mount Isa was offered at least one legitimate proposal of marriage every week.

"If you come back and see me in about three weeks I'll take you both on," said the jovial, sweating foreman of the Mines' Canteen.

All morning Diana and I had made enquiries for work on the mines side of the town, lured on by thoughts of a large bonus each week.

Three weeks! We had only reckoned to work a month in Mount Isa before pushing on to Alice Springs. Thanking the foreman, we made our way back across the river.

"Well it seems I've just got to be a nurse," Di announced. "Come on, I'm going to the hospital."

In the large verandahed hospital, whose age and woodenness was even more accentuated by the large modern block of nurses' quarters which overshadowed it, Diana was welcomed with almost open arms by the worried-looking little matron.

"Let's hope you'll stay longer than a month," she said eagerly as Diana explained our plans. "I'm so short staffed, I just haven't known what to do. The girls all prefer the coastal towns, you see. It's very hard on the outback townships. Now! You start tomorrow and your pay will be £10 for a forty-hour week to be done in various shifts."

She turned to me hopefully: "You are not a nurse, Miss Gardner?"

"No, a hairdresser. Do you want one on the staff?" I asked hopefully, for Diana would now have to live in the nurses' quarters and I couldn't live at Ernie's cabin for the next month. She shook her head.

"No! There's no position here for a hairdresser, but I could use you as a nursing aide. There's a thousand and one jobs you could do." She nodded delightedly as a thought struck her. "You could cut and perm all the patients' hair too. So many need it done!"

I had scarcely time to think and we were both fitted with half a dozen white uniforms each, shown over a large double room in the nurses' quarters and instructed to move in next day.

Diana chuckled as we made our way back to tell Ernie and Jack the news.

"Just imagine a Sister and a nursing aide sharing a room in England; they wouldn't even be in the same block." She grinned happily. "We're lucky, eh, Nurse Gardner?"

"How true, Sister Williams, and what I lose in pay as an aide I'll make up with haircuts and perms. I wonder how it'll feel to be a nurse?"

"You'll love it," Diana told me positively. "To-night I'll show you how to take a pulse and read a thermometer."

Diana was quite right. I did love it. It was wonderful experience to work for the next month amongst the hardy bush folk, ill in such dust-infested heat. In the women's wards, where Diana and I worked, blacks and whites lay side by side equal in their patience and courage.

I learnt, too, a great deal about Diana in that busy hectic month.

"Sister Willams is your friend, isn't she?" the patients began to ask. "Is it true you're both only staying a month?" Then, wistfully, "Couldn't you stay longer? That sore on my back's healing since Sister Williams came. I've never had my back done so often." "Yes, nurse, Sister Williams is taking the stitches out to-day: I don't mind having them done now."

I soon saw it was not always the big things that go to make a much loved nurse, but all the hundred and one small things, done well, that could make all the difference to a sick, helpless person.

Week-end uranium prospecting was still the rage since the discovery of the fabulous "Mary Kathleen" a few years earlier, and not many week-ends passed without someone making a fresh claim. So Diana and I were determined to try our luck.

Very early one Saturday morning, when the heat of the sun was already bouncing in waves from the tin roofs of the township, Matt Turner with an Aussie friend, Jim Pett, picked us up at the hospital in his vintage open Crossley and we headed out of town into the bush. Matt Turner was a young English miner who had been working in the Mount Isa Mine for the last eighteen months. He it was who had looked after the club for Ernie while he had been on holiday.

For twenty miles we rattled across the sun-parched bush, stopping only once by a freshly posted claim where Matt brought chunks of jagged dark grey rock to hold beneath the geiger counter and explain as the counter ticked fiercely.

"This is the look of the stuff. If you think you see any rock

45

or ground reminiscent of this, knock it off and test it for a count. Okay?"

When the track died out completely Matt bounced the old Crossley on over the parched earth, through slate coloured hills, jagged high ranges and sometimes rolling low bush as far as the eye could see. At last he said:

"Okay, girls, this is where we start walking. Jim, you carry the counter. We'll take a hammer each." Jim nodded. "I'll fill your water bags, sling 'em round your necks and you can drink as you go. It's a fair cow, this heat," he laughed. "Must be about 120° to-day."

On we slowly trekked in the broiling sun keeping a sharp look-out for rock, snakes and spinifex—the knife-like grass that could tear uncovered ankles to pieces. Wetting our lips every few minutes from our water bags we trekked on over the craggy, tortuous country, chipping off any likely looking pieces of rock to test beneath the geiger counter for any signs of uranium count, and always keeping each other in view. By the end of the day the men were exhausted, and Diana and I were utterly spent. When we reached the old Crossley again to make camp, it was the two men who cheerfully built a fire, cooked the meal and brewed many strong billies of tea.

Ten hours' solid sleep, however, worked wonders and after a large breakfast we set off again, this time towards the North. It was mid-day when we struck something: a piece of rock, which Diana had brought to test, swung the needle over on the geiger counter, and it ticked rapidly. In a flash the heat and weariness of the day was forgotten. Excitedly we all eyed each other.

"Know where you got it?" Jim and Matt asked quickly.

Diana nodded, and we followed hastily to a large, jagged seam of rock. For an hour we chipped and knocked and tested, but the geiger counter remained stubbornly silent as each fresh piece was held beneath it.

"Are you sure it was here?" Jim asked again and again.

Diana was adamant that this was the spot. At length Matt straightened an aching back, saying:

"If you're sure—can you show us the piece of rock you chipped this chunk from?"

"But I didn't knock it off, I picked it up amongst this rubble," Diana said, kicking at the pile of slate and rock beneath our feet.

After another half an hour and still no count, our enthusiasm melted beneath a cloud of depression. At length Jim switched off the counter and seated himself thoughtfully on a nearby rock.

"I've been thinking," he said slowly. "We're pretty near Dawson's beaut claim, aren't we?"

Diana and I wondered what was coming next, but Matt also had been thinking hard.

"I got an idea what you're thinking," he said quietly. "When they returned to Mount Isa in such a hurry they had a load of the stuff with 'em, didn't they?"

"Yep, and they could have come this way," Jim said. "And in their excitement to get to Mount Isa and stake a claim they could have dropped a lot of pieces, couldn't they?"

Matt looking ruefully at our sunburnt downcast faces, and threw an arm across each of our shoulders sympathetically.

"Yep! Diana, that's what you did. You found one of those dropped pieces. It would only happen once in a lifetime. *That's* what you'd call a real fair cow all right!"

We met Margaret when she came in from Moorestones station to have her baby in the Mount Isa Bush Hospital.

She was an English girl, so naturally we would often pop along for a chat. She had travelled out to Australia four years previously to work on a cattle station in a bush town in Queensland (small and shy, she looked the last type of person to do this). She had met Jack, head stockman on the station, they had fallen in love and were married and now Jack managed a station for an English company about one hundred and fifty miles from Mount Isa.

"You pass Moorestones station on your way to Darwin," she said as she was leaving the hospital. "It's sixty miles off to the right. There's only one road. It goes right on to Burketown up on the Gulf. If you can, come and stay a few days. I don't see many people right out there," she added rather sadly. "It would be lovely if you could stay."

We promised we would try and go if we could get a lift in that direction: I had always wanted to stay on a fabulous Australian cattle station, for I had heard in England of their weather and the wonderful swimming pools they always had.

But I'm sure Margaret didn't think she would ever see us again as she waved good-bye.

On our last week in Mount Isa we told Ernie about the invitation and great-hearted Ernie said immediately:

"I'll drive you out there. I know where it is. How about Tuesday?"

So, early the following Tuesday morning, we waved good-bye

to our ex-patients, black and white, lined up in their beds on the wooden verandahs, and roared out of Mount Isa.

It had been a hectic month of work and play, and we were looking forward to a week's laze by a beautiful swimming pool. We were also looking forward to seeing Margaret—but we nearly didn't get there!

It was a wonderful morning, the sun hot, the breeze cool, and Ernie let me drive. As we sped along the narrow bitumen straight as far as the eye could see to the horizon, the needle of the speedometer flickered past sixty, seventy and almost to eighty miles an hour.

"I shouldn't try to push it past eighty," Ernie said. "These Holdens have a nasty habit of swinging their bottoms round on you, if you do."

I had felt a slight wobble beginning as the needle hovered below eighty. Every time I tried to push it past, the very slight wobble of warning came, so I gave up and kept to a steady seventy. After about fifty miles Diana took over. Ernie didn't mind. He was quite happy as long as we were.

However, he didn't know that Diana had made a quiet bet with herself to push that needle a bit higher than I had. As soon as we had topped another slight rise the road stretched on again for a few miles, practically straight to the horizon, the low bush shrubland on either side. The scene repeated itself every time we nosed over a fresh rise. Diana picked up speed. Suddenly we seemed to be going at an alarming pace, the bushes were flashing by, the dust was whirling away behind like a dust storm.

"Hey, steady, old girl!" Ernie warned.

But the warning came too late, the off-side front wheel spun on a patch of bull dust just as the needle sat on eighty-one miles an hour—for one second only. But it was enough! The car seemed to be possessed; it careered, bucking and skidding, off the bitumen into the dust at one side, and then almost jumped the bitumen to plough into the thick dust at the other side of the road. Branches and leaves lashed the windscreen as we swerved and skidded like lightning away across the road again, missing a couple of trees by inches. Diana's unskilled pulling at the wheel made it worse.

I sat powerless; my mind was repeating mechanically, "You've had it! You've had it this time. This is the end." Diana must have forgotten to take her foot off the accelerator, and if Ernie hadn't been between us on the front seat, we *would* have "had it." Grabbing the wheel from Diana, he shouted: "Take your foot

48

off quickly! Take it off!" And with great skill he spun the wheel against the swaying zig-zagging of the car and gradually lessened the swaying. It seemed a year!

The back of the car stopped swinging round up to one side, but we still careered and bounced all over the road. At last I let out my breath. The needle dropped and we came to a shuddering halt, the noze of the car buried in a large bush.

Diana looked dazed.

"Gosh! Sorry!" she muttered.

Ernie wiped the sweat from his eyes and laughed shakily while I opened the door to climb out quickly and find out if my jellied legs could still support me.

It was the craziest thing I had ever known Diana do. She was usually so careful. I couldn't get over it.

"Never again will I be a passenger when you are driving," I told her. "I mean to go round Australia, not under it."

Ernie decided it was a good time to eat, and try to calm our shattered nerves. So we perched on a nearby boulder, pulled a cold chicken to pieces, surveying the noseless car. We all seemed very thoughtful: perhaps we were all thanking our lucky stars. Ernie drove the rest of the eighty miles to the station!

"Moorstones" was well named. The poor car had leaped and bounded over so many stones and rocks on a road that was barely a track for the last twenty miles that I was surprised not to see it collapse into a heap of old iron as we drew up by the cluster of whitewashed outhouses and one delapidated wooden building.

There was however, a sudden greenness about the place, rather like coming to an oasis. Behind the usual clutter of outhouses stood a high wooden coral and to the right of that stood, or rather leaned, the house. The main outline seemed to consist of uncut logs; in fact, that's just what they were—tree trunks with the bark stripped off. Lashed between these logs all over the house were closely woven latticed, wooden sunshades which gave a blind, withheld look to the place.

Margaret was delighted to see us. The introductions over, Jack, Margaret's typically lean, bushman-looking husband, went off to fetch the lanterns. There was no electricity. One long room which occupied the length and breadth of the house was divided in the centre by a large, old-fashioned, heavy wooden dresser, and one half used as a dining room while the other was a comfortable lounge. Upstairs there were bats in the belfry! We lurched with a flickering lantern up the creaking, uneven, wooden stairs to the upstairs verandah, through a narrow black alleyway and out of a door on to the back verandah and from there into our room at the far end. We negotiated the first part all right, but Margaret paused before the door leading to the back verandah.

"Keep your heads low and follow quickly," she advised. "They're only bats. Don't be scared."

As she opened the door, swishings and whirrings issued from the black roof above, and something zoomed down upon us, clutching at our hair and whistling between our legs. A hair-raising shriek from Margaret, swinging the lantern and beating the air, gave the room just the right eerie touch as we scurried across clawing at the air to ward off the flapping phantom-like shadows.

Breathlessly we reached the room at last, and pushing the rickety door hastily into place stood shakily against it, laughing shamefacedly. Phew!

"I'm sorry," Margaret apologised. "Jack laughs because I hate coming through there at night with the lantern. It attracts them. I try not to, but I always scream."

I felt like screaming at the thought of going back again.

"Sometimes they don't come down," she said reassuringly.

In all our stay at the homestead, however, never once did we manage to skip through the darkened verandah without bats trying to nest in our hair. And, as if that wasn't enough, the poinsettia bush outside our window produced weird scuffling noises and the sound of snapping twigs and branches all night, and insects perched themselves on the branch nearest the window sill from where they hurled themselves on to my bed. Many mornings I spat disgustedly from my mouth a number of assorted bugs.

We waved Ernie a sad farewell early next morning, wondering if we would ever see him again.

The swimming "hole" could be seen from the verandah at the back of the house, or nearly seen, for it consisted of a slightly wider part of the stream that flowed, sometimes, along the bottom of the overgrown straggly garden. We hacked our way through a tropical belt of high grass to see the glint of dull water through the taller, spearlike heads. There wasn't much water, and what there was, was covered by decaying leaves and twigs, odd pieces of bark drifting like half submerged crocodiles. So we hacked our way back again, without even getting wet.

"It is a bit low at this time of year," Margaret admitted. "In the wet though, about a month's time, it comes right up to the back door."

That didn't help at that moment and the day temperature was 102°. It was too hot to go out, so our days were spent lazing on the verandah reading and writing, or rather attempting to, between dodging away from the long-legged yellow and black hornets, which delighted in zooming blithely in amongst us and causing chaos as books, magazines and seats went flying, and we made a dash for cover.

"They won't hurt you, if you sit still," Margaret would say again and again, but my nerves would snap suddenly as one of the things seemed about to alight in my ear.

Betty, the aborigine cook-cum-everything, dashed out every time there was a scuffle to see if the safely netted-in baby had been awakened.

At the evening meal served by Betty, we were joined by Jack, Bill, the young jackeroo, who was learning how to manage the homestead, and Fred, the storekeeper, who—from Margaret's account—was trying to starve them out! There was a cold war going on between Margaret and him.

When Margaret wanted her weekly stores, she gave the list to the storekeeper, who was supposed to have a few months' stores locked away in his little white shed. He replenished the stores whenever he went into the nearest township, Camooweal, eighty miles away. The storekeeper was not employed by Jack, but by the company who owned the homestead and cattle and who had a scheme whereby, if money spent on provisions and outlay of the homestead could be cut down, his salary rose accordingly on every pound saved. Done in the right way, i.e., saving on the purchase of new fences where the old ones were still effective, was fair enough, but Margaret, ever a mild person, had not exerted her rights from the start, when he had grumbled at the few extra things she had ordered. (She certainly could never have been extravagant). And so things had gone from bad to worse, and by the time Di and I arrived meals consisted of beef, beef, beef—the bull had usually died from sunstroke—in various disguises certainly, but still just beef, with a few potatoes and sometimes a lettuce thrown in. He allowed her one bottle of squash a week, in a climate where one bottle lasted one person one day—if not too thirsty.

But now the feud took on a new angle for it was three to one and neither Diana nor I are particularly mild. The force of our attacks landed at lunch time when he was the only one of the three men to join us, Jack and the jackeroo having ridden off for the day to mend fences, number the cattle, or catch the wild "brumbies." Then Margaret would sit with bated breath as we stoked the ashes of the feud until the mean old thing would scuttle from the table, back to gloat over his horde of stores in the shed. But it worked, and gradually extra things made their appearance, a small tin of fruit, then a larger one, even an extra bottle of squash. Margaret was thrilled.

"I wish you'd stay for a month," she said excitedly. "We might be eating well by the time you left. But, of course, it won't last."

"You're an idiot!" I told her affectionately. "Put your foot down—*make* him give you the stuff; you're far too soft."

But she was Margaret.

"I hate bad feeling," she sighed. "He's practically the only one I see all day from 7 in the morning until 7 at night. I'd rather keep the peace, and go without food."

Meantime Diana's throat had been sore, and was steadily getting worse. Three days after our arrival she gave up trying to push salt beef down it and I woke in the night to hear strangled chokings coming from her bed.

Peering into her gaping jaws with a torch the epiglottis was hidden by swollen masses of yellow and green pus. No wonder she was choking! Braving the bats I fetched hot water and salt, and after gargling loudly in the bathroom, scattering sleeping cockroaches far and wide, Diana seemed slightly better, but she was worried.

"I may have picked up a bug from that native girl in the hospital," she croaked.

I shuddered, remembering the throat and face of bloated skin and poison that had made unrecognisable a young aborigine's face.

"Don't be silly," I assured her. "It's only tonsilitis."

"Well, ask Margaret when the doctor visits Camooweal in the morning."

The telephone system was a decrepit parody of an ordinary one. The call to Camooweal to enquire about the doctor took all the morning, and we were lucky—usually the line had blown down the night before a call was wanted and someone had to ride out and fix it first.

Later in the morning Diana shakily made her way downstairs, feeling a little better but looking like death: she could hardly swallow, though, and there was nothing for her to eat in the house.

"Maybe he'll have a blancmange or something over there," Margaret said tentatively, but she left it to me to storm the mysterious shed and its monster.

But as I made my way cautiously into the gloom, there was no sign of Fred. All round, however, the shelves were stacked with provisions: tins of peas, plums, apples, pineapples, custard, tins of meat, tins of beans, everything one would expect to find in a good store, so I helped myself. My arms full, I made my way gingerly to the door and there he was waiting outside—the monster! We saw each other at the same moment. His eyes bulged and he let out a strangled shriek.

"Di's ill," I exclaimed breathlessly. "She must have something soft. You weren't around so I helped myself!" and I took to my heels with him in hot pursuit.

I reached the house first and, throwing my spoils into a chair, panted: "Quick! he's after me—close the doors—lock the windows."

Margaret looked terrified as pounding footsteps came up the path and he burst in. No one said a word as he took a step forward, then he saw Di. At the sight of her drawn, white face, the accusations that were about to tumble forth ended in a gasp. He wavered—then turned and hurried out.

Ten minutes later, after we had luckily recovered from our aching hysterics, he returned, to thump down a bottle of squash and leave before we could recover from our amazement.

The doctor's fortnightly visit to Camooweal wasn't due for three days, and so there was nothing we could do but wait.

4

Off to Alice Springs

JACK drove Margaret, Di and me into Camooweal in the station Utility, where, at the Bush Hospital, the doctor took one look at Di's throat, sniffed, and immediately diagnosed "Vincents Angina."

"Penicillin for two days," he directed. So we booked a room in the hotel at the top of the one dusty road.

"Give England my love when you get there," Margaret said rather nostalgically as we bade them farewell. "But tell it, too, I wouldn't change this life for that one."

Camooweal consists of a dozen, wooden verandahed houses, a tin church, a small hospital, two pubs and three wooden stores.

Three times a day we went to the hospital for Di's injections. The rest of the day was spent in lazing on rickety seats on the verandah of the hotel, whilst the whole population of high heeled drovers' wringers, stockmen and jackaroos, mostly in from distant cattle stations, plied us regularly with "Aw come on, have a beer."

In the evening a crowd of cowboys took us on to the open-air week-end cinema show, where they proceeded to fall loudly over people as we clambered for our chairs. Everybody there, of course, knew everybody else. It was a family affair. At the front of the roped seats squatted the aborigines, who worked in Camooweal. Every five minutes the film broke down amid good humoured, ribald comments, but no one minded and everyone gossiped loudly until the film began again. Sunday became another Saturday as far as the cowboys were concerned. They drank on rowdily, lining up many bottles for us along the verandah, where we still waited patiently for any likely lift.

In the late afternoon a cloud of dust from the direction of Mount Isa came into view, and presently a much battered car deposited its two dusty passengers in front of the hotel. They were two men. The younger one was fair complexioned with blond hair which hung almost down his back; the older man mopped his red face and boomed loudly: "Phew! let's see if the beer's cold, Snowy!"

His tubby frame bounced up the wooden steps into the hotel. The younger man, after pulling a heavy swag from the back of the car, joined us.

"Good-day," he drawled. "What are you doing sitting out here in the wilds?"

"We're doing what you are, hitching," we laughed.

"Well, come and have a drink with Mac. It's his car," he said amiably. "I met him in Mount Isa. Going to Darwin with him. English, aren't you? So's Mac and I." He winked quickly. "That makes four. Shouldn't wonder if he makes room for you tomorrow. My names John Cadle, commonly known as Snowy." He grimaced. "It's my hair that does it. Come on and meet Mac, the old buzzard. He's quite likely under the bar already."

Mac greeted us loudly over a pile of bottles.

"Course you can come. You're welcome," he boomed. "Come to Darwin with us, but don't expect me to stay on the straight and narrow."

He mopped his streaming chubby face as he eyed us wickedly.

"Can you drive?"

"Well, a little," we promised him.

"Good. May have to," he roared, holding his shaking sides. "Have a beer. We'll go tomorrow, huh—maybe. The beer's good here!"

We awoke early next morning as we didn't want to miss this lift. After two days in Camooweal we felt it really was time to move. We had a hurried shower (the heat was already terrific), and, as soon as we had finished breakfast, with still no sign of either Mac or John, we strolled along the verandah, and had almost reached the end when a booming "Good morning" from behind made us both turn quickly.

Mac stood just outside his door, a beaming smile on his broad face, his hands on his hips.

"Come and have a beer," he called, "or maybe a wee drop of gin!" He laughed again, a merry, infectious laugh that started deep in his stomach and rumbled up to make you laugh with him. We accepted a shandy gratefully, perching ourselves on the verandah where the heat was already bouncing up from the dusty road, although it was only 9.30 a.m. A few moments later John appeared and downed a glass of beer in one gulp.

"You've certainly learned one Aussie habit," Di chaffed him.

"A good one this. You don't seem to be doing so badly

yourselves," he reminded us, pointing to our almost empty glasses.

"How's the old bus?" Mac asked, turning to John, who, we gathered, had been giving it a bit of a clean and general over-haul by way of payment for his lift from Mount Isa.

"Oh! fine. Could do with a day's rest, I think."

We both looked at him, shocked! But Mac chuckled. "Jolly good idea, I think we'll go tomorrow. Anyway it's too hot to travel to-day. How about that, girls? We can drink lovely ice cold beer in the cool, and that's the idea. Go on tomorrow. Let's fill 'em up again."

He disappeared into the room for another bottle.

"How could you?" We both turned on John wrathfully. "You know jolly well tomorrow it'll be just as hot. We thought you wanted to go on as well?"

"Another day in this place watching them all get drunk again and I'll die," Diana moaned dramatically.

"But it's so hot," John tried to clear himself. "What if we run out of water, or the tyre bursts," he ended lamely. "And what about my hair? You said you'd cut it, and you can't do that in the car."

He seemed to think this was the end of the argument. He badly wanted his hair cut: it hadn't been cut properly for the last six months and the back was as long as a girl's bob! From remarks last night I had gathered he had a weakness for really good hair cuts.

"I'll do your hair in ten minutes if you help us make Mac change his mind. Otherwise I won't do it," I delivered my ultimatum.

"You promised you'd do it," he flared.

"Well, you promised us Mac would be leaving this morning. And anyway, I thought he was in a hurry to get to Darwin."

"So he is, but he thinks the beer's good here."

"So do you," we both said together.

"Here we are! Where's your glasses. Whew! this heat." Mac rumbled out from the room, holding a beer bottle in one hand and mopping his streaming face with a huge handkerchief.

"Do you know, I think it'll be hotter tomorrow," John suddenly said. "It might be an idea to get on."

Mac looked shattered, pausing for a moment as he was pouring.

"Eh, what! D'you think so? Well, we'll stay till it's cool again," and, laughing merrily once more, he continued pouring.

The situation was getting desperate. We could see ourselves stuck forever in Camooweal.

"Oh, well, maybe there'll be a lorry or something through later to-day," I told Di resignedly. "That fellow going into Mount Isa yesterday said another one of his vans was on the way out."

She picked up the thread quickly.

"Anyway, thanks for the offer," she smiled at Mac. "We'll just hope for the best."

"You want to go now, to-day, do you? Really!" Mac looked utterly aghast for a moment as though he had only just realized we wanted to go that day.

"Oh!" he glanced from one to the other of us rather help-lessly.

"Would you go with the truck? I suppose it could be hot to-morrow," he muttered.

We drove in with the attack.

"The sooner we leave, the sooner you get to Darwin. Fre-wena's only 200 miles, we'd be there in a few hours. We can take plenty of bottles with us. They say the beer's really cold at Frewena." And so on until Mac's defences were completely down and five minutes later he thought it was a wonderful idea to go on.

"We'll get some petrol, and away."

I cut John's hair hurriedly, taking more off than he actually wanted. And we went to pack our few things.

Mac's car was an old Chevrolet with plenty of room ordinarily within, but what with most of Mac's worldly belongings in the rear seat, our two packs and swag in the boot, and John's pack and swag wherever there was space, all that was left was the front seat and one tiny space in the back, but we managed to scramble in and at last swung across the road to the petrol pump. Mac's steering seemed most peculiar, but we made the pump after a few attempts. He ordered ten gallons, mopping his streaming face and neck and casting every now and then a longing look about at the hotel, while we hurriedly opened a bottle and talked about the coldness of the beer in Frewena.

Then we found a soft tyre or rather the pump man did, and while everyone was humming and haaing I got him to blow it up and that meant he had to check the others! This was too much for Mac.

"Here, let me get in the back. John can drive," he declared. "I'm feeling sleepy. Wake me when we get there!"

He slipped a bottle down at his feet and, pulling out a gin

bottle from his hip pocket, uncorked it, licked his lips and drank.

"Want a drop?" he said genially. "It'll do you good." But we laughingly declined.

Twenty minutes later John put the car in gear and we lurched away.

There was very little traffic in the one dusty main street, just an odd station Utility parked in the blazing sun, a wringer lolling lazily against the wooden verandah of the other hotel, who waved nonchalantly, a few lean dogs cowering in the shady patches, and brightly dressed aborigine women with their shopping bags crossing the street here and there. We settled down, thinking of the next 290 miles to Frewena, when suddenly the car seemed to behave in a peculiar fashion. About two hundred yards had been covered, none too steadily, when a small wooden bridge with a sharp left turn just beyond came into view at the bottom of the incline. John suddenly seemed to be seized with a wild desire to go under the bridge instead of across it. Luckily I managed to grab the wheel at the crucial moment and we just managed to career across to the safety of the other side, the sharp left hand turn not helping very much.

"Phew!" John muttered, pulling up and looking a bit dazed.

"Are you sure you've driven before?" Di asked cautiously. Only then did we learn that they had been having a "party" in the hotel since 4 o'clock that morning.

After a battle of wits we at last stowed John as far away from the wheel as possible, and I took over the steering wheel. Mac didn't seem to mind, and so once again we started off. I had a peculiar feeling in the pit of my stomach. Neither Di nor I had ever embarked on a 300-mile drive before. The little we had done with Ernie seemed negligible compared with this marathon. Suddenly the next 280 miles seemed an awfully long way, and I had a wild impulse to turn the car and get back to the safety of the hotel. By this time, though, I had managed to find top gear, we were travelling at a steady 50 m.p.h., the road was straight and completely empty as far as the eye could see, and the car was going well save for a list to starboard every now and again. Suddenly a wave of heat came up to meet us from the floor of the car, sweat began to trickle slowly down our faces and eventually it dawned on us that this could not be just the heat, for there was quite a cooling breeze while we were moving.

"Mac," I yelled, "something's awfully hot. Do you think there's something alight?"

He heaved himself up from the back.

"She gets a bit hot. Don't worry," he said soothingly. "She's a good old girl, she'll keep going." And he sank once more behind the pile in the back. Di was now beginning to get very uncomfortable as well. The hot air blowing upwards was like a furnace blast.

"There's something wrong," I said definitely, and pulled up. After grovelling on the floor with Di for a few moments, we at last found the cause. The board that usually covered the dynamos had come off with the force of the air under the car, hence the hot dusty air blowing up. We wedged in the board and once more moved off with sighs of relief and a few remarks from John. But we were ill fated that morning for we had travelled about 200 yards when another hot blast sent me nearly into the back seat! I let out a yell which brought Mac hurriedly from beneath the pile.

"Good girl," he muttered as I pulled up. "Time for a drink. How far have we got? Good drivers these girls," he said confidentially to John. "Good, eh? How about a drink?"

Suddenly Diana and I went limp with convulsed laughter and John, thinking the sun had got us (I certainly felt a bit light headed) came to the rescue. Pulling a heavy brief case of Mac's from the back, he pushed the offending board into place and lay the heavy bag across with instructions to keep one foot on it as extra weight.

Mac by this time had managed to extricate a glass from somewhere and the now tepid beer and lemonade shandy went down very well, while the boys shared the rest of the beer bottle. Mac was less trouble asleep anyway, and he seemed quite happy with things as they were. All went well for the next fifty miles. It was now about 11.30. Straight on down the heat-shimmering, dusty road with nothing but a few rather barren trees on the horizon the road stretched away as far as the eye could see, so that the car at sixty miles an hour seemed just a crawling worm in some lost wilderness.

John by now was a bit more awake and we learnt that he had been in Australia for six years.

"I reached Australia with the Merchant Navy, then jumped ship and worked my way around doing almost everything and anything, a store-keeper for a homestead, a barman, a general hand on a cattle station, anything to make money," he told us.

"You've been to Darwin, have you?" Diana asked.

"Yes, and Alice."

Very rarely does anyone give Alice Springs its full name in the North: either "the Alice" or just "Alice."

"Are you ever going home?" I enquired, swinging the wheel madly as the car made another lurch to starboard.

"Oh, maybe! One day when I've made some money. I'm going to Rum Jungle with Mac. He's an engineer, so he'll get a good job, and there are plenty of jobs up there. You can save too: the money's good. £30 a week clear of tax, you know."

"Why didn't you save before then?" Di asked.

"Oh, I did but it soon goes." He grinned sheepishly, looking suddenly very young.

We knew what he meant. Life in the North for a man with very few women around and a climate that makes one long for something cooling was not very conducive to saving, for the average North Australian drinks quite a number of bottles of beer a day and night, and as much as we sometimes hated all the drinking we had seen, even we had to admit that once the temperature reached the 90s the only real thirst quencher was a "schooner" of beer, ice cold of course.

A long way down the road, we could suddenly see the reflection of the sun bouncing off what looked like a small huddle of corrugated shelters and one or two grey tents.

"Civilization!" John shouted, and I pressed my foot hard on the accelerator causing the poor, choking old car to give a sudden leap forward. The engine sounded as though it might give up the ghost at any minute. Mac struggled to life in the back, heaving himself up ponderously to inspect the view ahead.

"A road camp!" he shouted. "Here's a rest for you, girls. Good old bus this! Does well, doesn't she?"

We were prepared to agree quite cheerfully now.

"We'll stop for lunch. Maybe they'll give us a cup of tea," Di said hopefully. Mac snorted in disgust.

"Tea! Tea! What's that? They'll be so glad to see us they'll bring out the beer."

He was absolutely incorrigible, but instead of making you cross, his manner just made you want to laugh with him—not even at him, as at so many when they have had a few schooners. He was the kindliest, jolliest drinker we had ever met.

I drew the car in away from the road close to the huddle of tents. Suddenly a group of men appeared, deeply tanned and in need of shaves, most of them wearing nothing more than a pair of rather grubby looking shorts and a singlet. One came forward with a wide smile on his face as we all unloaded from the car and stretched our limbs.

"Hullo, there!" he called. "I wondered when you would be coming through."

He was looking at Diana and me, and we suddenly remembered one of the young men whose feet we had trodden on in the "picture show" in Camooweal.

"Well, hullo!" we greeted him. "Fancy you being here!" For he looked very different with a few days' growth of beard.

"So glad you stopped. Come on along and have a drink."

We all strolled across to the cookhouse, where a languid game of cards was going on. The men stopped playing to say hullo, and ask where were we from, and where we were going, until with everyone talking at once the babble of voices was suddenly interrupted by a shout of "Beer up" and there was a general rush to get glasses for us both. Mac just stood and almost licked his lips! The cook was then brought in and introduced as a "pommy," and ten minutes later, as we four sat eating huge sandwiches of corned beef and pickles and our favourite cup of tea, he sat and talked. And how glad he was to talk of the England he remembered. He had lived in Australia for the last twenty years and now, lean and tanned, hair iron grey, he sweated over a stove to feed a crowd of hungry men. "But I wouldn't go back home to stay for anything," he informed us. "Why, I'd freeze to death," he said half seriously. "But, mind, I'll go for a visit in a few years."

"What would he want with England?" the others all jested. Then, deadly serious, "This is God's own country." Again and again we were to hear this sentence all along the way. Sometimes we ourselves wondered about the truth of that comment, here in this heat and dust with their water carted from the nearest bore twenty miles away and a trip to town, eighty miles away, once a week, or even less, with very little to do at that except drink and gossip when they did make the trip. There was undoubtedly some strange something about this country.

At three o'clock we decided to make a move as we still had another one hundred and eighty miles to Frewena.

We were on our way again, this time with Diana at the wheel while Mac sank once more behind the luggage into another sleep. I dozed fitfully until we reached Soudan,

As we turned the bend, by the side of the road a huge board announced that we were now leaving the last water bore for another hundred and sixty miles. We had filled our two water bags at the road camp, and they hung beside the radiator at the front.

"Two boys died of thirst along this road a couple of months ago," John told us. "Evidently their motor cycle broke down and, as no cars came, they left the road to look for water, and a

61

car the next day saw the cycle by the road, took the news into town, and a search party from Camooweal found the bodies days later."

"How crazy to leave the road. There's surely an average of one car a day, even along here," I said, thinking of the two we had passed earlier.

"I suppose one can't think straight when one panics," Diana said soberly. "Someone was talking about them the other night at the hotel. They were evidently only kids, about nineteen I think."

"I wonder what we would do if this old bus broke down?" John said half seriously, and we all agreed to remember that there was water in the radiator that could be used as a last resort.

"Anyway, our luck usually holds good," I said, while Diana quickly touched wood.

We sped on and on into the unbroken haze. John seemed a sensible type now he was his normal self. Sixty miles, eighty miles on and we were parched again, dripping with perspiration.

"What would you give to be back in Mount Isa's pool?" Diana asked me.

"Quite a lot," I assured her, "but we'll be in Alice tomorrow or the day after at the latest. We'll have a swim as soon as we get there."

"I hate to say this," John put in very quietly, "but I don't seem to remember a pool in Alice Springs."

We both turned on him in horror and even the car gave another lurch to starboard in sympathy with our dismay.

"Oh! that's terrible! There must be!" Di moaned dramatically. "Surely you're wrong. I always thought they had a pool."

"I've always thought they had," I said. "I always understood Nevile Shute derived his ideas from Alice Springs, and his town had a swimming pool in 'A Town Like Alice'."

"Never mind! Cheer up!" said John. "I seem to remember a water hole some miles out of Alice, where people swim sometimes. You can go out there—that's if it isn't dried up at this time of year," he added as an afterthought.

"Oh well! we'll just have to wait and see," I said. "Something will turn up. Perhaps it'll rain!"

"Knowing how you girls seem to get what you want," John said laughing, "it quite likely will. I only wish I had some of your optimism."

"It's very easy really," I informed him. "You just expect the best and sometimes you get it."

He smiled, but Di knew what I meant, for hadn't we found it all along the way?

Now the scrub was the height of a man, interspersed with a few dead, barren looking gums. One or two flowering gums blazed in flashes as we drove on and on into a never-ending horizon of scrub and haze. A few more stops, a few more empty beer bottles left with the other thousands along the dry road, a moment of panic when Diana couldn't decide which way a lean looking cow was going. Then I took over again, and at six o'clock we reached Frewena eighty miles from Tennant Creek, an old army depot in the throes of being turned into a proper roadhouse, the usual wide verandah style place, high roofed and fairly cool.

There seemed to be one elderly weather-beaten man and a younger woman, evidently the owner's wife, who made us welcome with a shower, cool drinks, tea, and a mixed grill apiece. On enquiring about a room, however, they weren't much help. But the night was beautiful and Di and I decided to sleep in the swag out under the trailing creeper arch. John also decided it would be cheaper and fresher. But Mac found an old bedstead and mattress within.

The low rumble of thunder that we had been hearing intermittently for the last couple of hours seemed to grow louder and, as we spread our bedding and made ready to crawl beneath, the blinding flashes of lightning grew longer and longer before we were plunged once more into an even blacker star-studded night, while a great mass of tumbled cloud became more dense on the horizon.

"I don't like the look of this," I told Di. "It looks as though we may not be able to sleep out after all."

She sat with her arms around her drawn-up knees thoughtfully counting the seconds between lightning and thunderclap. Away in the night the wind was sighing and murmuring, an ominous sound.

"Maybe this will be our first tropical storm," Di said as John appeared from the garden with his sleeping bag, and another jagged fork of lightning lit the earth. The sky, the trees and every dim colour seemed for a moment to be painted with some vivid paint brush.

"I'll see no snakes or marauders harm you," John promised as he set down his bag a little way from us. A match spluttered and flared and the faint aroma of tobacco drifted across.

I lay for half-an-hour dozing uneasily after each clap of

thunder, trying to make up my mind whether it might not be safer to seek shelter inside. Suddenly the moaning wind in the distance grew until the noise was as of some great engine drawing ever nearer, but strangely there was no breeze. Then we were all sitting bolt upright in our sleeping bags. I heard John shout above the noise.

"Better go inside," he instructed as he started gathering his things together, but we sat fascinated, afraid and wondering. Surely this was no ordinary wind? Perhaps it was one of the willy-willys rushing down upon us. Faster the noise approached and still no leaf or bough stirred. It was deathly still. Nearer and nearer the rising wind came, and then suddenly, a hundred yards away to the north by the pale light of the clouded moon, the trees and stunted growth came suddenly to life, swaying and dancing like tormented things, the sand and dust whipped savagely against our skins and whirled off the loose articles of clothing and other treasures. The lightning struck again, followed instantly by a crack as of a cannon and all was dark again. As swiftly as it had come, the belt of wind moaned and howled its way on again into the night, leaving us bewildered and breathless in the stillness. A huge drop of rain fell on my face, then another and another, and all was mad skirmish to get into the shelter of the house. Pack, blankets, clothing, shoes and bags we clutched in a mad jumble and ran. The sky opened up and the rain lashed down, so that we were blinded and dripping by the time we reached the sheltered verandah, thirty yards away, John bringing up the rear and scooping up the odd bits and pieces as they fell from our overloaded arms.

We were all panting and laughing as we beheld each other, our pyjamas sodden and clinging to us, the rain still running in rivulets off noses and down backs.

Twenty minutes later, towelled down and dry, Di and I crept wearily into twin beds while the rain beat a deafening tattoo on the corrugated iron roof and dripped into puddles on the stone floor. John appeared noiselessly at the door, on his face a look of concern.

"Mac and the old boy have been drinking, but I'll be right next door. Shout if you want me," he said, and disappeared as noiselessly as he had come. In the dim light of a hurricane lamp we regarded each other uneasily.

"We'll both pile into one bed. We'll feel safer," I shouted above the rain. "Come over here—this one's wider." So Diana did, and we blew out the light. It was hot and sticky in the room, the rain tattooed on incessantly, and Di suddenly let out

On Magnetic
Island in the
Great Barrier
Reef

On way to Halls Creek, once
a famous goldmining town

Central Australian bush native

Making a boomerang
from a solid log

Goodbye to Alice Springs

SOME MEMORIES OF AUSTRALIA

Aborigine in Nullabor Desert

MORE MEMORIES
OF
AUSTRALIA

Jack cooks our lunch, Julia Creek, Queensland

Blow hole near Hobart, Tasmania

a yell. "Quick! The packs are on the floor, they'll get wet."

We stepped out into a couple of inches of water and, lighting a match, saw the two small mats almost floating out of the door. Grabbing the packs before they, too, followed, we pushed them high on top of the one and only piece of furniture—a worm-eaten wardrobe of some forgotten age, and hurriedly clambered back into bed. As my hand reached out to turn out the lamp it was arrested in mid-air. For a long space of time—it seemed—my breath caught in my throat, the hair on the back of my neck went stiff, and I heard Di give a gasp, for, staring through the wire mosquito netting at the top half of the door, was a face that in the half light of the hurricane lamp was shadowed and puckered wildly, parts gleaming with sweat, eyes bright and brittle with grotesque pools of shadow beneath. In the tattoo of the rain we had heard no one approaching and not until the bodiless spectre wavered and spoke did we realize it was Mac.

"Came to see if you were all right," he shouted above the rain.

Recovering somewhat, we answered him rather shortly, and told him to get to bed. Poor old Mac! He had evidently come along to see that we were quite comfortable and dry, and succeeded in giving us the fright of our lives!

Next morning all signs of the storm had passed away, except for great pools of water everywhere. We breakfasted early. Mac had the car tank refilled from the one and only pump, and in fine fettle we all piled in and away we went once more down the straight and narrow road.

Sixteen miles from Tennant Creek the bitumen broke away sharply to the left from the main road and on through to Darwin. Here the roads met from Tennant Creek, Camooweal and Darwin, and here, in the triangle of the roads, over stunted grass and spinifex, we came suddenly upon the recently erected memorial to John Flynn, the triangle of stonework holding high the gleaming white crosses, one on each side, dazzling our eyes.

I wondered suddenly how John Flynn would feel if he could once again travel through the outback and see such a monument in his memory. And I pictured him riding on his camel, dreaming all the while of doctors and medicine for the people on the homesteads hundreds of miles out in the bush, visiting them only once a year at the most, with his Bible and such little knowledge of medicine as he possessed. Out of his dreams he built the flying doctor service, and many hundreds of Australians have had cause to thank him in this so-called modern age of the outback.

Mac stopped the car, and we stood for a few minutes in the shade thrown from the monument, reading the inscription on the metal plaque. Mac, his usual booming voice for once subdued, said suddenly, sincerely:

"Must have been a great guy, this one. Sometimes wonder why we're all so different."

"Some have to make up for the others," John said half seriously, but Mac's face beamed suddenly:

"That's it!" he said, taking no offence. "I guess that's it."

We reached Tennant Creek at 11.30 a.m., dusty, hot and thirsty.

5

Aborigine Artist

FOR two hours we enquired along the dusty main road about a possible lift and drew a blank.

"Hey, girls, see what I see?" John said as we came into view of the hotel.

"Yippee, a truck!" Diana gave a shout.

A young man sat under the shade of the hotel, glass beside him, haversack at his feet.

"Good day," we all greeted him. "You going to Alice Springs?"

"Yes."

"When are you leaving? Where's the driver? Do you think there'd be room for us?"

He answered our questions unperturbed, saying at last, "The driver's inside." We found him, introduced ourselves and explained where we wanted to go.

"Shure thing, girls," he said easily. "I'm Stan Laywood. We're leaving in an hour. There's thirty eight feet of empty trailer out there. You can take a stroll occasionally. Don't keep me waiting," he called as we rushed out to join Mac and John and grab a hasty meal at the café-cum-milk bar opposite.

The hour fled on wings. A couple of photographs were taken, adieux exchanged with promises to meet in Darwin, our haversacks were swung up to us; and then we were off. Waving good-bye through a cloud of dust and heat from the back of the trailer we jolted out of Tennant Creek en route for Alice Springs, the centre of Australia.

With shorts, large hats and a good breeze created by the moving truck, things both looked and felt good. (Mike, the other hitch-hiker, had chosen the stuffy cab).

A little later we investigated the trailer. There was a monster spare tyre, a huge pile of rope, a large empty petrol drum and a swag well done up in a heavy tarpaulin on which we perched for another few miles, until Stan signalled us to unroll it and use it if we wished. This may sound easy enough, but a swaying and speeding trailer with no sides is never the best place to start humping things around. A sudden lurch to left or right often sent us perilously close to the edge. Eventually we managed to unfold the thing to find, as well as blankets and a pillow, a single spring mattress. Laying this lengthwise across the trailer, with rucksacks behind to stop too much breeze, it made a resting place fit for a queen. Diana promptly fell asleep, leaving me to contemplate the barren landscape and blue sky.

Diana woke as we reached Wauchope at 4.30, exclaiming at our increasing tan. "Crikey, we'll look like a couple of 'abos' soon," she laughed.

We drew in beside the one and only building, a small hotel of unknown vintage, and made a rush for the waterbag hanging in the shade at the side of the verandah. A few large mugs of cool water just takes the edge off a thirst, when one is ready for a few iced lemonades or shandies, and only then does one begin to "think straight" again.

In the cool interior of the hotel the owner greeted us warmly and so did two young men sitting on the high, dark wooden bar. "Hullo, where did you blow in from?" they asked, eyeing us appraisingly and immediately ordering two drinks. By the time Stan and Mike joined us (on arrival they had discovered a puncture to mend in one of the huge inner double tyres) we had learnt that they were bore-drillers.

"Sometimes it takes twelve months to discover fresh water," Alf, the fair one, explained. "Salt, salt and more salt, then, when you begin to wonder what the real stuff tastes like, wham, you get a break."

"Other years it's not so bad—it makes up and over for the bad ones," Ted, the other stranger, hastened to say, seeing our dismayed faces at the thought of years of work pounding the earth miles from anywhere, in the ever blazing sun.

"Does it take long to drill a bore?" I asked.

"Months and months if you have to go through rock," the second driller said, "but then others are easy. It all depends."

We left at last in the late evening, to drive on a few miles before stopping for the night, Mike crawling into his sleeping bag, Stan into his swag and Diana and I into ours, all spaced out on top of the empty trailer as a precaution against snakes.

Half way to Alice Springs we came to the Devil's Marbles. Strewn over the flat, dry earth for about two miles were gigantic, perfectly round rocks, mostly two or three times the height of a man, some balancing precariously on top of narrow ledges and others reminiscent of giant golf balls perched on minute tees.

They looked as though one breath of wind could send them rolling over. But although we pushed with all our might at a more precariously balanced one, it would not budge.

Some stones lay open as though split asunder by one clean stroke of a giant knife. Later we learnt this happened in the winter when heavy frosts made them crack and split wide open. There have been many theories why they are there but no one really knows.

Nine miles from Alice Springs, the road suddenly began to twist and wind through fairly well vegetated country, getting greener and greener.

After the hundreds of miles of flat desert country we had come through, the town, with its small bungalow houses set in squares of green lawns and fruit trees in abundance, was like no other township we had yet seen.

"It's more like a suburban town, isn't it?" Diana said in surprise as we viewed it from the back of the open trailer.

At last round the corner from the main street we drew up opposite a large modern luxury hotel, still in the process of being built. This hotel, we learnt later, had been built practically single handed by Stan's brother-in-law, whose mother owned it and who immediately offered us permanent jobs.

We were running low on funds but, having planned to stay only a few days and wanting to see as much of the place as we could, we declined the offer. The hotel was, of course, far more luxurious than we dared afford, and Diana gave me a strangled look when I asked Stan, out of curiosity, how much it cost a night.

Mrs. May's, on the outskirts of the town, although still more costly than we had expected at 16s. 6d. each, bed and breakfast, had to do. Mrs. May, a charming-middle-aged woman with a young daughter, soon had us drinking large cups of tea whilst the water heated outside in the laundry for a much needed bath.

Next day the Alice Springs thermometer soared to 103°. Even the local inhabitants suffered, and Diana and I, coming from the more humid coast to the dry heat, could do no more than sit languidly on the two easiest chairs, supplied regularly with iced coffee and lemonade by Mrs. May, and catch up on belated sewing jobs. Even this was an effort.

Next day the thermometer went back to the normal temperature for that time of the year—95°. But still the dry heat was making us feel limp and lifeless. I couldn't seem to think straight any more. It was Diana who had the idea of seeing if we could talk our way into the not quite finished Alice Pool.

The three men working by the pool behind the barricaded front entrance would not let us in, saying it would be officially opened in a few days, but at that moment the boss, who was also the owner, appeared and, hearing we had come all the way from England to have a swim in the pool, he not only let us swim but showed me completely round the filtering system which he had planned and built himself.

With renewed energy we climbed Anzac Hill at the southern end of the town, where the gleaming marble War Memorial to the town's War Dead, stands high above the town.

Again the suburban atmosphere struck me, except for the hundred yard stretch of sandy, dried-up river bed which stretched north to south and reminded us that here was Australia, with all its dryness.

A few days after we left The Alice news came that a mighty torrent of water had swept through the town, causing much damage, but the wide, dried-up river bed had looked harmless enough to us.

Next morning at breakfast we asked Mrs. May if the old coloured gentleman we had seen yesterday riding in a taxi and smoking an enormous cigar could have been Albert Namatjira, the famous aboriginal artist.

"That's him!" Mrs. May laughed. "He never walks now, always rides in that taxi."

"Is it possible to see him working, or view any of his paintings?" I asked.

"Well, if you go to the Hermannsburg Mission where he lives with the Arunta tribe, you could see the natives painting. They do have tours out there, I know."

That there was more than one aborigine artist was a surprise.

"But why not see Mr. Battarbee? Perhaps he can help you. He's Albert's agent and I know he has many paintings at his house."

Most people have heard of Albert Namatjira, the first aboriginal artist to become world-famous, but few people know how this came about. We didn't, but we wanted to. So, following instructions from Mrs. May, we made our way to the bank of the wide river bed and plodded across slowly in the blazing sun, our feet sinking into the loose, fine sand, making speed an impossibility. It seemed strange to see the great gum trees growing from the bed of the Creek, affording here and there a little shade as we plodded on, swotting at the swarms of flies that clung to the back of our blouses in black patches. Reaching the opposite bank on the west side of Alice Springs at last, we found the luxurious, pastel-coloured house of Rex Battarbee.

"Mia Mai," Diana read out the name on the gate. "I bet that's aboriginal."

The door was opened by a youngish woman with greying hair who listened to our explanations and invited us in, saying in a very English voice, "It's very nice to know you are both interested. Rex will be back from town shortly, so have a look round."

On the walls of the lounge and sun room were hung many pictures which I, like Diana, immediately took to be Albert Namatjira's work, but Mrs. Battarbee laughed softly.

"All those who have never seen Rex's work immediately credit it to Albert," she said. "You see, it was from my husband's paintings that Albert took his style. Rex came to Alice Springs twenty years ago," she explained, "and while he was painting at Hermannsburg, fifty miles from Alice, a young aborigine became intensely interested in Rex's paintings and offered to be his donkey boy, carrying all his equipment and helping generally all free of charge, if Rex would only teach him to paint.

"Rex was glad of the help. Albert was a bright young man, with quite a gift for colours then, although up to meeting Rex he had only been using the colours that he could mix from the natural stone and flowers around Hermannsburg—that only the natives know how to mix."

At that moment Rex Battarbee returned, mopping the perspiration from his brow as he entered the room, a tall rangy man with a quick, nervous manner. After being introduced, we followed him through to another room, where he began opening drawers in the low cabinet and placed a pile of smallish water colours on the table.

"These colours!" I said in amazement. "Do you really see these startlingly beautiful colours as you paint, or is it only in a few places that you can see them? For quite honestly the country we have come over in the last few days—to me—has just a yellowish, fawnish look, a bit blue at times, but nothing like the colours produced in both Albert's and your work."

Diana nodded in agreement.

"I understand you have not yet been to Hermannsburg, At that moment Rex Battarbee returned, mopping the paintings. That's good."

Rex Battarbee paused to straighten his long back from the cabinet.

"Many have been, and say exactly the same as you have just done. Let me explain. I may go to one spot many times and see

71

no colour, nothing at all. But one day, maybe I arrive as the sun is setting or in the right position for where I am standing—and suddenly the whole scene is charged with colour, reflecting and bouncing from one rock to another, from one gorge to another until the whole scenery before me is a suffusion of half tones—pinks, yellows, blues and majestic purples."

We nodded in silence and he went on excitedly, "I know this will only last, say, half an hour at the most that day, so I must paint and return a little later each day to the same place, day after day, to capture the colours." He paused. "So you see you must *look* for this beauty, otherwise you will never see it—and leave disappointed—like so many."

A few weeks later, one early sunrise, we saw such a riot of colour as Rex Battarbee had explained, and wondered at the glory of it. But just now we watched as he and his wife held aloft for our inspection, the many beautiful (some primitive) paintings of the seven other aboriginal artists—for those of Albert Namatjira's that were for sale, were, as we had thought, much too expensive for us.

Eventually Diana and I decided on two each, both as usual finding our tastes coinciding, and choosing one each of a new artist with very much the same style as Namatjira's, the other completely different, in the flowing curves characteristic of the artist's tribal symbols, with a boldness and clarity that was intensely striking, although at first sight I had been slightly repelled. Later, this painting became my favourite.

We left Mrs. May and her family with instructions to look us up if ever they came to England. Mr. May drove us the little way into town to the hotel, and, as we waved good-bye, said:

"Don't forget to come back if something goes wrong and you can't get away."

"We'll sleep in the creek for the night," Di told him, "if they shouldn't be going till the morning." And she meant it. Our cash for Alice Springs had run out.

"This may be our last chance to get a meal for four days though," Di said. "How about a slap-up meal? We shouldn't need more than a few pounds for living on the way to Darwin."

The thought of food was no sooner formed than we dumped our haversacks and were round the corner to our little café. We could get a three-course meal and coffee for 6s. 6d. with a sweet of apple pie and custard, or the like. We had been there three times before but not till this evening did we meet the proprietor. As we sat waiting, a small chubby boy of about seven ran out from the kitchen in hot pursuit of a tiny kitten. We helped him retrieve it and he very proudly let us hold it, telling us shyly that his name was Tommy. He chatted for a while and then suddenly said brightly: "Where are you going?"

We told him Darwin, and he said very proudly:

"I came all the way from England," and to a smiling woman who appeared from the kitchen, "Didn't I, Mummy?"

So we met Mrs. Black who joined us as we ate, telling us how the doctors had all agreed that Tommy, the little boy, would not live very long in England with asthma.

"Take him to the sun, they told us," she said. "So we emigrated. It was a wrench, I can tell you. I loved England and the thought of never going back sometimes made me sick. But we came, and here we've been ever since—for five years.

"Alice Springs is a wonderful place. He's grown bonny and healthy. No one would recognise him for the weakly, little white thing he was."

We told her of our trip, where we had been and where we hoped to go, saying we intended to return to England next year.

"Well, take my story home," she said, very sincerely. "And if any child is sick, get the parents to bring him out to Australia. It's a grand place, and there's so much space—you've seen enough to know anyway," she laughed. "I don't need to tell you!"

As we made to leave she presented us with a huge bag of oranges and apples. "They'll keep you going on the trip," she said, scooping up into her arms the brown child, who had just run in from the pavement. We left them smiling, and waving on the step—a happy woman and a healthy child.

We waited an anxious twenty minutes at the hotel, sitting on our haversacks and eventually the young man, whom we had met the evening before (with the driver who had said he would take us), turned up. Our sighs of relief didn't last long, however, for the unloading hadn't been finished from the train (known as the ghan) that brought up supplies from Adelaide, and anyway his friend wouldn't be able to take us after all as he had just realized he wasn't insured for passengers. A fortnight before, Mervyn told us, there had been an accident with two girl hitch-hikers involved. Luckily they hadn't been hurt much but the company had forbidden any more lifts by the drivers.

Seeing our crestfallen faces he kindly suggested: "Look! I work for Ted Styles in Darwin, so I do as I want. It's just possible that I may be loaded by tomorrow. It wouldn't be till about 7 o'clock but I'll take you if I'm ready."

It was a lot of ifs and buts, but what could we do but thank him very much?

"It looks like the creek for us to-night, after all," I told Di laughingly and Mervyn chuckled, saying: "You really are doing it the right way. That's good. The road to Darwin is long, hot and dusty. It'll be rough and you'll need all your sense of humour."

Just then Stan Laywood appeared from the hotel and, on hearing our news, suddenly said, "I'm a fool. I should have thought of it before. I've an old caravan at the back of the hotel. You can use that for to-night. Ly's been looking for you, wants to see you both. There's a crowd of American Met. weather officers here and he wants you both to entertain them."

The evening turned out to be one of rather happy discussion: this time England versus the U.S. versus Australia, ending by the crowd of us eating cold chicken and sandwiches at 2.30 a.m. on the roof top and Ly promising: "If you ever want to come back and work here, hairdressing, Eunice, I'll rent you the shop in the hotel."

At 6.30 p.m. the next day we waved farewells to the boys on the balcony of the Alice Springs Hotel, heaved our haversacks on to our shoulders and turned our backs on "The Alice" to head out of town and find Mervyn Farrell's truck.

The truck and trailer, a huge 38-footer, was ready to leave, piled high with a jeep, two cars, and on close inspection, we discovered a couple of refrigerators, a new piano straight from England, many, many cases of beer, sacks of potatoes and various other things in the way of provisions for Darwin. After Di and I had decided it was not light enough for the owner of the orange trees just behind the fence to see us, and I had relieved him of a few oranges, Mervyn appeared. (Incidentally, the oranges grown in Alice Springs are some of the sweetest in the world). He apologised for keeping us waiting, inspected the truck thoroughly, backed the huge, clumsy machine and trailer expertly through a very narrow lane on to the main road, and we roared away into the night.

It was cool in the cab, the night sky black with a million sparkling stars, the powerful lights picking out the long, straight, narrow road as we swallowed up the miles. After a while we ate sandwiches, oranges and chocolate that Mervyn produced, and, taking it in turns to help keep him awake, one talked while the other slept. By eleven o'clock Diana was snoring and it was as much as I could do to keep my eyes open, the flashing road beneath the lights mesmerizing me into a sleepy numbness. Then, a long way away, a speck of light appeared on the horizon.

"That's a couple of the boys returning from Darwin," Merv said. "I wonder who?"

Fifteen minutes or so later, we drew up abreast of each other and Merv left the cab to stretch himself, talk and have a cigarette. The low murmur of voices was joined by the approaching roar of another mighty engine and a third truck came to a standstill behind us.

After a while Merv clambered back into the cab and waited while the truck behind nosed past and the tail light grew dim as he drew away in the distance.

"He seems in a hurry," I remarked, glad of something to think of to keep me awake.

"That's the 'perishables' truck. They have to get to Darwin before the stuff aboard starts to rot," Merv drawled. "They left Alice at 8 o'clock and should be in Darwin on Monday in time for the shops to open with the stuff for sale."

"Monday, but it's Saturday—nearly Sunday now," I said rather surprised. "Can they go faster than the usual 38 m.p.h. average of these trucks?"

"They shouldn't," Merv laughed, "but they do! There are two drivers. They only stop to eat. Otherwise they drive solidly day and night. It's the provisions truck that's usually smashed up, if any. They try to break the time record and sometimes they get very tired towards the end and off the road they go. The last two girl hitch-hikers were on the provisions truck. That was a mighty smash up—but luckily they were all all right. Anyway, that's why they aren't allowed to take anyone now."

"Why does your boss let you take people?" I asked. "He must have a lot of faith in you."

Merv glanced round in the dim light of the cab, his young face rather solemn. "I guess he has." It was more than just a statement.

Twice I dozed and woke, dozed again and was awakened by an unfamiliar rattling and jolting. Stunted tree branches lashed the side windows and closed in all around, but with great dexterity on Merv's part we at last lumbered our way back on to the smooth bitumen again.

"What happened?" said Di, awake now.

"We took a walk," Merv laughed. "Don't worry. I often go to

sleep: only for a few seconds, mind, but that's when we do a little detour."

Half an hour later it happened again. It was 2 a.m. and I was beginning to feel I would be violently sick if I couldn't just relax into a dead sleep.

"O.K., we sleep," Merv said, bringing the huge truck to a standstill. We pulled down our swags, lay down and I remembered no more. I awoke stiff and cramped.

"My back will never be straight again," I told Di.

"We've got company," Di said. "Another driver turned up in the night. Merv and he are checking the trucks."

Tired as we felt, the heat of the sun was already too great to lie around in, although my watch showed it to be only 7.45 a.m.

"It looks as though we'll have to do without a wash for a while until the next bore. Let's find out where it is."

We staggered to our feet and the two men appeared from beneath the truck as we approached.

"My word! Some people can sleep," Merv laughed. "Meet Billie Meecham."

We shook hands with a young faced man with laughing eyes, wearing the newest looking Stetson I had seen for months.

Wauchope was another half-hour's drive and Mr. and Mrs. Vernon made us all welcome. We showered and ate a huge breakfast.

"Better get the girls to Darwin soon," George Vernon said to Merv. "Otherwise the Wet will see they get no further. Drinks all round! Have a good time—maybe we'll see you again," and our two trucks roared on, leaving their trails of dust rising slowly in the still, hot air, this time one of us in each truck as company for Merv and Billie.

At about one o'clock we roared again through the sleepy main street of Tennant Creek, out past the Flynn Memorial, and with their noses towards Darwin, seven hundred miles away, the trucks lumbered steadily on.

"One of the really good things the Yanks did was this road," Merv said. "Without the war, I guess this would still have been a baked up track."

As it was, the narrow line of dark bitumen stretched away unendingly through the sandy, stunted and uncivilized looking landscape.

At this time of day the horizon was a heat-hazed shimmer, the inside of the cab would have been impossible without the slight breeze we created as we travelled. Dust lay on bare arms and legs, and where the sweat had trickled, little lines of white skin appeared. Even my sunglasses didn't quite keep out the glare of the sun. We drove almost straight into it.

"You have a sleep," I told Mervyn.

He hadn't had much sleep in the last two days.

He wouldn't let me take over completely on account of the complicated double gears, so we compromised, I steering while he kept one foot ready for any declutching. It was monotonous—mile after mile of flat straight road, the flatness of the road calling for a gear change about once in two hours. The very boredom of this sort of driving lulls one to sleep. And sleep Merv did, as soon as he realized I could steer straight enough to keep somewhere on the road. His head lolled back and he snored rhythmically with the engine. Occasionally I remembered to glance in the side mirror to see that Billie and Diana were still following. Once their truck veered crazily across the road behind and I chuckled sleepily. Diana was "driving."

Later a nerve-racking whoop brought me to with a start from a semi-conscious state. From a group of ghost gum trees a little off the road, some way ahead, two almost naked brown bodies came shrieking and running towards the trucks, one brandishing a long spear in one hand and what looked very like a shield in the other. For a moment my mind went blank. I couldn't recollect where I was. All I could think of was native head hunters and poisonous darts. The startling spectacle charging towards us made my hair stand on end.

My hands froze to the wheel! I forgot I was in a nice safe truck with Mervyn beside me, as the gleaming bodies, the spear flashing higher in the air, leapt and bounded towards the lumbering truck with terrifying howls. Suddenly I found my voice and, shaking Mervyn wildly, I shouted and pointed in the direction of the aborigines. A sleepy Mervyn sprang to life and, pressing his foot hard on the accelerator, at the same time hanging half out of the open window, he shouted and gesticulated, as we pulled away slowly from the two figures. Then he lowered himself back on to the seat, laughing. "Give you a fright, did they?" he drawled.

I mopped my face.

"What on earth did they want? I thought the aborigines were civilized these days."

"Oh! they only wanted cigarettes and beer. They must have come from the Alice Springs' reserve on a day's hunting I guess. Get them always trying to stop the trucks and ask for cigarettes. Once you stop, you never get away," Merv explained. "Boy!

they talk, all their troubles in pidgin English. On the reserves and hunting, of course, they wear their native things. That's why they had the spear. They didn't mean to give you a fright!"

As Merv took over the driving once more, I wondered how Diana had reacted and I settled back to have an uncomfortable nap.

I woke for the sixth time with another crick in the back of my neck as we approached Renner Springs.

Renner Springs consists of a store and a number of outhouses on the lonely road, literally a hundred miles from anywhere. The owner and his wife, who turned out to be English, came out to greet us as we pulled in. They had been waiting for their stores and beer which was a day late. Inside the store the usual opening of bottles commenced until we had all slaked our tremendous thirsts. Then, while the boys unloaded some of the stores, Diana and I made our way quickly to one of the outhouses for an exhilarating cold shower.

Once more refreshed, we were glad to tackle the usual two eggs balancing on huge steaks that Mrs. Emrick had prepared for us.

Then, because the house was still very hot from the day's sun, we ambled out under the star-studded, night sky. Sitting on the mudguard of Merv's truck or on the warm earth, we talked of far-off England for Mr. and Mrs. Emrick, who, as usual, wanted the latest news, although quite content with their lonely yet very full life. For as Mr. Emrick said: "We meet more people passing through each week here than we would ever meet in England living in the centre of a town. Here folks are friendly, they have time to talk. At home everyone has so many neighbours and odd people living almost in their lap, that they aren't really interested in 'people' any more. The outback teaches one to like the human race as it is. With over-population that feeling for people is somehow lost!"

"It's the same thing," Di said, "when we meet one car after driving for a whole day perhaps. We both stop and have a talk or at least shout and wave like maniacs who haven't seen a human being for years. There's a feeling, a bond, between every one here, brought about, I suppose, as you say, by a scarcity of people."

We got Billie talking of his life as a buckrider (he had been the champion for three years).

"Two days before I shoulda gone to the States to ride," he said ruefully, "I broke a leg! Still I guess I made quite a packet as it was. I wouldn't change this life now. Next year I'll buy another truck and hire a driver. Then I can buy as many hats as I want!"

We laughed. Billie had a passion for hats, which he wore at such a cocky angle. As soon as one got a particle of grease on it, and this happened frequently—the boys were always changing tyres or fiddling with the great engines—it would be kicked blithely over the nearest gum tree and replaced by another from the back of his truck, where he seemed to keep a store!

I shall never forget the peace of that evening. As we sat on, talking and laughing drowsily in the warm night air. Mervyn softly played a mouth-organ he had bought in the store. The black velvet sky was pierced by a million twinkling stars. The warm soft breeze that caressed our faces was like an answered prayer after the broiling heat of the day. There was a feeling that time stood still, no rush, no hurry, a tranquillity and peace that not even the weird notes Diana started producing later from the mouth-organ could shatter! We sat on in a kind of void of time: there was no future and no past, just complete contentment of the present.

But these times don't last. So, at about 10.30, the boys decided to drive as far as possible before camping down for the night. Adios said, the two trucks roared away again, with four very sleepy people aboard. Trying hard to keep awake, we kept going for another three hours before stopping, and at last collapsed on to our swags, practically falling from the cabs straight into a dead sleep.

The heat of the sun woke us at 6.30 and, after a quick wash at the water bore, we were off again with promise of a good breakfast at Elliot, fifty miles on. "Another store, owned by a German," Merv told me.

I had only time to notice a handful of wooden houses as we reached Elliot, then a tanned figure, looking like a Greek god, in shirt and shorts, came running from the "café" towards the slowing trucks.

"Now what's wrong?" Merv said urgently. "Joe Skinner! He should be nearly to Darwin with the provisions."

"It's about time you turned up, where the hell have you been?"

The newcomer's handsome face looked cross and worried, and the word bloody cropped up even more than usual.

"The bloody provisions trucks broke down yesterday afternoon. I got a lift back a hundred miles last night, expecting to meet you all the time. I thought you'd had some trouble too. We'll have to drive like hell to get the stuff to Darwin even on your truck. It must be bloody well stinking now!"

Then, before I knew what had happened, Diana and he were crushed into the cab with Merv and I: we had waved good-bye to Billie and his truck and, without even a cup of tea, were roaring off again, first stop Mataranka, a hundred and fifty miles away.

Merv drove his engine flat out, and as they talked we gathered how serious it was. All the stuff on the provision truck was perishable food, which was why it was driven practically straight through, so as to arrive in Darwin still fairly fresh, even after two days' heat blazing down on it. Already a day had been wasted.

"I thought they'd have a spare part in Mataranka. So we limped it in and wasted hours hunting. Then, as I knew you were coming along next, I thought I'd come and hurry you up. Now I see you had other troubles," he said, turning his attention to Diana and me for the first time.

"No trouble," said our gallant Merv. "Meet Eunice and Diana." Which was rather ludicrous as we had been practically sitting on each other's laps for the last fifteen minutes!

The cab held three people fairly comfortably, but four in this heat was sticky, to say the least of it.

There was only one thing to do, and that, to keep going. Mervyn's engine could do no more than thirty eight miles an hour, so, after reckoning we would reach Mataranka at five o'clock that evening without any stops, no more could be done till we arrived there—and we all suddenly felt hungry.

Luckily, Diana remembered a couple of tins of beans in a pack, and, after a perilous journey over the open back of the truck, Joe found them, opened them cunningly with a blunt penknife and, with the help of an odd fork and spoon, retrieved from the depths of a front compartment, we consumed the lot shakily, dropping dripping beans left and right as we swayed and roared on in the ever growing heat, taking an occasional drink from the water bag, which Merv slung to the side windows so that we need not stop when anyone needed a drink.

Mataranka is another small outcrop of wooden verandahed houses in line with the road. It boasts one large hotel, however, for Mataranka is known for its mineral springs.

Merv swung the huge trailer into the gravelway of a small café and we came to a standstill beside the "invalid" provision truck. A man in shorts and the usual shirt—with the sleeves

Deep-sea fishing brings its rewards.   Near the Monte Bello islands

On Green Island, off Cairns in Queensland

Crossing the border from India to Pakistan

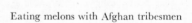
The walls of Babylon

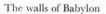
Eating melons with Afghan tribesmen

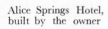
Alice Springs Hotel, built by the owner

ripped out—came hurrying from the café. This was Syd, another of the "boys." He had evidently been trying to do some fixing on the broken trailer and I don't think I had ever seen any one quite so covered in grease and dust.

As the three men stood discussing what was to be done, an elderly woman, her cheeks pink with rouge and wearing a once elaborate but now faded and battered garden hat, came hurrying from one of the bungalows. As she approached, she threw her hands in the air dramatically and screeched:

"Ah! it has come at last, my piano!" and as she patted and touched the bits of piano that were visible, she muttered and crooned to herself over it.

"I've waited so long," she sighed. "Now I can play, play—as I used to long, long ago."

She seemed a little mad to me, but the disappointment that spread unbelievably over her face when Merv explained that it was not for her was almost terrible to see, and made us realize again how much of a life line the trailers are to these lonely people. For the railway line ends before Mataranka, and the trailers are the only completely through transport from Alice Springs to Darwin. So, many things, small and large, are brought by them from far-away places, on the last lap of their journey, and the boys who drive on this life line are known and respected by all the folk in the townships along the 1000-mile road.

By the time Diana and I had washed under an open tap behind the café and drank our fill of tea, the boys had coupled the two trailers with a huge length of twisted wire, the thickness of a man's wrist, and off we went again—but at a snail's pace now, with the double load to pull for Merv's poor hot engine.

It was 6.30 when we set off for Katherine, ninety miles away, where it was hoped the spare part would be found. Travelling at never more than twenty miles an hour we crawled on, over humps and detours in the road, making the gears crash jarringly at the unaccustomed extra work, over occasional snakes that wriggled and twisted across the road in the piercing headlights, or lay curled and sleeping on the hot road; keeping a constant watch for kangaroos, who, as usual, attracted by the lights, came leaping almost on to our laps into the cab. The boys didn't like hitting them if they could help it.

Merv, Diana and I had slept for about four hours out of twenty four, and Joe and Syd in the limping trailer behind had not had much more. When at last we reached Katherine at

11 p.m., I felt my eyes must be popping from my head in the effort to keep them open.

Drawing into the gravelway, opposite the first hotel, we made a rush for food and drink, only to find the place shuttered up for the night. Everywhere was closed, even the small café at the end of the township.

"You'd better both try and have a sleep," Merv told us back at the trailer.

"If we can't find a spare, we'll have to fix the provisions trailer to my engine, leave my stuff and all go on to Darwin as quickly as possible."

But before following the other searching two, ever thoughtful Merv heaved his swag down from the trailer (ours had disappeared under the other packages) and quickly laid it out by the side of a wall fairly near the truck. This we gratefully sank on to while he hurried away.

But we had reckoned without the Katherine mosquitoes that breed so thickly in the swampy parts of the Katherine River! They buzzed in a cloud above us, their stings painfully piercing our thin clothing, even through the thin narrow sheets which we hastily pulled completely over us although this made breathing almost an impossibility in the hot, airless night. We slept for half an hour and then sat up simultaneously to count the huge, egg-like bumps that were mounting rapidly all over us. Diana seemed to have fared the worst. Swatting, and sinking even further under the sheet, we tried vainly to sleep again, tossing and turning in an attempt to escape the venomous jabs until, with a sharp roll on Diana's side, the sheet ripped—with a sound like a rifle shot—clean down the centre!

"Crikey! Poor Merv!" Diana said, now fully awake.

"It must have been rotten," I said. Exasperated and furious from lack of sleep and mosquitoes, I wasn't particularly caring what Merv would think.

"This is hopeless!" Diana said, still swatting and waving her arms vigorously to ward off attacks, then in desperation, "Let's try the cab of the trailer."

Leaving the swag, we staggered wearily across to the trailer and climbed in, quickly shutting the doors and winding up the windows.

By the light in the cab, I was able to see Diana's left eye, (or rather not see it, for the swellings that were rapidly rising round it) before we dozed off again. I let out a piercing shriek a moment later as another thrust from a sly insect's fang pierced my arm.

By this time we were both fighting mad. Grabbing anything that lay near, we flung open both doors, fanning and swatting in desperation to clear out any lurking insect, then, with a pre-arranged shout, we slammed both doors violently together and sank back exhausted, to listen with frayed nerves and a sickening weariness for another faint buzz.

After this had happened more times than I could count with the betraying buzz still persistent, we grew hysterical. Then, utterly spent and beaten, we dozed fitfully between bites.

Never was I more glad to see the dawn break in a golden glow for, with the coming of light, the attackers vanished. The boys appeared and inspected Diana's bites with dismay.

No spare part had been unearthed anywhere so they set about changing over the trailers, which Merv informed us would take a good four hours. So we dived into the nearest shower which we found at the back of the hotel and hoped the proprietor wouldn't mind! It was quite a modern affair after the taps and bores we had grown accustomed to. Refreshed but ravenous, we set off down the main street to eat a huge breakfast in a neat little café.

Back at the trucks we found there was nothing we could do to help in the complicated job of unscrewing the bowels of the trucks, and Joe suggested that Merv take us, in the nearest handy vehicle, the mile to the Katherine River where we could have a swim.

Grabbing our costumes from our packs while Merv borrowed a nearby empty station wagon, we were soon deposited by the clear, sleepily flowing river and left, with a sudden thought of Merv's that "he didn't think the crocs came down that far!" After seeing a few local inhabitants luxuriating in the water, we quickly followed suit, until a large green under-water weed, shimmering and floating in my direction, made my heart sink like lead, as the seed of the thought of crocodiles already planted in my mind sprang to life—and I sprang for the bank!

Deciding a sleep might do me more good, I didn't need the rustle of the shady green leaves and the languid, peaceful strokes of Di ruffling the water to lull me off.

Later we both wakened from a dead sleep, to find an odd character offering us an armful of food and cigarettes, saying he had seen us earlier and thought we might be hungry.

He then went on to inform us casually that he would like us to stay on in Katherine where he would set us up in our own businesses! That he was a South American (which was quite unusual even for cosmopolitan Australia), and that he liked us both so much we could take it in turns to be his "girl friend!"

Diana told him she would think it over, for he insisted on giving us his address and the food. We thanked him warmly, but sleepily, for his offer, and ate the food—as there was no sign of Merv or the other boys who had promised to bring food. Both promised him again we would think it over and were fast asleep once more before he had disappeared down the road. Three nights' short measure of sleep was catching up with us.

Late in the day while we were again floating languidly down stream the roar of Merv's truck announced their arrival.

Syd's greasy figure had been clean by comparison with the three filthy, bedraggled bodies who entered the glade, their arms full of beer bottles and sandwiches, eyes red and bloodshot from dust and lack of sleep.

"You must be starving," Merv said apologetically. "It took longer than we'd reckoned but it's fixed now." And we could see up on the high road the stacked-up provisions trailer that was now coupled to Merv's engine. Joe's engine and Merv's trailer were left in Katherine to be retrieved on a later journey.

Soon the clear water was developing into a dirty muddy colour as the three of them stood in the river, and scrubbed madly at the dust and grease. The cool water soon revived them. The original idea was to get going as soon as they were reasonably clean, eating the sandwiches en route. However, Syd had already had quite a fill of beer, judging by his merry state, and was quite content to laze a bit in the green coolness. The idea was catching!

"Aw! I guess a couple a hours later now won't rot the stuff any more than it's already rotten!" Joe said, handing out a bottle of beer each, while Merv chuckled and hastily unwrapped the sandwiches. Syd took the rest of the bottles and laid them deep in the water to keep cool.

"Boy! What a trip! It's turning out a bit of everything. Never had one like this before. You girls are leading us astray," Merv said with his eyes on Diana.

Much later, when the moon had painted the river and glade with silver shafts and frogs croaked hoarsely along the bank, Merv put away his mouth organ and Joe rather reluctantly, announced that, if we didn't go now, the shops in Darwin were really going to be furious in the morning!

A much needed Land Rover for Darwin from Merv's trailer had been added precariously behind the provisions, and with three in the cab of the trailer, two were to sit in state in the Land Rover's two empty front seats. Merv wanted to drive first.

"Can't trust Syd in his state—with this load," I heard him say quickly to Joe.

"Sure thing," Joe affirmed. "Eunice and I'll take the back. Syd can go with you and Di in the front."

The swaying Land Rover balancing, as it was, on the edge of the trailer was not the place I would have chosen to spend the next few hours, but listening to Joe's soft, drawling voice talking of Darwin I soon forgot to worry.

"What makes people, girls especially, want to know what's in the next place all the time?" he asked. "Why not be content where you are. I am. Of course I might have wanted to travel if I'd been born in foggy England," he chaffed, good humouredly, though without the usual sharp sarcasm. We had grown accustomed to remarks like this however. I don't think he heard any of the answer for his head dropped to my shoulder and he slept.

Ninety miles on, at Adelaide River, we all stretched our limbs as a great drum of kerosene and crates of beer were unloaded. It was 12.30, the night cool and clear—but inside the dim store flies and mosquitoes buzzed in a swarm below the kerosene light, as we all sat round the huge, scrubbed, wooden table and thirstily drank more iced beer.

With Syd still in the cab, Joe drove as we set off again while Merv climbed up on to the provisions for a sleep, Syd still in front; they were afraid he might fall off the top, and Diana joined me in the Land Rover. The moon was brighter than ever and suddenly the scenery changed from the stunted dryness to a jungle-like thickness of trees. The road began to twist and turn, uphill and steeply down again, through the maze of thick vegetation on either side. Night birds called and strange sounds came from the black trees and thick undergrowth as we lumbered on.

Two hours later we came to a clearing in the jungle where the lights gleamed from the verandah of a small, wooden building set back on the fringe of black trees. Joe's dim figure appeared beneath us.

"We've a hundred and fifty miles still to Darwin, so we'll have some food here," he said, helping us as we jumped down on to the dark road.

It no longer seemed strange that two women and a man were still up and ready to serve steak or chops at 3 o'clock in the morning. But steak needs to be very tender at that hour, and unluckily those steaks were the toughest we had ever tackled. More adieux, and we were on the last lap to Darwin.

6

Ruined Romance

AT 7.30 a.m. with bleary, tired eyes we beheld the first flat, bungalow type houses of Darwin, balancing daintily on their high wooden stilts set in clearings of the still thickly vegetated jungleland. Everything looked vividly green and a short deluge of warm rain was soon steaming up from road, roofs and jungle.

Earlier, Merv had asked: "Where you gonna stay, girls?" And grown silent at our: "Wherever we can."

Now suddenly he turned, his usually quiet face bright with ideas.

"You know I work for Ted Styles," he said. "He has a bungalow here where all his drivers can stay a night or two before going back to Alice. Well, Ted'll be away for a coupla nights. He won't mind. Why don't you take over his spare room till he comes back; you wouldn't have to pay anything, and if you want to, you can cook a coupla meals for the boys. They've forgotten what food that's not out of a bottle tastes like!"

He laughed. "So have I."

The idea was heaven sent and, seeing our brighter faces, Merv swung the trailer in the direction of Rapid Creek.

"It's seven miles out of Darwin, but Joe and I have a Ford Customline. You can use it to get into town anytime."

Soon the trailer was ploughing along a mud track and, through the banana and palm trees, we could spy the glinting blue sea.

The mile track ended abruptly in a shady clearing set on the elbow of land between the open sea and a crocodile river complete with mangrove swamps.

The clearing was a jumble of empty drums, old trailers, pieces of engines, huge old tyres and mounds of empty beer bottles, and, in a small "garden" of banana trees and cactus, a house of corrugated iron and wood which made us exclaim: "Gosh! Where's Robinson Crusoe?"

The boys laughed and followed us into the large, stone floored kitchen, sweeping up armfuls of empty beer bottles that lay on the chairs, the radiogram, the refrigerator and even sticking out of the huge, old, iron range in one corner. These they promptly aimed through the back door to join a huge pile under the mangrove trees.

Merv said apologetically, "Sorry about the mess. We'll clear up when we get back. Here's your room. You'd better both have a sleep," he said, pulling aside a curtain.

So, first slaking their thirst from the store of beer in the fridge, the only supply it held, they roared away into Darwin, with our instructions to bring back some provisions.

The thought of having to waken to this mess was impossible. We therefore got to work with local equipment, hosing the place through, sweeping out first the geckos and small hermit crabs asleep under almost every piece of furniture, while frogs croaked in alarm and leapt from rafter to rafter in amazement.

Outside in the palm trees, great clouds of brilliantly feathered gallahs (a mixture of parrot and pigeon) swept upwards into the tropical sky. My shriek brought Di quickly to the back garden and together we surveyed the thrashing body of a crocodile looking as though any minute the flimsy wire cage around it would give way.

"Strange pets they have," Di muttered in awe.

"How are we going to sleep with that thing around?" I asked, very worried.

But, once beneath the huge mosquito net in Ted Styles' room, having at last showered the sweat and grime thoroughly off and crushing on the net any mosquitoes who had also found their way within, we slept to the wonderful murmur of the sea—a hundred yards away.

We woke at 3 p.m., sticky with perspiration, to the ear-splitting sound of a broom handle being dragged across the corrugated iron wall. A record blared out full throttle and Merv appearing in the doorway with two huge cups of tea.

The boys had returned—with a few others!

Even the semi-cold shower did little to revive us, but the boys seemed not to need sleep, contentedly sitting with feet up before half-a-dozen open beer bottles and tins of tobacco, and talking and laughing above the noise coming from the radiogram.

We prepared a hasty meal for all, hurriedly ate it before the mosquitoes could eat us first, and then, with Joe and Merv, started out to look at Darwin in their Customline.

A large proportion of the shops had Chinese names above the fronts and inside one could buy groceries as well as all sorts of other wierd things from the same counter.

D.C.A. (Department of Civil Aviation) seemed to cover a good part of the town while Government offices were very much in evidence.

As we circled the glinting harbour I was amazed to see so much evidence of ruins, the aftermath of wartime Darwin. Out in the bay many buoys marked the treacherous sunken hulls that lurked beneath the serene blue water.

And, overlooking the bay, the large modern "Hotel Darwin" gave an air of tropical luxury.

By the time Di and I had purchased a few badly needed things, I felt limp again, and Di's forehead was covered with beads of sweat from the terrific humidity. We were glad to get back to our "jungle house" and share another shower with a couple of bright green frogs.

Later in the evening, as Di sat fanning herself and I was leisurely sorting out the latest records, Merv said casually to Joe:

"Let's give them a party at Ludd Millers!"

Joe caught my eye as he looked up from the pile of notes he had been sorting.

"O.K.—It'll complete their education!"

Soon the car, with four of us aboard, was heading away through the trees. "Ludd Millers," a smallish open air restaurant, nestled in a cloud of bougainvillia on the top of a rocky arm of land, jutting high above the sea. The faint strains of music greeted us as we entered the softly illuminated garden, passed the shadows beneath the trees, passed the dimly lit concrete dance floor and, seated above the whispering moonlit sea on either side, we sat lazily sipping glasses of Pimms, listening to the soft murmur of voices that drifted across on the scented air.

"This is the life for me," I whispered contentedly, the glorious tropical night beginning to cast its spell.

The spell continued as I swayed in Joe's powerful arms across the dance floor—two solitary figures beneath the star filled sky, and, from wherever we looked, a golden pathway shimmered across the dark water from the low, full moon.

"I think I should like to live in Darwin," I said to Joe. "It could be a real paradise with someone you loved."

He laughed rather cynically, but clasped me tighter and, his body close to mine, he said: "Why don't you stay? I need a wife in Darwin."

I wanted to believe him, but something in the way he paused before saying "Darwin," or maybe the strange secretive part of him that appeared frequently made me know instinctively he didn't fully mean what he said. And as we walked back to the table he had once more assumed the casual, withdrawn manner that nothing seemed to pierce.

"Eunice thinks this is good," he told Di and Merv, who sat, hands touching, awaiting our return.

"Let's show them a real moonlit beach."

So again we jolted along a sandy mud track through the darkened palm trees and, leaving the car on a bluff above the beach, scrambled and slid down to the soft, warm sand. Taking off our shoes we strolled, two isolated couples, hand in hand, along the water's edge. Each tiny wave shimmered with light and the wide lonely sand, at first bright and golden with the full moon-light, stretched on into the night, the shadowed cliffs seemed to enfold the beauty all around and the soft warm breeze was gentle.

"Now I know what moon magic is!" I laughed softly.

As the other two figures wandered on, the murmur of their voices floating back to us, Joe drew me into the shadow of the cliffs.

"We'll wait. I'm tired of walking."

Then his mouth was hard and hot and his hands a part of the wonder of the night and although I tried to reason with him, I began to realize the reason for the lack of morals we had been amazed at in even this little while in a hot tropical climate.

But, as one thing leads on, so another balances it! A soft scraping on the sand made me look up—straight into one eye of an enormous crab a foot away who regarded us steadily and ready, it seemed, to move in at any minute. Then I saw another and then another till I realised they were all around—huge 9-inch crabs, their pincers waving for an attack. Horrified, I aimed a sandal at the nearest, which sent them all scuttling sideways as fast as lightning across the sand. Joe laughed at my horror, and when they returned enquiringly a few moments later, he streaked after one which he brought back to show me, to prove how harmless it was. But it didn't look very harmless to me with its pincers still waving menacingly and its baleful eyes peering out from beneath the large shell. The beauty of the still night was shattered.

Ruined Romance

Two shadowy figures returned, and Diana said:

"We've been chasing crabs, huge things, 2 feet long!" And we laughed together, but Merv and Joe were quiet. They hadn't realized how crabs could react on those who weren't used to them!

Home at last! The tiny hermit crabs—balancing their shell homes precariously on their backs as they staggered drunkenly in their dozens across the floor to totter blindly over the high step on to the ground outside—were stranger than pink elephants.

"Thank heaven they can't climb," Di said as we climbed sleepily into bed.

It must have been about 2 a.m. when Di, giving me a shake, said softly:

"A trailer's just arrived. I think Ted Styles has returned—I hope he doesn't want his bed!"

We lay listening to the murmur of voices floating through the wide open windows. Merv's dim figure appeared in the doorway.

"Ted's back. I told him there were two girls in his bed," he chuckled, "but he says it's O.K."

I must have slept again, for suddenly I woke as the light snapped on. I could see through the fine mosquito netting a thickset man of about forty, who stood in the doorway surveying us and holding aloft in each hand a dish.

"Well, I'm damned!" he exclaimed. "Merv's found a coupla white ones. Last two he brought back were black!"

Merv's shy face appeared round the curtain:

"Don't believe a word," he drawled. "I told you what he was like—the greatest practical joker."

Di and I sat up in the high bed, finally disentangled ourselves from the netting and were introduced.

"Thought you might be hungry," Ted went on. "Have some supper." And, placing a huge dish of crab ! ! and a plate of thin brown buttered bread before us, sat on the foot of the bed and talked. It was a crazy hour to eat crab and have a discussion, but this was a crazy place. We devoured the lot, and, thanking him for his bed, settled back once more.

"Anytime! Stay as long as you like," Ted grinned. "Now I'm tired. So move over."

Seeing our faces they hooted with laughter.

"Oh, well," Ted said. "Never mind." And still laughing they left us to dream uneasily of crabs and practical jokes.

Once, when all the boys were away, two acquaintances

promised to take us crocodile shooting, and we sped along in David's sleek Riley to the coastal ship in the harbour to join Roger, the first mate, on the deck, who was already watching the small dinghy being lowered to the calm blue water below.

It was late afternoon, and away to the North-West the distant rumble of thunder echoed ominously from a piled-up mass of clouds on the horizon.

"Do you think we ought to go?" Di asked nervously, watching the jagged distant streaks of lightning.

"Oh, yes! It's only one of those short tropical storms. It's way out to sea, won't come this way," Roger said positively.

So down the rope ladder we scrambled into the swaying dinghy, where David was already checking bottles of beer, steaks, a must with any Australian day-out, a couple of guns, oars and a powerful torch, in the tiny prow. We drifted for ten minutes before the boys eventually started the popping engine and then headed away from the ship, while a sailor called over the rail laughingly:

"If you get stuck, give us a signal with the torch—we'll come and rescue you!"

For an hour and a half we chugged merrily across the harbour, not particularly worried that the engine failed twice again. David explained the plan:

"We'll get to the other side of the harbour, have a barbecue first, as it's no good going too early, and then we'll follow one of the creeks inla nd to where the crocs breed."

"Fair enough," Di said as we lightheartedly watched the jagged lightning.

But later I remarked:

"I somehow think that this is no small storm brewing." The thunder and lightning were gaining strength and the swell of the sea increased, and as at last we drew the dinghy up on to the sandy beach a slight rain had begun to fall and darkness was closing in.

We climbed the bank armed with the steaks, beer and a small rug which Diana had thoughtfully brought, and quickly sought shelter beneath the trees beyond the beach. Scattering to collect wood by the light of the moon which was still visible in the clear half of the sky, we soon had a good fire blazing away, while we each held a sizzling steak on a stick over the dancing heat.

"Boy! that was real good," Di exclaimed in a good Australian tone as she wiped the grease from her fingers on a nearby tuft of grass and, edging away from Roger's encircling arm, exclaimed:

"Oh no,—you men! This is supposed to be a crocodile hunt, not a woman hunt—remember!"

Leaping to her feet, Diana led the reluctant boys back to the dinghy after we had all scuffed the fire well out.

The outboard, for once, started immediately and Roger turned the nose of the dinghy towards the distant low line of coast, saying:

"This current's very strong but we'll get there in about an hour, and as long as those bloody clouds don't keep piling up the moonlight will make it as bright as daylight. Watch out, crocs, here we come!"

"If we do manage to get a crocodile there's really not much space for it in the boat, is there?" I asked diffidently. Suddenly the idea of even a dead croc at our feet was a bit disconcerting.

"We'll think about that later," David said, and even as he spoke, the engine stopped again—and, with the suddenness of the tropics, the storm burst.

Roger's prolific abuse was drowned by a mighty clap of thunder and a jagged fork of lightning illuminated the now dark, swelling ocean all around. Heavy drops of rain began to fall.

"Better start rowing," Roger shouted above the wind and, as David and he tried valiantly to start the engine, Di and I began to row clumsily in the choppy sea.

"We'll have to get back to the ship," David shouted at length. "It's going to be bad. Try and keep her nose towards those lights!"

All thoughts of crocodile hunting were now gone. Half an hour later the distant dim lights from across the harbour seemed further away than ever, and the boys were still crouched in the stern of the dinghy struggling to get a spark from the outboard.

Then, as Roger took a turn at an oar, he shouted, his voice harsh: "We're caught in the current that flows out between the heads. Rowing's useless in this direction. We'd better try and get back where we came from—pull for all you're worth. That bloody engine must have water in it," he exploded. "If we get carried out past the heads into the Timor—we've had it!"

For another two hours we rowed in turns and tried to keep warm but, lights and land far away on either side grew dimmer

93

and the flashing light of a lighthouse on the head grew steadily nearer.

"How long can we last if we do drift out into the Timor?" David shouted to Roger anxiously.

"We've enough water for a coupla days," Roger shouted back.

"But surely they'll know on the ship. They'll come after us, won't they?" I asked.

I wasn't going to be panicked if I could help it.

"No one's ever been found before, and several boats have been lost like this!"

Roger seemed to have given way to panic. I was crossly surprised, though pretty scared myself by now as the tiny dinghy seemed to be slipping back all the time, despite our furious rowing against the wind and current. Once David had the idea to try and send a message back to the ship by the powerful torch.

"They must be wondering where we are," he shouted to Roger. "You said we'd be back by midnight."

But, although he signalled repeatedly for the next half hour, there were no answering flashes. It was doubtful whether anyone aboard so far away could see our signal in the rolling swell of the sea.

Diana unfailingly kept to her tradition in an emergency and fell fast asleep in the prow. Even the boys were pretty exhausted after pulling for four hours against the current. It was getting on for 2 a.m.

At last Roger, breathless and leaning heavily on his oar, shouted:

"There's only one way left. Near the West head the current slackens. We'll drift to there and, if luck's on our side, by rowing like mad again we might make the last few yards of beach—it's a chance in a hundred—but it's the only way."

Di woke, and for another half an hour we were swept shivering and fearful in the rocking dinghy towards the mouth of the harbour. Then, with about a hundred yards to go to the open sea, the current suddenly slackened.

"Now!" Roger shouted wildly to David. "Row for your life!" And as the shore grew gradually nearer the cross current began to drag the small craft swiftly towards it. In the dim light—for the moon still shone ghostlike from behind the stormy clouds— the shore looked dark and rocky and beneath we could see the white swirl of angry waves dimly as we tried vainly to peer into the darkness for a place to land.

"God! I'd forgotten the rocks!" Roger sounded grim. "They'll tear the bottom of this thing to pieces. I'll have to get as near as I can, then, when I drop the anchor and shout, get out and swim for it."

Suddenly I was terrified.

"Get out and swim!" It wasn't the swollen sea I was scared of but the thought of lurking sharks and Portuguese men-of-war that thrived below in the black, unfriendly water. But there was no time to pause and think too long as the dark shore loomed ahead and we seemed to be racing towards it.

"Now!" Roger shrieked as he threw out the heavy anchor, and with a prayer on my lips we three slipped over the side of the boat.

The water rose to our chests, and suddenly, as I was about to lunge forward and swim, my foot touched the bottom.

"It's O.K! We're on the bottom!" I shouted hysterically to Di. "It's O.K! We can walk!"

And then, at last, we floundered and stumbled over the rocks to David's outstretched helping hand. Roger, still standing in the swaying boat gauged the distance, and threw the folded blanket with a shout towards David's dim figure. Luckily he caught it and we all made our exhausted way up the beach. My teeth were chattering and I was shivering violently as Diana exclaimed:

"It's the first time I've been cold for months. Doesn't it feel awful?"

While we huddled in the blanket, Roger went in search of shelter, returning twenty minutes later.

"Can't see a sign of anything," he said. "We'll have to wait till morning and explore."

So we all lay down in line for warmth under the thin blanket in soaking shorts and shirts, and dozed fitfully till morning, while the mosquitoes and sandflies feasted on us, adding to our misery.

In the morning we were amazed at our luck for we had landed on the only flat piece of beach along the rocky shore. Less than fifty yards from it the arm of land ended abruptly and we should have been swept straight out into the open sea.

Later the launch sent out to look for us (Roger's ship was sailing at noon) picked up four very scraggly, sorry looking, swollen and bitten figures, and towed the small dinghy in its wake back to the ship.

We left Roger to an irate Captain who was waiting to give him a dressing down.

"Anyway, we're damned lucky to get back. We nearly missed that beach!" was his parting speech as we politely thanked him for the trip and returned to our jungle home.

The only thing we caught that night were severe chills!

7

" . . . Nor a drop to drink"

BITTEN to death by mosquitoes and sandflies and finding no one was travelling West, for the Wet had set in and the rivers were flooded and impassable, we booked seats and flew out of Darwin at 6.30 one morning, just as the sun was rising.

Diana hated goodbyes.

"It'll be a change for us to be waving goodbye to somebody one day," she said sadly. "The one who goes on never feels the parting so much."

Merv's lonely figure was soon obliterated by the blazing reflection of the sun.

Penny and Sally were on the 'plane. We had met them in Darwin on the point of giving up their third attempt at getting through the North West. When they learnt we were going on, naturally they couldn't turn back: it was against human nature. Penny, a New Zealander, had chummed up with Sally on her arrival in New Zealand from England. Together they had hitched round Penny's native Island and then set out for Australia, where they had been now for three years, working their way round. Twice they had tried to get through the North West, but the Wet had beaten them each time and they had returned South.

The same would have happened this time, but our idea of getting to Wyndham quickly and from there shooting South again with the Wet behind us had fired their enthusiasm.

Nosing our way through a ceiling of pink cotton wool, we could occasionally see the green jungle-land beneath. Crocodile rivers with their network of creeks glinted in the sunlight, worming their way to the rim of blue ocean. The scene was dense, torrid and achingly lonely. Then came the North Kimberley Mountains reminiscent of the Arizona Mountains with their long, flat topped plateaux.

Three hours later we circled a flat plain below, where a single air drogue flapped vaguely at the end of the runway. We could

97

see only one building, its corrugated roof glinting below. This was Wyndham, but where was the town?

"It's been swept away in a flood," I said pessimistically, and the three of them upbraided me laughingly.

The town sat along one road. Ten houses and three "pubs," six miles from the airport, behind a high, flat topped mountain range of salt flats at the foot of the Gulf.

Once landed, we watched the plane, now a silver speck, disappear, with mixed feelings. Those aboard would reach Perth to-night. If the rivers to the South were already flooded we would be there many months later. Then, in the Airport Utility, we were sped into Wyndham, dumped by the one hotel, and left.

No town would have been there at all but for the Wyndham Meat Works which employs the small population. The cattle are driven many months overland across the Southern Nor' West by the lean, hardy cowboys, to be "canned" and shipped to the South and then abroad. There are quite a few meat works round the coast of Australia. If the cattle were driven too far South, they would arrive lean and bony, so to save the loss of poundage on too long a journey, these meat works have been set up. They were quiet at this time of year but still throwing off a meat works' own peculiar odour.

A hotel was always the first place to enquire if a truck might be going South. So we all trooped into the bar. At the sight of four invaders, two old timers nearly fell off their stools and, whether we liked it or not, it was drinks on the house and keep-'em-coming. Wyndham hadn't seen so many girls all at once in its whole history. After our early rise the heat and the excitement that comes with a new place, we felt pretty tired.

"Can we have a nap on your back lawn?" Di asked the bar-keeper.

The greenness through the doorway looked wonderfully inviting.

"Well!" he paused. "Dunno what the old girl would say."

"Never mind her," broke in one of the old timers. "There's a row of camp beds on the verandah, go and have a doss there. I'll make it right with the old girl."

He led the way as the four of us straggled after him up the creaking, wooden steps. On the shaded side of the cool verandah the camp beds stood in line, and staking our claims, the four of us were soon fast asleep, twice to be woken to have iced drinks pushed into our sleepy hands while odd characters, disbelieving the news, came to peer round the corner of the verandah at the strange newcomers. But we hadn't reckoned on the "old girl." We woke to blink, through a barrage of accusation and blasphemy, at a large, ruddy faced woman who was addressing us. We gathered she was very put out: surprise still registered on her face as she shouted at the top of her voice. The gist of the tirade was, "no one had told her we were there. This was her hotel and no nice girls slept on men's beds, even at 3 o'clock in the afternoon, *even* on an open verandah. We were never to darken her verandah again."

As we couldn't get a word in edgeways, we all slunk down the creaking steps again, just in time to grab the old timer back from where he was fast disappearing through a door.

"You said you'd make it right!" I accused. He grinned sheepishly.

"I looked for her, but she'd gone."

As she seemed to have gone again, we bought him a shandy, and asked him to direct us to an address of a friend's brother-in-law that Penny had.

Peggy and Ron Hankin, when we found their stilted bungalow at the end of a salt flat, were soon laughing at our account of the day, with their four young children jumping all over them.

"We couldn't ask for a loan of her back lawn for the night after that," Penny finished, "so we came to see if you had one!"

They hadn't, and if they had, they wouldn't have dreamed of our using it. Ron laughed, "You wouldn't stay long outside at night with these salt flat mosquitoes! We'll be glad to have you stay."

So our sleeping equipment was laid in line in the airy kitchen that night, with all sorts of extra padding beneath. After all the strange places we had grown used to, it was wonderful to be in a real home again, with children's laughter and love; this was a real family.

Ron's job as electrician at the Meat Works kept them far out in these lonely wilds, away from civilisation, but they were complete in their small family circle.

Next night the increasing Wet let up long enough for the weekly open-air film show. After ten minutes the film stopped for re-winding and Chu-Chun-Chow, who was, so it said, the Chinese tailor down the road, showed, in slides the perfect Savile Row suits he made, just the thing for the outback's heat! Another ten minutes and he was back to show the de luxe American ultra modern heavy Desotos, that were just the thing for a day in the country. We couldn't have been more in the country. Anything that was completely useless to Wyndham from a pink elephant to a white mink stole he proudly showed on slides at regular intervals. We sat amidst smothered howls of laughter enjoying the unexpected "side" show much more than "The Thousand Eyes of Night" unwinding at intervals, and at least a thousand years old.

Ron came back from "town" two days later to tell us that Les Wilde's carrier had come up from Hall's Creek, and we were welcome to go back with him.

"He said his will be the last truck going South West until after the Wet's through," Ron said laughing. "You sure cut it fine, you gals!"

Hall's Creek, a ghost of its former gold boom days, was two hundred miles due South. On the trip we learnt a few more things about the rugged Australian truck drivers. When a now flooded river crossed our path, we drove upstream until we found a fairly shallow width and then drove straight in. The water rose above the wheels and the four of us, glad enough for its coolness, waded up to our waists to give a helping push as the spluttering engine objected loudly, but we always made the opposite bank. Three rivers were thus negotiated.

In the middle of the third we had a great surprise.

In the flooded Bow River, as we swam and waded across, a hundred miles from anywhere, who should appear swimming from the opposite bank, but Jack.

"Howdee," he laughed, wading up.

We yipped our amazement, introduced Sally and Penny and very ludicrously shook hands in mid-stream!

His "lift" was on the far bank trying to get across. They had been there for two days for the "Aborigine Welfare Officers" small van wasn't built up as high as our truck.

The three of us were glad to see each other again. The first time since Mount Isa. We had known we would catch up with him one day.

On the further bank we sizzled a panful of eggs and sat talking.

"I got to Wyndham by ship from Darwin," Jack said. "There I worked a few days unloading the ship, then went on to Halls Creek, but there's no work at all there. No one was going on to Derby, my money was running out, so this lift back to Wyndham seemed a good idea!"

"Why not come on with us?" Di asked. We had missed his merry humour. "Les won't mind another passenger."

But, though Les insisted he was welcome, Jack decided he must return to Wyndham.

"If I come back with you and there's still no truck through

we'd all be stuck," he said. "At least the ships call at Wyndham for unloading. I've a friend there who'll put me up till I get some cash."

So eventually we left him and the inspector by the bank, hoping the river level would drop before their stores disappeared and, as we drove away, he called, "See you in Broome one day."

At the last river only a trickle of the flood to come was seeping down the bed of the river. This is an easy one, I thought, but ten yards from the opposite bank the back wheels spun madly in the slimy mud, and there we stuck. Les dug the mud away uncomplainingly—and quite ineffectively. With no trace of irritation in the scorching heat he toiled on. Later he began breaking off the boughs of nearby gum trees.

"I'll lay these under the wheels, then they'll get a grip—and off we go," he explained. But not until we had stripped the nearest ghost gums almost bare to lay a ten-yard strip of branches and leaves over the thick, slimy mud to the opposite side, did we eventually roar up its bank.

The road all the way was a mere dust track, which often, after a cloudburst, faded away altogether. Les seemed to travel by the sun—and intuition.

Our meals were barbecued in the shade of great bottle trees, and our water-bags replenished from the swollen rivers. But one thing worried me about this trip and I sank into a black gloom. I seemed to have lost my sense of humour! As the four others laughed and joked—I just sank lower and lower into a deep depression.

Two evenings later we arrived in Hall's Creek. Bob Wainwright's 38-foot trailer was leaving for Derby next day on its last trip that season.

"The more the merrier," Bob grinned attractively, when we had unearthed him. "But don't forget your water-bags—well filled!"

So we knew we had beaten the Wet!

As we set off next day, all sitting beneath our battered sun-hats on the back of the trailer, Di exclaimed:

"Eunice! What on earth are those red bumps on the back of your leg? They look like boils!"

I was aching all over so I hadn't noticed any one place. The track was the worst so far, corrugated, dry and jolting. Penny let out a gasp.

"They're not boils," she exclaimed. "They're tropical ulcers.

You've been scratching sand-fly bites, and they've turned septic." Who could help it, I wondered.

"I had two in Darwin last year," she grimaced. "Poor old thing, no wonder you've been feeling low."

Although I could soon feel the gnawing gatherings drawing and pulling horribly all down my leg, and I ached in every bone, the next part of the trip took on a new colour. I hadn't lost my sense of humour—it was temporarily missing.

The track was so corrugated that Bob drove at about five miles an hour and even at this pace we jumped and bounced all over the back, our flesh shook on our bones, our teeth chattered like four high powered machine guns. A large 20-gallon drum of petrol bounced from its corner every two hundred yards. Small wonder that our light frames (in comparison) were soon complaining. When we couldn't take any more we jumped off and walked alongside, but we were soon dripping with sweat and back on again, even if it meant having no flesh or teeth on arrival in Derby. Many times the track not only faded out but ended altogether. Bob seemed to be another traveller by the sun, for no matter how many hours we cleaved our way through stunted bracken around bottle trees, gums and creepers—no mean task with a 38-foot trailer—we somehow managed to land back on a track in the end.

Di was worried about my ulcers which were now bulging with yellow heads.

"They've got to come up a lot more than that," Sally told us cheerfully. "I did Penny's when she had them!"

So at each barbecue, Diana applied primitive fomentations, boiling the water in a clean used milk tin, then Magsulph plasters from our depleted first aid kit. There were five ulcers on the inside of my leg and one monster on the knee.

But we all had reason to remember that trip!

Now came the part which we always referred to after as the "horror stretch." Diana, Sally and Penny sat jolting in the blazing sun for five hours on the open trailer behind, with their large, but very battered, sun-hats. They preferred it to the stuffy cabin which was hotter, but in a different way—it wasn't the heat of the direct sun rays. I sat with Bob in the cab, to save my leg getting banged. Occasionally, when our tongues began to feel like strips of leather, we all stopped for a few mouthfuls of water. Bob had a bag. The girls had one each, and Di and I had a large one between us. The water was pooled, however.

Nookamba Homestead was to be the first stop, where we were to pick up a load of empty petrol drums. By the time we arrived, at 4 p.m., the girls had taken more sun, dry heat and jolting than ever before while Bob and I were sitting in a permanent puddle in the front seat. As we pulled in at last beside a small, thatched shelter of branches and leaves, and a huge pile of heat shimmering drums, the first thing I noticed as I clambered from the cab was Penny's rear portion heaving over a nearby fencing.

Di and Sally, their faces glowing green beneath their tan, staggered without a word into the shelter. Bob was busily wiring up the drums and seemed not to have noticed anything. The cluster of whitewashed out-buildings of Nookamba Homestead glinted in the sun about a mile further on.

So, grabbing a water bag from under the trailer, I rushed to Penny and practically dragged her after the other two. Inside, she swallowed a mouthful of water, smiled feebly, and passed out! Di and Sally looked as though they might join her any minute. Going mad with the water, I sprayed the contents of the bag over the three of them. It was too far to walk on to the station, although I reckoned a shower would have helped matters a lot, if we could have got there. As it was, we'd have to carry Penny, so instead, we all collapsed exhausted amid the beetles on the floor. It was that sleep that saved them, and when we woke later, picking beetles out of our hair, they were white but recovered somewhat.

Meanwhile Bob, with the help of an aborigine, had stacked the glistening drums into a large pyramid on the trailer: how he had worked in the heat has always been a matter of incredulous wonder. If any Australian truck driver deserved a medal, it was he. A whoop indicated he was ready to move on. We straggled from the shelter with thoughts of a cool homestead in mind, and took up our positions on the hot, smooth drums, where Bob had left a small space after the first layer.

"We'll drive on to the station and fill the water bags," he said cheerfully, as he dived into the cab. I read the others' thoughts and said quickly:

"He didn't only mean fill the bags. Naturally he'll stop, we're bound to be invited for a meal, or at least a shower." For hadn't we always received wonderful hospitality from these lonely outback stations?

But for once, when we most needed it, luck seemed against us. As we filled the water bags from a solitary tap at the side of an outhouse, Bob explained:

"They're all away here in Derby, one of the kiddies is sick. That's why I didn't bring you along before loading up."

So there was nothing to do but fill our dusty, sweating bodies with tepid water until it practically spurted from our ears, then, for good measure, we took off our sandals and in turn let the water gush over the outside of us as well. With our clothes wringing wet reasonable coolness returned, and we piled back on to the hot drums, relieved at the promise of a stop in half an hour to eat and boil the billy.

We left the last but one water bore between Wyndham and Derby late in the afternoon, drove on until midnight and started again early next morning, after showering nakedly like four sylphs in a murky puddle in a lonely, dried-up river bed.

Not long after, we stopped for a drink of water to find that our large water bag had rubbed on the wheel in the night and there was not a drop of water left in it! Flabbergasted, we checked the three others. We had been using these, leaving the larger bag for the hot day ahead and there was barely one small bagful left. The sun blazed down at a temperature of 114°. We checked this later. There was fifty miles to cover before we reached the next bore! At under ten miles an hour we bumped on, daring only to wet our tongues with a dribble of water now and then. Between five people one small water bag seemed a mere drop. Tantalizingly all day mirages of beautiful pools shimmered at a distance around us, in front, each side and behind. My tongue and mouth after two hours was coated with slime, the hot air hurt my nose as I breathed, and the ulcers throbbed.

After the third hour we all started on tales of shipwrecked sailors which carried us through the next hour when Bob stopped, came round to the back and we swallowed our last mouthful of water each.

"Only another twenty miles," he said encouragingly. "You O.K?" We nodded. "Two hours—we'll soon be there," and we bumped off again.

The tank stood at last before us. Tall, round and full. With trembling eager hands we helped Bob throw a narrow hose over the top; we heard the splash as it hit the water inside. Bob put his mouth to the end of the tube to syphon it out, and as it came —as quickly spat it out. It was salt! Not too salty for the cattle, but enough to make us pretty sick. The disappointment was intense. No one moved, a kookaburra laughed jeeringly from a nearby gum tree. We had another six hours of driving ahead— even by night the heat was pretty bad.

"We can do one of two things," Bob said very seriously. "Wait here in the shade—or go on—as quick as we can shake our tail! If we wait, you'll be a little cooler, but still as thirsty. If we go on—we'll have water in six hours. But it's up to you!"

Six hours to our perspiring bodies and leatherlike tongues seemed as long as six weeks. But it was better to be on the move, with a slight breeze, than hanging around. Bob filled the semi-trailer's tank with the salt water, we soaking ourselves thoroughly, and so we began the last lap of the journey, which soon began to take on a nightmare quality. The mirages now closed in on us in the afternoon heat, while the four of us humped the heavy, coarse grain sacks over and round us as extra protection from the sun, and watched the heat bouncing off the glistening drums, while we sat amid them—frying!

A mile from Derby at a cattle dip, at midnight, the cattle mooed in surprise as five ghostly bodies took a running dive into their dip and then began a whooping dance of glee.

There by the water we thanked Bob for the eventful ride, and he drove on to his wife waiting in Derby. We curled into our sleeping gear and slept the sleep of the dead, oblivious to the mosquitoes for once.

With morning came the flies along the salt flats, buzzing and settling in clouds above and over us. We hurriedly washed, making sure no soap went into the cattle trough, an unforgivable thing, then headed into Derby.

No such four comical figures could ever have straggled into town before.

Diana's monster straw hat was now frayed all round the brim, pieces of straw floated down into her face, gradually disintegrating before her eyes. Her pyjama coat, fraying madly where we had torn out the sleeves, hung loosely outside her short shorts, the bottoms of which were only visible occasionally. The long brown legs encased at the extreme end in flapping sandals were a smooth chocolate brown. Her rucksack bulged from her back like an ungainly growth. She was beginning to look like a marching tinker's circus. A black bottomed billy can clanged at every step against our battered frying pan, a pair of thick crêpe shoes dangled alarmingly from much knotted thin laces, swaying rhythmically with a long, sausage-like string bag with odd things poked through the many breaks where the string had been tied again and again, only to come apart elsewhere.

Penny and Sally in their khaki shirts and shorts, leather belts dangling with purses, penknives and assorted pins, looked like a contingent from the local Girl Guides. From the neck up, however, Sally might have been going to a Dutch garden party. Her brightly coloured straw hat tied beneath the chin like a poke bonnet was held down with red ribbons, while Penny's beloved sun helmet, firmly resting on her ears and casting a green hue down to her neck, made her head look as though it had got lost from a tiger hunt. Usually we had to lie flat on the ground, on our backs, to see her eyes up under the brim, and although she was now bent double beneath her pack her view of feet only was not strange to her. Last, but not least, came myself. My straw "donkey hat," as the others called it (for when I had acquired it, two large ear splits had already been hacked out of the crown) was now curled at the brim like a Trafalgar Admiral's tricolour with the heat. My pyjama top, even more frayed round the armholes than Diana's, was practically rotting off in shreds. Each time I hitched my pack higher on my back an earsplitting rent came from over my shoulder. The sole of my left sandal had almost parted company with the rest and slapped the road loudly at each step. Strung out between us were the odd trifles we were unable to cram into our packs: the portable radio, the swag, sleeping bags and assorted magazines.

So the odd circus jigged its way up the main street. We had reached civilization. It was good to be alive on this sun-soaked morning and a shower would complete our love of life.

Dumping everything at last outside the one hotel in sight, we asked for one.

"You gonna book up here?" the owner asked.

We had no contacts here so we booked in, and Di and I won the toss for first showers.

As we appeared ten minutes later, mopping the water from our streaming heads, a coloured woman was just departing down the steps of the verandah where Sally and Penny were sitting.

"Wasn't that nice of her!" Penny exclaimed. "She saw us arrive and came along to say if we had nowhere to stay we were welcome at her house."

"It's a pity we booked in here," Sally said thoughtfully.

"Well, we'll just book out!" I cried. "It *would* be a change to stay in a coloured woman's home. Wouldn't it be fun!" As their faces registered agreement, I took a flying leap down the steps, towel flapping out behind me, and sped to where the woman was about to leave in a huge, battered, old Ford.

"The girls told us of your invitation," I said breathlessly, "May we change our minds and come? We'd love to!"

The flat Malayan face broke into a broad grin as she nodded a fuzz of black hair.

"That's wonderful," she beamed. "Tell you what—you wait here for a while and I'll be back to pick up you—and your goods.

Won't be long. My kids are gonna be so thrilled," she cried, a flash of teeth grinning from ear to ear. "Now don't go way." And the large old car banged and clattered off, to return as noisily fifteen minutes later.

Jessie Coleman's house was the strangest looking place any of us had seen. Built for a dusty, stormy, hot climate, all round, between the roof and the high stilts, the exterior was covered by many layers of wooden louvred shutters about two feet long and a foot wide which now, as they all partially jutted out open, gave the house an appearance of a square Chinese pagoda. Behind the louvres was a fine mosquito netting, behind that, an all round verandah and, in the centre, the living rooms. The shutters could be opened or shut at will, together or separately, at any side of the house according to how the day's sun, dust, or rain was shaping. Jessie's was a mixed marriage, herself a quarter caste Chinese Malayan, Aboriginal, Australian, she was married to a big laughing Australian. Three of their six children, between the ages of two and fourteen, were like their mother with flat, wide noses and a hint of elongated eyes, while the others were typical little Aussies.

In Derby there were many mixed marriages—they were accepted—and that night there was another.

Jessie's brother married an Australian girl, so, of course, we were invited to the feast. Practically the whole population of Derby, including the children, sat down in the garden behind the bride and groom's future house, at long loaded tables groaning under their stacks of delicacies. Most of the population was related in one way or another, and the children plainly bore witness to this as they scuttled between our legs and beneath the creaking tables, shrieking with delight.

It was a happy place, where everyone did their share in the small community, from making ice cream at home, to selling at the small stall in the main road, to cheering on the girls' netball team when they played every Saturday night by floodlight. A small swimming pool was nearing completion, all done by willing unpaid workers.

We were sorry to leave when a party of Wapet geologists headed through for Broome, and took us on with them.

8

Sharks and Pearl Diving

BROOME is the pearling port of Australia. We arrived in the middle of its second boom equalling that of the '20s.

Coloured pearling crews and divers were again gambling for high stakes. £1,000 changed hands one night before our eyes.

The deep blue water of Roebuck Bay laps on the thin white line of fine sand which stretches for miles on either side of the township spreadeagled behind the mangrove trees.

Down in China Town, in their two-storied tin shanties, live the coloured population, Japanese, Chinese and Malays, who outnumber the whites in their spacious low bungalows at the top end of Broome. Here live also the master pearlers who own the pearling luggers.

Japanese aircraft had bombed and strafed the waterfront twice during the war. Broome was evacuated and became an R.A.A.F. base.

Before the war between 700 and 800 tons of mother of pearl shell was fished up from the waters of the township in a year. It was worth more to the master pearlers then the pearls themselves, selling in America for nearly £800 a ton. Now the search for shell had started again.

White men had nothing to hide as they took their half caste beauties home after a night at the one picture house in China Town, or from a night's drinking.

White women were escorted by one of the coloured men from the luggers.

The worst problem for Broome seemed the aborigines or binghais. About two hundred lived in camps within a few miles of the town. Below China Town, on the sandhills amid the mangroves, is the largest camp with no sanitation and no water. Natives have to carry their water from the township. Several native babies had died of gastric enteritis in the tin makeshift homes, and it looked as though nothing was being done about it.

One of the three pubs, "The Governor Broome," was owned by a woman, Molly, who had a voice like a sergeant major and a heart of gold. In the evenings, as couples sat drinking schooners of beer with husband or boy friend, she would lift her skirt above her knees and dance a can-can round the bar that would have done justice to Montmartre, singing stridently, "Oh you beautiful doll."

Down in China Town in the hotel that used to be unsafe for white men to enter alone, Diana and I would watch as the pearling crews roared in straight off the luggers—here sometimes, and if they were lucky, to roll their pearls down the length of the counter for us to inspect and envy. Many of these were worth between £50 to £300 pounds each, and many that should have gone to the master pearlers were sold to the barman who smuggled them away. In a couple of tin shanties by the rickety China Town pier, the shells were sized and sorted, and the shell fish hung on long strings to dry for sale later.

An empty, unfurnished bungalow was put at our disposal by the kindly barman of "The Governor Broome."

Penny and Sally continued next day with the party of geologists to Perth and Di and I were left to await another lift going through. Broome intrigued us: we wanted to see more.

From our hard sleeping bags we would rise before the sun grew too hot, boil the billy and a can of beans for breakfast over a fire in the garden. We couldn't make the old range in the house burn, however much we tried.

Then we would stroll under our large, ragged straw hats, our towels under our arms, down to the shark-proof enclosure for a swim. Most of the inhabitants of Broome, white and coloured, came down at least once a day, when the tide was in, to laze in the warm, brilliant, azure water.

So we met Johnny and Jeff. Johnny was a Dutchman and making a small fortune with his taxi. (There are no buses in Broome). Everyone paid a fixed rate of 2/- anywhere about the township. There were a dozen or so taxis, usually all packed to suffocation, for no one dreamed of walking in the hot sun.

Jeff, an Australian, was the merry-eyed barman at the China Town hotel. He had come West a year earlier after his wife's sudden death in a car accident, leaving his small son and daughter in the care of his parents. Together these two were the craziest couple in the Western boom town.

One day we ambled along to the curve of the beach where a high red stone bluff continued from the green mangrove trees that bobbed in the limpid blue water. The bright colours in the sunlight were an artist's dream, but we were soon busy knocking and chipping off the oysters that clung to the rocks beneath the mangrove trees.

"We can swim here," Jeff said suddenly. "It'll save going all the way back to the enclosure."

Johnny didn't look keen and said dubiously:

"I guess if we keep around the rocks, and don't swim out—it'll be O.K."

Diana and I at first were adamant—our greatest dread was sharks.

"You go ahead and commit suicide if you want to," we told them. "We'll sit here and watch—and eat all the oysters."

But it was torture to see them and hear them teasing us from the clear water which lapped invitingly at our toes over the rocks.

"My word, see those two binghais back there swimming?" Jeff called. "Bet your life they wouldn't be out there if it wasn't safe to-day!"

We couldn't stand it any longer, the craving to lower sun-soaked bodies into the cool water was too much.

Nevertheless I swam fearfully, keeping near the rocks and gasping for breath as Jeff tried to duck me, but Diana was feeling venturesome and swam with Johnny about ten yards out.

Suddenly, about twenty yards away from them, a school of shimmering flying fish broke the surface in panic and flapped towards them. They submerged and then, nearer this time, rose again quickly in full flight and fear; it was easy enough to see that they were scared of something: something that made them swerve and panic from one side to another in a great arc. A shark! I could see it from beyond the fish. All this we saw in a few seconds. I could not shout a warning, my throat was dry and dead.

"Get back!" I heard Jeff's strangled cry as I held my breath and watched helplessly as Johnny and Diana cut the water madly towards us. Then I turned and the fin had disappeared. The flying fish had passed us. Diana and Johnny were still a few feet from the rocks.

"Oh God! Let them get here," I prayed quite unconsciously for my mind was blank and paralysed.

Then Johnny was bravely pushing Di ahead up to Jeff's craning hands and as he, at last, scrambled from the water, the blood flowed from his cut legs as we all hauled him to safety over the coral. Beneath in the clear water a grey shadow slipped away.

There was no time to tend gashed arms and legs for Jeff let out an exclamation: "The binghais! Quick!"

Sharks and Pearl Diving

We stumbled to the other side of the rocks, the boys shouting: "Shark! Shark!"

The binghais swim well at any time, but these two shot through the water as though they had been fired from a gun, reaching the beach and safety two seconds after the first warning shout.

Three days later this nine-foot monster was caught off the end of Broome Jetty and hung up for all to see. It was then, as we inspected the ugly head and saw the three rows of razor-like teeth jutting back one behind the other into the mouth, which hung open a foot and a half wide, that the delayed action and real shock hit us, and Diana's and my sun tan turned an awful yellow.

There was an unspoken colour bar among the permanent residents and we might have had to conform to it had we not just been passing through.

"Betty and Ludo, the two Thursday Island folk you met the other night, are giving a party for you both," Johnny informed us one day. We were thrilled.

"Jeff and I'll pick you up at 7 o'clock. So pull yerself into gear." This meant, be sure to be ready. Johnny had so many of these quaint sayings.

Betty and Ludo's house was a corrugated iron shanty, a couple of scantily furnished rooms and a large stove. We were introduced to half a dozen coloured friends of theirs then, while Betty fussed over us and Ludo poured out a large schooner of beer for each of us. We all sat down at a bare, wooden table on the narrow verandah, and as Betty brought in the many dishes of weird looking meats, a Malay sang softly to his guitar in the corner.

"It is wonderful that you both come," Betty said, pinching Di's cheek.

"Don't talk, woman!" Ludo cried. "Bring them the Sarti," and he sent her with an affectionate slap on the bottom to fetch it.

This was small chunks of mutton skewered on to a thin wire and cooked in a mild curry. Holding one end of the wire in each hand we followed the way they ate, tearing off the meat with our teeth. There was rice and boiled turtle, sharks' fins and oysters, roast chicken and some sort of boiled eels, and a lot more of which we didn't catch the names, but it was all delicious.

"Give us one of your Thursday Island songs after dinner,"

Johnny asked Ludo, who grinned from ear to ear but said shyly, "If you and Jeff do something, too."

So, as soon as the table had been taken away, the guitarist started up a lively tune, and the quiet night air was broken with howls of mirth all round as Johnny and Jeff swung into a weird hula-hula-cum-bull fight dance, prancing and gesticulating like a couple of tormented souls. The Islanders and Malays loved it. Beaming and stamping their feet, they egged them on, while tears of laughter came to our eyes.

At last, exhausted and soaked with sweat, they sank on to the seats beside us.

"O.K." Johnny called. "Your turn."

From the doorway Betty weaved to the centre of the verandah luring Ludo behind her. They held a large handkerchief in each hand which they used expressively to lure or repel the other.

"He number one, good-looking fella,
    But he no like me no more," Betty sang.

"'Nother fella lika me too," teasingly she lured him on, while Ludo, pretending to beg forgiveness, sang back:

"I like you some more 'nother fella,
    Not lika me
    I number one good looking fella
    You lika me some more!"

It was a catchy little tune and their infectious happiness was wonderful to watch.

Diana and I sang "The Happy Wanderers," our favourite song—but it sounded just as ghastly as it always did whenever we sang together.

The guitarist still strummed away in the corner while Ludo refilled his glass again and again. Now he began to strum a new melody, weird and melancholy.

"That's the one," Jeff called, his eyes gleaming. "Listen to this," he said urgently, taking my hands. "It's beautiful, but you'll want to cry."

The high pitched woman's voices rose above the men's as they leaned back and closed their eyes, forgetting their surroundings, to sing of their lovely Thursday Island in the north.

"Oh T.I. my beautiful home,
    That's the place I long to be,
    Oh T.I. wherever I roam
    I'll come back to you, T.I."

The haunting melody stayed with us long after we had thanked Betty and Ludo for a wonderful evening, and had left, much against their will. They would have gone on singing all night, and so would we, but the boys said the police would not be very happy to find us all there after midnight.

It was too warm to go to bed, however, so we collected our costumes and were soon swimming in the enclosure, the phosphorus rippling and falling over us like so many diamonds as we swam and dived.

"Have you ever seen such phosphorus?" Jeff exclaimed. "No wonder you had to come to Australia. You can't moonlight swim in foggy old England."

We had—once—but he wouldn't believe us.

It was too lovely a night to argue, the moon floating full and high, the diamonds in the cool water and, from over a sandy ridge the haunting strains of soft voices and a guitar and "Oh, T.I."

Most of the coloured boys knew Di and me now and greeted us with a flash of white teeth in the moonlight as we dragged Johnny and Jeff over the ridge and they made room for us in their circle. Time meant little. Here was a guitar, here were coloured people and wherever they were they naturally sang.

Their luggers were in high and dry in the mangroves for a few days, so they sang until the sky was streaked with approaching dawn and only then did they wander home. Di and I were glad we didn't have to get up at 6.30 a.m. to tear round in a taxi, or be on duty at 9 a.m. like Jeff. We were getting thoroughly lazy.

Although money was getting low and there was no sign of a lift South, we didn't mind: we weren't ready to go yet.

But one day the beer and goods supply arrived, brought in by one of the ships that plied between Perth and Darwin feeding the townships up and down the West and North-West coasts.

"That ship's going to Perth," Di announced suddenly, as we sat precariously on top of the wooden poles of the shark enclosure, watching it unload at the end of the jetty, a few pearling luggers bobbing at anchor nearby. The activity on board meant that they would soon be putting out to sea again for a few weeks. We were wishing we could go with them.

"Let's go down this evening and see if we can stow away."

Neither of us really wanted to leave Broome yet, but Diana had promised her parents in Tasmania, 2,000 miles away, that we would arrive for Christmas dinner, and Christmas was barely two months away!

"O.K., we'll go to-night. They don't sail until tomorrow."

That evening the hotel did an extra roaring trade—it was

always time to celebrate when the new load of beer arrived. The noise of stamping to the rickety old piano flowed out in a rush between the swing doors of "The Governor Broome" as men bobbed in and out.

The warm orange light spilled out from above and beneath the swinging doors inviting us in, but we passed on quickly and were soon picking our way over the uneven planking of the jetty. The water swished softly beneath, and behind the yellow lights of Broome splayed out around the Bay like a twinkling necklace.

The jetty was very long, for the tide had a 28 foot drop in Broome, but eventually we reached the end and paused in the shadow of the unloaded goods a little way from the ship. Two gang planks were down, and unloading was still going on from the stern end.

We walked slowly by, weighing up possibilities and discussing all sorts of plans in low whispers.

"Hullo there," a voice startled us from above. "If you want to have a real look, come on up."

So we clambered along the gang plank and soon a red headed engineer named Mike was plying us with iced beer and questions.

"Want to get to Perth, eh? All our berths are full—there's only twelve of them anyway. Sorry, wish I could help," he said. "If you're still here next time we call, there may be some room then."

"When do you call in again?" Di asked.

He paused. "About eight weeks."

We explained about getting to Hobart for Christmas. Mike whistled:

"Boy, you'll have to get weaving, especially if you have to do it all by road."

As if we didn't know!

Now was our chance to see if there was any place to stow away, so we gleaned instructions as to where the toilet was and off we went to explore. We peered hopefully into the air funnels but they seemed to have a clever wire netting over them, which wouldn't budge. It was as we were discussing quietly the possibilities of the third lifeboat, for the tarpaulin wasn't so tightly battened down on this as on the others, that a quiet voice asked from behind:

"Are you lost, ladies?"

We swung round in dismay, trying not to look too guilty. I breathed a sigh of relief, however, for this man was dressed in shirt sleeves, no cap, no gold braid or medals. I had almost

Sharks and Pearl Diving

been expecting it to be the Captain, and I could see us being taken down to Perth clapped in irons instead of going as decent stowaways.

"Ah, well, actually yes," Di stammered. "Ah, we've lost the ladies' toilet."

I was still trying to disentangle my hand which seemed to be stuck beneath the tarpaulin. Luckily I managed to wriggle it free and follow as the low voice escorted us to the toilet. Inside we held a whispered discussion. "If we brought all the gear down to the ship at about 3 o'clock," I said, "the moon will have gone." I remembered the time it had sunk a few nights earlier.

"It would be darkest then. We could creep up the plank quietly, and, before they know—hey presto!—we're under the tarpaulin. We have some cans of food and we can pop out at night when all is quiet."

"Well, we can try," Di said a little dubiously. "They can only make us walk the plank if we're found. It may be an idea to try and gain Mike's help though."

We hurried out and along to where Mike was still sitting.

"Thought I heard the Captain with you," he said.

"Oh no!" Di answered. "We got lost and a gentleman helped us but he wasn't the Captain. He had no cap on!"

Mike listened quietly to our plans and then he chuckled.

"Sounds fine," he said, "but we sail to-night not tomorrow. Sorry, gals, I might have helped too."

We cursed the idiot who misled us into believing the ship was in port for two days, and then settled down to wait for the ship's departure, resigned to our fate. Di even seemed rather glad. She forgot her parents momentarily at the thought of a few more days with Johnny.

At last the activity on the jetty ceased, and one gang plank was hauled in. It was time to go.

"Anyway, thanks for a pleasant evening," we laughed to Mike.

"Maybe we will still be here next time you drop in—better look out for us."

A uniformed figure appeared up the deck steps and, as Mike sprang to attention, a low voice said,

"May I escort you to the gang plank, ladies?"

There was a low chuckle.

"I'm sure you'd hate to be left behind when we sail."

Our helper had been the Captain.

There was a slight trace of sarcasm in his voice. Yes! he knew all right, for he didn't leave us until we had meekly stumbled

115

down the gang plank, and then stood and watched as it was pulled in.

"Oh well," I said to Di as the ship pulled away and the lights aboard grew smaller, "at least he thought we were game enough to try. Otherwise he wouldn't personally have escorted us off."

But Diana had made a discovery.

"Have you missed anything this evening?" she enquired slowly. "You must have noticed something missing about the whole evening, something we've lived with, eaten with and slept with for months!"

One thing only filled this category—mosquitoes, I thought instantly.

"No mosquitoes!" I cried. We hadn't slapped at the blood-loaded, bulging suckers for a whole evening. Even now as we stood no warning buzz floated round our ears, the gentle breeze was broken only by the lapping of the sea against the wooden legs of the jetty.

"Of course—it's the breeze that keeps them off."

She was right, and it wasn't a cold breeze: we never once felt cold in Broome; it was warm, soothing and gentle.

"I'm going to sleep out here," Di announced. "I want to remember again how it feels to have one long night with no black, bulging creatures clinging all over me."

So an hour later we returned plus sleeping bags and breakfast!

Next morning two wharfies who had come down to collect the last of the township's stores were amazed to find two tousled headed, white females sitting up in their sleeping bags, at the end of the jetty, busily eating large platefuls of cornflakes!

My tropical ulcers needed special attention, hot water and fomentations and regular food, so drawing again on Di's diminishing bank balance, we moved into "The Governor Broome" with Molly and the boys. My empty bank book I had stuck way down at the bottom of my pack back in Darwin. As I owed Di about £30 we reckoned a little more wouldn't matter. We both knew I could make it up again in a few weeks as soon as we started work.

One evening as we sat on high stools talking to Jeff at the counter of the China Town bar and Little Bepo, the coloured yardman, serenaded us on his battered guitar winking as he strummed softly singing "Gonna Buy A Paper Doll," there was a feeling of excitement. The Malay crews were talking, making plans for the morrow. Tomorrow would see the last run out of the season for the pearling luggers before "lay up": from

December to April the tropical storms and willy willys, gushing fountains of water, batter the North West Coast and make pearling too dangerous for the small luggers to put out.

Turning to Jeff, I asked: "Surely you know some captain who would take us out with him: rack your brains!"

"But they'll be out from two to three weeks. You'd never get back to Tasmania by Christmas if you went. They don't stay in the Bay remember, they go miles out to the pearling grounds."

Presently Kelly came charging through the swing doors, grinned amiably through a growth of beard, and hauled himself up beside us on a stool. Kelly, a young Australian, had his own pearling lugger. Tanned and bright eyed, he was the only white pearler now in Broome: we knew him through Jeff.

"Fill 'em up, Jeff, and for the girls. Last night's drinking for a coupla weeks. Make mine whisky," he drawled.

Jeff plonked down the drinks.

"What time you leaving—early I s'pose?"

"Mid-morning, soon as the bloody tide's high enough," Kelly laughed, downing his whisky in one gulp—pushing the glass across the bar for Jeff to refill.

"Come on, girls, drink up," he chided.

"We're doing fine, thanks," I said, my mind on other things.

"Do you ever stay in the Bay, Kelly?" I enquired. "Or do you always head well out to sea the first day."

"Oh, my word!" he roared. "Usually well out, but tomorrow I'm gonna try out that reef just off the north peninsular." He swung on Jeff. "You know the one where there's supposed to be so much shell, but no one ever finds it? Well, I had a mind to try it last time out but didn't, so I reckon I will tomorrow."

Di spoke quickly: "Do you want an extra couple of shell openers?"

"Free service, of course," I laughed.

He regarded us quizzically with intense blue eyes for a moment, while Jeff explained casually:

"You could have 'em rowed back to the peninsular and we'll pick 'em up three same evening. Go on, take 'em," he bantered cheerfully. "Give the crew a change!"

Kelly's eyes twinkled.

"O.K. Just to give you the feel of a rolling lugger—come to the China Town jetty at 10.30. God help you if you're sea-sick," he laughed, and tossing back another drink, he rose, exclaiming:

"Gotta say goodbye to someone. Don't forget, 10.30 and, my word, don't forget to make him pick you up," he said seriously, stabbing a finger at Jeff. "It's a fair cow of a walk from that forsaken bit of peninsular."

Soon after ten next morning Di and I picked our way along the rickety China Town jetty in blouses and shorts and a loaf of bread and can of beans under our arms. We sprang into the small dinghy half full of Malays, and were rowed expertly through the swaying, water-logged mangrove trees, and hauled aboard Kelly's lugger anchored out in the Bay.

Around us in the sunlit brilliant water the other luggers were at half sail, making for the open sea. And what a beautiful sight they made, their sails billowing in the hot breeze as they skimmed gracefully away between sea and sky.

Kelly's lugger was about forty feet long and smelt of salt water and fish. We stood on the deck with Kelly and the other diver, a friendly, slant-eyed and stockily-built Jap named Sotoo. Instead of following the line of luggers out to sea, we were heading across them in the direction of a peninsular which could be seen sharply outlined to the North West.

By late morning we were anchored way off the dun coloured shore.

The heavy diving equipment was brought up by the crew and Sotoo prepared to dive. Wearing only trunks, he donned the heavy suit and huge wooden boots bound with leather and iron. Then he placed a thick woollen cap on his head and the helmet was gently screwed into place. Air pipe, thick ropes, a large knife, the roped basket, and he was ready. With a last wave Sotoo was lowered over the side. Kelly, with a couple of the crew, gave a final check to the modern air pump as the sea swallowed the shadowy diver. One of the crew sat on by the pump ready for any emergency if the diver got into difficulties.

"Usually I go down as well," Kelly explained. "But it's not necessary to-day. Sotoo will explore below and see if it is worth staying here for a few days: if so, we'll both go down tomorrow. If not, we'll go on to our last bed."

The spirit of adventure sang in our blood.

"I'd like to go down and find out how it feels," I exclaimed, "but"—and I could not withhold a shudder—"sharks would always keep me on top."

"Sharks," Kelly nodded, his face serious. "They don't always attack though, it's the gropers that have always been the divers', especially the skin divers', worry. To divers they're worse than any other underwater creature. They're a round headed, whitish fish who usually attack on sight. About 300 to 500 lbs. in weight, they're a fair cow, can bloody well swallow a man whole—

they've such a whacking gullet," he said, his eyes all the while taking in the activity on board and over the side.

"I don't think we'll make divers anyway," Di laughed thankfully. "We'll stay on top and grab the pearls when the shells are opened."

"Of course besides gropers and sharks there are octopus, whales and giant clams," Kelly said, his eyes twinkling mischievously. "If a diver gets his leg in a clam you can cut his life line and leave, because he's had his lot, then—"

"O.K! you've convinced us," we gasped. "We promise not to want to go below."

The lugger sat easily in the smooth swell of ocean as we ate our bread and beans on deck with Kelly while the crew had a large plateful of rice, some sort of Chinese mixture and strong black tea.

A shout from the man at the pump and the first basket of shell was hoisted from the depths. Some were quite large but they mostly ranged between five and eight inches across, the shell flat, whitish and still covered with remnants of greenness from the living world below. Another basket was quickly lowered, then the shells were tipped from the first basket on to the deck. With long, sharp pointed knives the crew and Kelly began opening them, sliding the razor edge between the clamped down shells' lips and forcing them open. The shell fish were scraped from inside into a small heap to show the gleaming iridescence within the shell. A few of the shells were almost half an inch in thickness each side, but Kelly was not pleased and we had seen many larger shells in the sorting shanties in Broome. The opened shells were laid to one side and the fish strung to dry, skewered on long lengths of twine. In the third basket which came aloft Kelly opened a seven-inch shell to find within a cluster of iridescent pearls. As we exclaimed in wonder, thinking he must have hit the jackpot, he snorted disgustedly: "Only this tiny one at the end's any good," he explained prising it off skilfully and holding it aloft. "It'll bring about £30. The rest are barrack, see!" He pointed with the knife tip to where the four other lumps were round only on one side, the bottoms flat and tight to the shell.

"You know how a pearl's formed! The poor old fish picks up a grain of sand or something that lodges itself in its flesh. As it irritates he covers it layer by layer with a secretion and there's yer pearl! But blisters and barrack are the irritants that stick right on to the shell and only get covered on one side by the secretion. So these are no bloody good, even the shell's poor quality. Here!" he exclaimed. "Keep it as a souvenir."

We were delighted.

"Maybe we can have them made into a ring each, the flat bottom of the pearl won't show," I said excitedly.

He winced.

"Better keep it as an ash tray, I reckon, for all the good it is," he grunted.

"How many pearls do you find in a season?" we asked.

"Last season I found a £300 pounder," he boasted. "Some seasons you find none at all, other seasons a few small ones. It's all in the luck of the game."

There were no more that day at any rate, although Sotoo sent up many more baskets.

As the sun descended towards the Western horizon of sea and sky Sotoo was hauled aboard. When the helmet was unscrewed and he could speak, he explained briefly to Kelly: "Not good, the shells are too small, eh?" and wiped the sweat from his eyes.

They agreed to sail the next day, and as dusk fell we spoke our grateful thanks, waved farewells and were rowed by two of the Malay crew to a sandy beach of the peninsular, where the headlights of Johnny's taxi flared above the beach and promised us we would have no "fair cow" of a walk back to Broome.

9

Tasmanian Christmas

SUDDENLY there was barely three weeks left to Christmas and still not the faintest whisper of anyone going South.

There was nothing for it but to fly to Port Hedland, two hundred miles South. There, tied up at the end of the short jetty, was a small coastal steamer, the M.V. "Kintoo." We had learnt that the officers aboard were all either English, Welsh or Scots. The "Kintoo" was to sail South at 3.0 p.m. that afternoon.

Feeling rather desperate at the thought of the 3,000 miles we had to journey before reaching Tasmania, half of which was barren desert scrub, we marched determinedly up the gangplank and asked to see an officer.

An officer in his mid-thirties, with the biggest thatch of hair I'd ever seen, soon appeared, bowed merrily and exclaimed in a rich Scots accent:

"Ma goodness, what have we here?"

He seemed to be in rather high spirits.

"We came to see if you could help us to get South," Di began, but before she could continue he let out a roar: "You're English —both of you? Och, you're as brown as gins—you must come and meet the rest of us. We're having a small celebration." He winked broadly. "When we get to port we like to test their beer, man. Come on now!"

He led us up the narrow iron steps to a small cabin where two other officers were rowdily celebrating.

"This is Thomas Owen—Spanks to you—and this Tom White, Chief Engineer. Spanks is Welsh, as if you didn't know, and Tom's English. By the way, I'm Laurie Thay, First Mate."

He turned to the others: "They're English, man! They're stuck and want to get South. Can we help 'em?"

"Get the girls some glasses," Spanks roared. "They've come a long way. We must celebrate. First time we've ever found two strays up this godforsaken coast."

Tom rushed off to get more glasses and we made ourselves comfortable in the tiny cabin. They seemed a good crowd, although a trifle inebriated after two days in port. We recounted to them our adventures of the last few months.

"So you see," Di finished hopefully, "we've got to get to Tasmania for Christmas and here it is the 2nd of December already. There's just no one going South overland, and when your agent told us all your berths were full, we decided to come and see for ourselves."

Laurie chuckled.

"All our berths—we've only twelve, man, and they're a weird assortment if you like: couple of abo missionaries, a dipsomaniac who hasn't been out of her cabin for four days. Ah, there's a spare berth there," he exclaimed, "and a bunk."

But as quickly he dashed our rising hopes.

"Ah, I forgot though. The Captain said he'll need those South at Onslow, and when he says we're full, och! it needs a minor earthquake to make him change his mind."

The situation seemed pretty hopeless; although we had enough money for a berth each South, we just hadn't enough to fly. The "Kintoo" was our last hope.

"Oh, well," I said forlornly to Di, "it looks as though we'll be eating our Christmas dinner on the Nullabor Plain—let's hope we can get another wild turkey."

Some while later, as we all still sat talking, Laurie said suddenly, "Do you know, Eunie, you speak like my wife does. Do you by any chance come from Kent?"

I nodded.

"That's right, the garden of England. Maidstone to be precise."

"I knew it," he slapped his great hands down on his knees with an exclamation. "Why you're practically next-door neighbours. My wife's home is Tonbridge."

His eyes gleamed suddenly and there was a mysterious air about him as he rose.

"I have an idea," he said. "Excuse me, I must have a word with the old man."

He returned, grinning amiably to lean against the door of the cabin and listen quietly to our tale of the shark. Only when we had finished did he speak.

"Well, we can only offer you the sight of a few whales, perhaps a few sea snakes, and, of course, deep sea fishing is verra exciting when you hook a 20 lb. Barramundi or Barracuda every hour."

122

He chuckled as the four of us gazed uncomprehendingly at him. He was enjoying himself thoroughly.

"Och man!—When I told the Skipper the next-door neighbours of my wife had turned up—a thousand miles from anywhere—och, what else could he do but make room for you both. You see—he's a little scared of my wife!"

Dear, incorrigible Laurie. "You're the first angel with a strong Scots accent we've ever met," we told him jubilantly.

Deep sea fishing down the West Coast was like no other fishing—it was done by finding a few odd hooks and lengths of rope, to the end of which we attached any pieces of meat over from the galley. The bait, having been thrown over the stern and the end of the line affixed to the rail, we would wander off to join Laurie on watch at the bridge, or try our hand at the complicated job of steering the ship, or pore over maps and watch for the many islands marked, including the Monte Bello group, or watch as from a distance a lonely whale 'blew,' or gaze in astonishment as the small ship ploughed through a white sea of plankton. Then, when we returned, maybe an hour later, to our lines to pull them in, there always on the end was a 20 lb. Barramundi or Barracuda.

Three days later, six hundred miles south of Port Hedland, at the small coastal township of Carnarvon, we waved goodbye to the "Kintoo."

Laurie had said:

"Och, now don't forget you've my address in Perth. It's six hundred miles, and overland you'll probably be there a day before the "Kintoo" berths. I've written to my wife and she'll want you to stay a few days to hear about the old country. So we'll all meet again in civilization!"

The road three hundred miles south to Gerathor from Carnarvon was little more than a lumpy track.

Two kangaroo skin sellers, Ken and Dick, their large semitrailer piled with dead kangaroos, were the only ones travelling South. In fact they were travelling right to Perth and cheerfully offered to take us along saying casually, as they stowed our packs on to a clean part of the trailer, "You may have to hold your noses all day tomorrow when these skins get high, but if you can stand it we'll give you one each to take home to England with you when we get back to Perth."

By the end of the next day, Dick, having learnt we could both drive a little, drawled quite seriously: "How would you both like a job? We've another semi in Perth—get your licences and

I'll pay you £25 a week each to take it to Carnarvon, pick up skins and bring 'em back to Perth, roughly a week's journey each trip?"

"You mean to say you'd trust us on these roads with a semi trailer?" we asked laughingly. The corrugated surface of the road made talking almost an impossibility, then, as we hit a smoother dusty stretch, he said with an Australian assurance: "Fair dinkum. No man wants to do this trip—that trailer's been just sittin' there for the last two months. So now I'll start offering the job to women. It's yours if you want it!"

"If we'd meant to stay in the West for a few weeks, we would have taken up your offer," we said, "but we're reckoning to stay only three days in Perth before trying to cross the Nullabor Plain to Adelaide, Melbourne and thence to Tasmania. But thanks for the offer."

How different the country looked from Geraldton to Perth, the latter half of the trip. Through golden wheat paddocks stretching as far as the eye could see on either side of the smooth bitumen roadways we drove for the next three hundred miles: the fields and trees seemed lushly green to our eyes, accustomed as they were for the last few months to stunted yellow bush and sand, and now there were many small townships. We laughed gaily as a few of the thousand rabbits, that frolicked by the side of the roadway, scampered and somersaulted merrily out of the way of our lumbering trailer.

Fifty miles from Perth Di said softly: "I wonder how civilization is going to feel after five months outback?"

I was wondering exactly the same. We had grown used to the easy "time-almost-doesn't-matter" feeling that one acquires outback. Would the rush and bustle of a busy city make us long for Darwin or Broome again?

"Do you know, I think I'm a bit scared," I admitted.

Di laughed. "Well, the only reason I'm longing to get there is to see how much mail has accumulated."

"And anyway," I said, "even if we do like civilization again, we'll only have it for a few days—and then the Nullabor!"

Perth, as we entered over the wide Swan River, looked as bright and sun washed as I remembered it, but a lot larger. Large open areas, which I remembered on the day's trip from the ship when I first arrived, were now covered with houses and shops. Indeed Perth suddenly looked twice the size of a year earlier. When I mentioned this to Di, she chuckled: "That's only because we've not seen a city for so long. I feel rather like a gin coming into town for the first time."

124

Outside the large main Post Office Ken had difficulty with the large trailer. The busy cars piled up behind as we blocked the road trying to edge it into a space to park while we collected our mail.

"Come on, get in, mate," called the irate driver of a taxi. "You're not in the bush now, you know."

"No, if I was I'd get some help," Ken called back.

Di and I stood hesitating at the kerb. The sun-tanned jostling throng looked pink and pale against our deeply bronzed limbs clad only in shorts and shirts still. They eyed us wonderingly. From many cars there came low whistles.

"Where you from—Hawaii?" called a voice.

"My word, someone's been sun bathing," issued from another.

"Quick," I muttered to Di, "let's collect our mail and get out of here."

When we woke next morning in the large, soft guest bed of Mary and Laurie's attractive house on the outskirts of Perth, a fine soft drizzle was streaming down the wide window panes. The day beyond was dull, overcast and grey. Suddenly I was ten thousand miles away from where I lay. Back in England. Any minute now I must rise, dress and eat breakfast with the sound of the rain beating against the house. Then on with a heavy mac and thick shoes, up with the umbrella and hasten, head down, through the windy morning to work.

"Oh, what a terrible day!" the customers would exclaim all day, "I don't know why I bother to have my hair done, do you?"

"Come on, you two lazybones," Mary called as she entered the room, dispelling my thoughts. "It's been pouring—but the sun's coming out now. The "Kintoo's" berthed and Laurie will be here in an hour. Then we're all going sight-seeing."

As we dressed I said to Di: "Let's make sure we sail home early enough next year to catch the summer. After so much sun an English winter's going to be even harder to take straight off."

She chuckled. "You, too, evidently saw the rain this morning."

Three days later we left Perth after battling our packs through an array of reporters and flash bulbs, a couple of buses and three kindly lifts. We reached Kalgoorlie late on the same evening, having followed for three hundred and fifty miles the long pipeline which supplies Kalgoorlie, the famous gold mining town, with its only supply of water from the great Mundaring

Weir near Perth. Mr. Connor, the man who thought out and built the fabulous scheme of supplying water to the distant goldfields of Kalgoorlie, never saw his dream come true for he shot himself two days after the Weir was opened, believing the project to be a complete failure.

Next day we reached the small township of Norseman, on the edge of the Nullabor Plain and the last township for seven hundred miles.

There were ten days only to Christmas.

After three days of watching and waiting we began to despair. Being near Christmas the few cars which were going on across the Plain were all loaded with families going East to parents or relations. In the friendly little township everyone seemed to be looking out for a lift for us. and everyone wanted to "Get you girls home for Christmas dinner." As Di and I sat thoughtfully one morning on a shady seat in the main street with a merry new acquaintance, Ken Scott, the young English Sergeant of Norseman, Bill Savill, drew up in his small car.

"I put out a broadcast last night," he told us cheerfully, "so if anyone's coming through empty now they're bound to pick you up. Oh! by the way," he said looking rather pleased with himself, "there's a crowd of men up in 'Bracks' café waiting for a haircut, Eunice. Bob, the barber, is sick so I reckoned you'd like to do something while you're waiting. Diana can sweep up the hair and collect their money. If anything comes through I'll come and collect you both."

Not for a moment did we think he would call on us, but I was only half way through cutting the hair of the sixth shaggy headed man when he rushed in.

"Drop everything and come," he ordered. "Something's come through. They're waiting for you now. You're going to get your Christmas dinner after all."

Back in the main street he pulled the car in behind two enormous stationery furniture vans already covered with layers of dust, and introduced us to four very dusty young men. Wally, Ken and Bob were Australians. Jock, the fourth, was well and truly Scotch. Laughingly they told us:

"Of course you're welcome to come with us, but this is how dusty you get after a hundred miles in our old dustbins, so you can guess how dusty you'll be when we reach Port Augusta, a thousand miles East. You'll be lucky if you can still see! Oh, and you'll have to split up of course—one in each van."

The Nullabor Plain is flat, sandy, dry and unvegetated except for low, yellowish looking bush and weird dry roots which snake grotesquely over the unlovely landscape. The road, still a mere track for the next seven hundred miles, shook the huge empty vans until every single piece of metal seemed to clatter and shriek for mercy through the long, dusty, heat shimmering days. But the evenings were cold and the nights bitter. Each evening the boys built a large blazing fire and produced a wonderful meal by opening a dozen assorted cans of food and tipping the lot into a large billy over the fire. Our supply of cans was naturally added to the boys' store of food.

Dull and monotonous as the days were, however, the evenings we loved: we soon discovered that Wally was a wonderful singer, and after the evening meal he would stand in the light of the flickering fire and sing for hours on end, imitating perfectly the voices of Al Jolson, Bing Crosby, 'Fats' Waller and half a dozen others, and, spellbound, we forgot that we were tired and covered in dust, our hair standing on end, dry as straw, and that we were hundreds of miles from anywhere beside a lonely desert camp fire. Then, much later, we would pile back into the narrow cabs of the vans and clatter on into the dark night. They only stopped for about four hours' real sleep each night— the rest was caught up with by cat naps during the day.

On the third day we reached the lonely Nullabor Homestead where the four boys, known well by the station owner, were soon sitting, feet up, round the large table in the cool outhouse kitchen drinking large glasses of beer and homemade wine and listening intently to the Test Match being broadcast from Adelaide. Diana and I went for a swim in the deep, salty sheeps' water hole and returned refreshed to hear from a jubilant Jock that, for the first time in many years, the "Ashes" were once again ours.

Two nights later, a hundred and fifty miles only from Port Augusta, Jock, who was driving, took a wrong turning in the bush and Ken, Bob and Diana passed us on another side track without our realizing it. When they had still not caught up with us by 11 o'clock next morning, a rather unhappy trio turned back to find out what was wrong with the supposedly delayed second van and lend some assistance. Only after re-covering sixty odd miles did Wally and Jock come to the conclusion they were wasting their time, that the second van must somehow have passed in the night without their knowing. So, furiously and for the third time, they clattered the great van slowly back over the sixty unnecessary miles. Fifty miles from Port Augusta we met the others coming back to look for us. Everyone was tired, hungry, and cross and everyone tried to talk at once, but eventually, after a hot shower and large meals at Port Augusta, frayed tempers were forgotten and spirits returned to normal.

Next morning we breakfasted in the small city of Adelaide, then lumbered over the chain of high green mountains which rise sheerly behind the nestling city and on towards the border of Victoria. Thirty two hours later, on a sunny Christmas Eve, the early morning passers-by in Collins Street, Melbourne, watched in amazement as we unloaded our gear from the vans, smothered Melbourne's Main Street with a thick haze of dust, and waved farewell through it to our four homebound drivers. We were besieged by more reporters and cameramen.

"You've been all round, haven't you? 13,000 miles! And you're pommies, too! You came across the Nullabor? What do you think of Alice Springs?"

Plenty of questions—plenty of answers—but no vacant seats to Hobart with any airline.

"You should have bought your tickets three weeks ago. Christmas is always a bad time," the agent reproved us.

"Three weeks ago we were three thousand miles away in Broome," Diana told him with a sigh.

He eyed us with new interest.

"My word! Are you the two English girls I've just been reading about in the paper? I recognise you now! You've promised to be home for Christmas dinner. Ah!" He tapped his chin thoughtfully for a long while, then: "Do you think they could hold dinner over till 8.30?"

"Of course," Di said quickly. "Any time as long as we arrive before midnight tomorrow."

For half an hour we watched in trepidation as he 'phoned and rephoned, altered charts and then adjusted them again. At last he returned with a gleam in his eyes.

"You know it's amazing what one can do if one tries," he said with a laugh. "It's all set. You arrive in Hobart at precisely 8.30."

After paying our fares Diana held aloft our last ten shilling note and, grinning, exclaimed:

"Well, we've made it but this won't get us a bed to-night."

"Who cares? After tomorrow we'll have your soft bed for a few weeks. To-night perhaps we'll sleep on the beach, eh?"

"Come on then, It's Christmas Eve and the sun's hot. Let's go for a swim."

At the rear of the yellow stretch of sand at Sandringham Beach were many delapidated beach huts. Many of the sun-bathers and swimmers were using them as changing rooms. So we followed suit. Later, as we lay drying on the fine sand Di said, thoughtfully, eyeing the crumbling beach huts:

"You know most of them do have a roof and one or two have really only a few missing boards at the sides."

I nodded.

"And to-night will be warm and then we shall have money for an evening meal and perhaps enough for breakfast."

So we slept again that night with the sound of the surf in our ears, on the wooden floor of someone's forgotten beach hut, to rise with the sun on Christmas morning, and to be the first to plunge into the crystal sea while Melbourne was still busy unwrapping gifts.

Late that afternoon as the D.C.3 soared gracefully over the green mountains and valleys of Tasmania, Diana's excitement grew with each valley we crossed, and as we finally nosed over Mount Wellington to see below the tiny nestling brightness of Hobart, she drew in her breath in a long, happy sigh.

"Look!" she exclaimed, her eyes gleaming with excitement as she pointed away up Mount Wellington. "Half way up there, there's a small piece of England. Dad will have found something to make into a Christmas Tree; he'll have it decorated with tinsel and lights and make-believe frost. There'll be paper chains in all the rooms and balloons, and Mum will serve the turkey and plum pudding, and we'll pull crackers, and Dad will tell you all the jokes that I've heard so often for so many Christmases before. Then, because it gets chilly up the mountain, we'll all sit round the fire and crack nuts and eat oranges and—" she paused and her voice trembled a little as she said softly, "Oh, Eunie, they'll be so glad we made it for Christmas dinner."

She was so right about everything, and somehow it brought closer to me another lonely couple far away on the other side of the world who were sharing the same sort of Christmas, just the two of them now, with their children scattered far and wide over the world.

I hoped sincerely that our thoughts winging back to them at this special time would make their memories bright and ease their loneliness.

10

'Copy' for John Arlott

A week later we had no difficulty finding a job each in Hobart; Di nursing once more and I hairdressing, for Diana had promised to stay for two months with her parents before leaving with me for Sydney, to sail in June or July for England, I to return home and Diana to join two friends for another year's work in Europe.

With over £100 to save each for fares we bluffed our way into evening jobs as waitresses at one of the three luxurious hotels around the lovely Hobart Bay.

Our wonderful tan soon provoked many questions, and Diana made Hobart's elite circle laugh by saying to a party in desperation on our first evening, which happened to be New Year's Eve and consequently a very busy time: "I'm sorry I've forgotten how many wanted fruit salad. Will all those who want it put up their hands?"

Obligingly and hilariously the smart set did so, and the unusual ordering became the friendly joke of the week, while invitations for yachting and swimming barbecues poured in.

One hot week-end, a fortnight later, we sat beneath Mount Wellington on the green smoothness of Hobart's cricket ground and excitedly watched as the M.C.C. and Hobart Cricket Team batted against each other in a friendly match.

"Do you know," I told Di, "this is the first time I've ever seen our team in action?"

As the field of players readjusted themselves we glanced around at the gaily dressed crowds. Suddenly a familiar face caught my eye as a large man in his early forties, wearing a dark, very English suit, ambled towards us.

"I remember that face," I said to Di. "When I served him last night at the hotel, he insisted I was Swedish. I had a hard job making him believe I was as English as he sounds."

Di laughed. "Well, it looks as though he's coming to make sure again."

As he drew level he greeted us charmingly.

"Ah! I was hoping you'd both be here to-day," he continued in his deep, rather slow voice.

"This trip you've just done. It might make a good "off the Test" story for my paper at home. Now tell me a lot more about the adventures you had."

Taking out a notebook he seated himself comfortably beside us, and wrote quickly as Di and I talked for the next hour.

During a pause I asked: "By the way, may we know your name?"

"Arlott," he said slowly. "John Arlott."

"Who? John Arlott, the cricket commentator," we asked, puzzled.

He eyed us quizzically.

"I can see you need proof of my identity," he chuckled. "Look, it's nearly time for lunch. Come and meet Len and the team. They'll be pleased to see two English faces—and there's a farewell party next Monday evening before we go back to the mainland. You must come to the party and tell them all about the rest of Australia. They'll want to know how you two have taken over their column in the paper—next week at home."

Diana's eyes sparkled with suppressed delight, but we both felt a little overawed, but that feeling quickly disappeared once we met our victorious friendly team. And what a wonderful few days we had with them!

After six weeks' work we were able to pay back into Diana's bank book the money we had borrowed for the last part of the trip, and which she was keeping strictly for her return fare from England. We now had another £20 each towards our fare to England, and we knew we could get higher wages in Sydney, where we planned to work hard for three months before sailing home in June.

One early February morning we bade farewell to Diana's parents in the little house half way up the mountain and set off towards Barrie on the North West coast, there to pick up the boat, the "Taroona," to Melbourne and the mainland.

With two fast friendly hitches we reached Barrie at twelve o'clock the next day and at 7.30 that evening boarded the "Taroona." All night we pitched and rolled across the Bass Strait. We woke only once, however, when, in the middle of the night, a crescendo of falling and breaking crockery shook the ship as it rolled over and over for what seemed to be an eternity before righting itself again. We docked early next morning in Melbourne beneath a glowering, overcast sky, and thinking longingly of far-off, exotic Broome, set off quickly in the opposite direction towards the East and Sydney.

Two days later we reached Cooma below the snowy mountains in a small utility owned by an Irishman, Paddy, and his Czech friend Bill, who were returning after a few days' leave to their job on the great stony mountain's Hydro Electric Scheme, soon to supply Victoria and New South Wales with all their electricity. We had, of course, heard a lot about the colossal scheme and they both knew how much we wanted to see the great dam and tunnels which they had helped to build.

"You'll be glad you've seen this project, if you can spare two days before going on to Sydney," Paddy told us with a true Irish brogue. "The first camp's six miles up into the mountains. If you like to come on with Bill and me, we'll arrange that you stay there for a night or two. There are small chalets for anyone who comes to view the scheme." Bill nodded his blond head agreeably.

"Yes, good, then tomorrow, Saturday, we take them to see dam and to top of highest mountain in Australia, Mount Kosciusko. See wonderful sight—roof top of Australia—Ah, Paddy."

"Begorrah, yes, and we'll have dinner at their famous chalet on Kosciusko tomorrow where everyone comes to ski in the winter. It'll be nearly empty now, but honest to goodness, it's the only place I know in Australia with any real atmosphere. Wait till you see it. It looks like a mixture of a medieval English castle and a Swiss mountain lodge."

"Say no more. We'd love to come," we told them. "After that build-up we'd even walk up the mountains to see everything."

As he turned the car towards the distant mountains, Paddy said:

"You've been to Mount Isa so you'll appreciate the camp. Most of the workers on the scheme are New Australians like Bill and me, Czechs, Irish, Dutch, Norwegian, German and a few Americans and Aussies. Once we get to the camp, you'll almost forget you're in Australia. They're a grand crowd, doing a great job of work."

And so they were.

We reached Canberra at mid-day on Monday in a fast Holden.

"You say you've never been to Canberra before?" our driver drawled pleasantly. "I'd like to show you round but I gotta get to Sydney real quick. Shall I drop you off in the centre, so you can stay and look round, or you gonna come on with me? You're welcome."

"Thanks. We'll drop off and have a look round," we told him. Canberra, as a newly built city, we thought surely worth seeing.

Canberra kept up its reputation for strangers and within five minutes our driver was well and truly lost in the network of avenues and spacious parks.

"Well, if this isn't the craziest thing," our driver exclaimed with a short laugh, as for the second time in ten minutes we came into view of the great white Government buildings and Parliament House.

Canberra is certainly an architect's dream with the most modern colourful buildings. We had a good look at nearly everything twice, as we tried vainly to assist our driver in looking for the right roads for the next hour. Then suddenly we were out on the opposite side of the city without knowing how we had got there. Before us lay the highway to Sydney. Our driver braked the car to a standstill and turned to regard us with a highly amused expression.

"Well, gals, I guess I showed you Canberra whether I wanted to or not. So now for Sydney, huh!" Laughing merrily we sped on our way.

Late next day we beheld Sydney, a somewhat smokier Sydney than we remembered but nevertheless it was wonderful to see it again after so many months.

I had done what I had set out to do—made the full circle of a great continent—13,000 miles of friendship and adventure—and suddenly I felt a deep thankful humility as I looked at Diana. It had only been possible with her understanding, humour and friendship, and the help and friendship we had been given so willingly by everyone we had met on our journey.

As we rattled by train once more across the Harbour Bridge towards friends who lived on the North Shore, a great white liner sailed serenely beneath us and going towards the "heads" at the mouth of the brilliant Harbour on her way to England. I turned to Diana:

"And now for a flat, and a job."

"And then—England," Di echoed serenely.

A week later, half way between Bondi Beach and the city, we found our small flat. I was welcomed back to my previous job with the family of hairdressers opposite Hyde Park as though I was part of that family, and Diana very soon was nursing again.

The World at Our Feet

It was good to see Audrey and our many friends. Audrey was sailing for England the coming October.

Our wages were extremely good but not enough to be able to save £125 each in the next three months before the winter came. So one day we presented ourselves timidly at Sydney's leading hotel and asked to see the head waiter about evening work.

"Naturally you've done waitressing before," said the suave head waiter. "Spoon and Fork?"

"Yes," we said looking at each other, and mentally crossing our fingers. What on earth was "Spoon and Fork?"

"You will start next Monday evening," said the head waiter smoothly, a twinkle in his eye.

That evening as we watched the other girls serving delicacies with silver spoons and forks from large silver platters expertly balanced on one hand, we realized what we had let ourselves in for!

For the next few evenings the floor of our flat was littered with broken china and food, but practice tells, and our bank books soon looked the better for every extra hour we worked at 6s. 4d.

"Only six weeks left before we sail," I remarked to Diana one humid sticky evening as we sat on the back steps outside the flat.

She was flicking absently through a newspaper.

"Sometimes the trip seems like a dream," I mused. "Even after this little while."

Diana eyed me over the paper.

"I know, and you're thinking again you'd like to go home overland from Colombo, all because of that article we read by that Australian fellow and his wife who did it by car. But look, Eunie, they had their own transport. You'd need a man around on a trip like that. We'd have currency changes all the time, visa troubles, language problems—anyway, I doubt whether any girls have ever travelled through that way alone before."

"I suppose you're right—you're the sane one," I said with a shrug. "But wouldn't it be fun to try? I've always wanted to go through the Khyber Pass. We could buy a gun—or knives in case of any trouble with the tribesmen."

"We'd never get through by ourselves," Diana said conclusively and retired into her paper.

Only that morning she had received a letter from England from the two friends who she had planned to join on the Continent once we reached England. Cupid had intervened: one had suddenly married, and the other had become engaged and was, therefore, saving too hard to make another Continental trip.

Diana was disappointed, but it made no difference to her plans save that there was now no rush for her to get to England.

In the midst of my musings ten minutes later she gave a sharp exclamation:

"I'll be damned! Listen to this—Reuters correspondent reports "To-day two English girls on their way to Australia left Folkestone with their bicycles. They plan to cycle 12,000 miles overland to Colombo via the Continent, Middle East, Khyber Pass and India.""

A great excitement welled suddenly within me.

"There's your answer. If they can do it, so can we," I exclaimed.

But Diana, always the more careful, reliable one, later had an idea.

"I still have the address of that Australian who wrote the article we read," she said slowly. "He lives here in Sydney. We'll go and see him and, if after that we think we could make the trip alone—well—" she paused, a sudden gleam in her eye, "well —we'll go!"

Two days later we made our triumphant way back to the flat complete with a list of strange sounding names and addresses, and an even longer list of do's and don'ts for the forthcoming journey. Diana was now as thrilled as I as we began to plan.

"We'll cancel our passages on the 'Orsova' and re-book on a ship that goes to Djakarta, Singapore, then Colombo," I said. "We may as well see all we can."

"Right. I'll get two dozen photos each, and see about visas."

"We've three lots of injections to have—smallpox, cholera and typhoid. We can get those free at the University. I'll ring them tomorrow," she said.

"I'll see about travellers' cheques," I continued. "They'll have to be endorsed for every country we're going through, won't they?"

"Yes. Now we'll make a list of all the countries we'll have to travel through, and another for clothes and things we need, and we'll have to save every penny we can until we sail, if, as we were told, we may not be able to hitch-hike until we get to Turkey."

The next five weeks passed in a mad jumble of work, injections, consuls, officials, photos, visas, shipping offices, banks, shopping, tax claimant sheets to fill in, travellers' cheques to sign and all fitted in between two busy jobs each.

A few days in Tasmania for Diana to say 'Au revoir' to her parents and, on the clear sunny morning of June 15th, we stood on the deck of the "Surriento" waving farewell to the many friends we had made.

My eyes grew misty as the ship slipped quietly out beneath the Harbour Bridge.

A thousand wonderful memories crowded my mind and I vowed to myself that one day I should return again.

It was Geoff, an amiable Irish doctor, whose love of a joke nearly caused one of us to be sold to an Indonesian.

When the "Surriento" docked one morning we had four hours in which to explore the Indonesian town of Dakaha.

With Geoff, Diana and I made our way through the dirty looking paddy fields, passed the straw-hatted coolies, and eventually into the narrow streets emblazoned with many red, hammer and sickle posters. Accosted on all sides by dark eyed streetsellers and vendors we reached the queer smelling bazaars and paused before a rickety stall on which were beautifully carved wooden heads.

"Velly pleety," shrilled the cheeky Indonesian owner eyeing Diana and me. "You have two velly pletty vives."

Geoff, always ready for a spot of fun, let out a roar.

"I've a hundred more at home—want to buy one? Let's see what he offers," he exclaimed with a chuckle as the gold-toothed Indonesian came from behind his stall.

"I give—tlo heads for one," he said excitedly, seizing them from his stall. "See velly lovely—take many moons to carve heads. I give tlo!"

"Gosh! You old devil," Geoff roared. "They take ten minutes to carve—many moons indeed. No sale."

Laughingly we made to move on through the crowd that had gathered.

"Stop, don't go—velly solly!" the Indonesian shrieked, barring our path. "Velly well, I give tlo sheep's heads," he said that being in his eyes a fair price for a wife. "Tlo sheeps' heads and tlo wooden heads."

"Sounds a fair price," Geoff mused.

"Yes, good," said the Indonesian, and before any of us could stop him he disappeared quickly into the crowd.

"Ass, come back—no sale!" Geoff called after him, but his voice was lost above the chattering throng.

"We'd better go before he brings the heads back on a silver platter," Di laughed uneasily.

The joke was getting a little out of hand.

Suddenly a young uniformed Indonesian policeman, who had

been watching lightheartedly until then pushed his way through to Geoff.

"He go find sheep to kill," he said obviously worried. "Once he kill sheep—you must sell." He smiled brightly. "You wait, me tell him no sale, huh?"

Geoff laughed, albeit a trifle ruefully.

"Good man—go tell him quickly before he does the deed," and thrusting the required price for the heads into the hands of the young stall urchin, we seized the heads and beat a hasty retreat back to the "Surriento."

In Singapore, in the tinsel finery of a glittering bazaar, we haggled like locals and bought a long sharp dagger each, since everyone on the ship insisted that we must be very brave to venture through the Khyber Pass into Afghanistan and were beginning to make us feel more shaky each day.

Midnight at the deserted wire-fenced dock of Colombo was not exactly the best beginning to a strange journey, and as Diana and I watched the fast disappearing lights of the launch which was carrying our friends back to the ease and safety of the ship, we were both feeling a little miserable and apprehensive as we made our way to a small hotel, wondering what lay ahead of us.

We woke next morning with a mixture of wonder and disbelief, as we realized we were really beginning the unknown journey ahead, and were now alone in a strange country. After a very civilized breakfast of bacon and eggs we were greeted at the desk of the hotel by the Sinhalese manager himself.

"You stay one night only, I hear, because you travel north to India," he stated.

His dark eyes stared dramatically as we explained why we could not stay longer.

"It is too early yet to stay a while. We must first see how our money lasts."

"This is terrible," he exclaimed, washing his brown hands in the air, "that you should want to pass so quickly through our beautiful Island. This cannot be—I shall at least see that you enjoy one day in Colombo. To-night you can catch the train north to Talaimanar. But to-day you shall be my guests—Come!"

So saying, he shouted loudly to the Sinhalese workers who padded around barefoot, and then swept us out of the cool hotel into the blazing sun and into a tiny battered Austin.

"You call me Henry," he said merrily as he swung the car

along between the gaily coloured crowds, missing taxis, buses and oxen carts by inches.

"Now it is my duty and I am pleased to do it," he said quietly. "You must visit Buddhist Temple—the Museum and our famous Zoo. These you must see before you leave—and other things if there is time."

Diana and I eyed each other wonderingly; however much we hated organized sight-seeing, the thought of offending this friendly, helpful little Sinhalese was out of the question.

Henry was as good as his word, and after an extensive tour of the large Museum and spacious Zoo, exhausted and weary with the heat as we were, he still insisted we visit his Temple.

Inside the flower filled, cool temple we stood barefoot, gazing in wonder at the high statue of Buddha as Henry explained:

"I am a Buddhist. Many people of Ceylon are Buddhist. Buddha is the God of all Gods, 18 feet tall; he was the son of an Indian King. He lived 501 times to eventually gain perfection," Henry told us softly, but proudly, "and he gave us a very strict moral code."

The wonderful fragrance of the Temple flowers dying on the altars all round filled the air and also attracted a thousand mosquitoes and tiny insects. By the time we finally left the Temple Diana and I were badly bitten. Henry was very concerned about the large red bites, but promised us cheerfully :

"To-night I shall pray to Buddha and he will heal you quickly."

But probably he forgot, for days later we were still scratching at the bites. We scratched our way through Anuradhapura, the country of ninety kings, and we were still scratching when we reached the lonely mud village of Talaimanar in the North where we left the clattering train and boarded the small steamer for India.

11

Back Door to India

IF Bombay is the gateway to India then Diana and I, landing at Dhanushkodi, had entered by the back door!

Dhanushkodi, in the extreme South is a long, flat, white sandy shore and low woven palm leaf huts, set back a little way from the water's edge. We saw a few cement buildings, part of the shipping and train service.

The train for Madras stood at the end of the pier, but we had three hours before it left and as we had already bought tickets on the boat, we went exploring.

A sense of the unreal grew upon us as we strolled along the wide sand shore. It was as though we were the only two white people in the world.

The natives were so dark skinned as to be almost black. The women who were spreading huge fishing nets all along the sand to dry wore rings through their noses and earrings, not one or two but half a dozen on each side, and the weight of the bottom ones had in most cases pulled down the ear lobe to their shoulders leaving a gaping hole in the centre. It was hideous, but their eyes were large, liquid and some very beautiful. The stench of stale fish and human waste hit us in waves. Men sat in the long, narrow fishing boats, shaped rather like large war canoes, which had been drawn on to the beach, and cleaned the nets. A little way out to sea the dhows swung in full sail, long poles sticking out from the sides like outriggers, on which the natives spread themselves to act as human weights against the breeze. As we picked our way between the dingy, palm-frond huts and boats a few women and children began to follow us at a distance, their filthy rags flapping. We watched as large piles of huge fish were sorted, cut and boned expertly, then thrown into a salt pit to be dried and later packed and sent for sale in Madras.

Naked black babies, their eyes and noses oozing, played happily in the burning sand and paused to regard our white faces in amazement. The glare as the sun hit the white sand made us shade our eyes despite our sunglasses.

It was like a forgotten corner of the world. The touches of civilization in the small ships and the trains seemed not to have affected them at all. As we returned slowly along the beach, trying to avoid the huge nets that now almost completely covered the long stretch of sand—there must have been miles and miles of it—the crowd grew more curious and jabbed and pointed as they followed us. They didn't seem particularly friendly. Suddenly a child, whether boy or girl we never knew, with lustrous, moist, black eyes and carrying a cane basket, broke from the crowd and perched itself in the sand before us. Magically it crooned and an old bottle top in one tiny, black hand became a frog, in the other it suddenly became a bird, flapping its wings madly to be free: an old key became a baby pelican, a piece of filthy cloth a lizard, as it chanted and muttered weird sounding words. I thought I heard "abracadabra." The crowd closed in to laugh and watch as interested as we were. Having finished its performance, the child tucked all the bits and pieces into the basket and extended a small dark hand, the voice changing to the pleading whine that we were to hear so often in India.

We had only a few annas in change between us and the small magician didn't think it enough! There was a loud whine in protest and the crowd was no longer laughing. We backed rather fearfully as the muttering swelled among the wild looking mob, and, turning to go, Diana's toe caught in the edge of a half-buried net, ripping a large, gaping hole in the mesh. Aghast we could only stand and stare and the crowd rushed forward to inspect the damage. We had no way of saying we were sorry, we had no money to pay for it, we were outnumbered ten to one and the only whites in Dhanushkodi. There was only one thing to do: we took to our heels and fled—ran until we were back within sight of the train and comparative safety.

"Sparks," the Indian wireless officer from the boat, was travelling on leave on the train with his wife and two children. He popped along from his carriage now and then to see how we were and at Trichinopoly he rushed us off for a meal in The Railway Vegetarian Restaurant. These restaurants are a common sight on any large railway station. Inside the restaurant each person sits at a small individual wooden table, lined all round the room, so that everyone faces inwards.

"Just follow what I do," Sparks said, for we felt rather self-conscious as we took our seats. There were no other women and the thought of eating rice with our fingers with two dozen onlookers was a bit nerve-racking! A large banana leaf was placed on each of our tables by the waiter who then sprinkled water on it. This was evidently to wash the leaf, and any surplus water we tipped to the floor. A large mound of rice was plopped on to the leaf, followed by a number of vegetables running with ghee and burning with curry. A milky substance, which turned out to be yoghourt, came next with two large, round flat chupatties. Breaking off a piece of chupatti Sparks began neatly picking up pieces of vegetable with it, which he then dunked in the yoghourt and ate. I tried this and my mouth suddenly felt as though it had caught fire: my eyes watered while I fumbled for the glass of water but this, as I shot it down my throat, only made the burning worse.

I sat there in agony, looking like a fish coming up for air. When I had at last recovered from the shock I managed to look round self-consciously, sure that all eyes must be staring pityingly but, thank goodness, all heads were lowered. Everyone was too busy eating to have noticed my antics. Diana seemed to be enjoying hers as much as Sparks. Finally, I found that, if I took the minutest piece of vegetable well padded with a mouthful of chupatti, I could just manage, but it took a long time and we nearly missed our train!

In Madras we could contact no lift.

The monsoon was at its height. In the heat those with money fly, those without go by train! We might have got a lift on one of the many filthy local lorries but, having already had dealings with the poorer class Indian mentality, we decided on the train. The fare was cheap enough—from Colombo to Delhi cost £6 each—for a distance of roughly 2,000 miles.

With Buddy, an Indian engineer from the hostel, we clawed our way through the raging mass of humanity on the long platform. By the number of people milling around, every passenger's relative, right back to their great-grandmother, must have been there to wave them off! Above, every few yards along the length of the platform, large fans flapped lazily, but for all the good they were they might have been electric heaters. Perspiration dripped in puddles everywhere. The only space anywhere on the train was in the Ladies' Compartment. It should have held thirteen, but by the time our packs had been jammed in after us the number in the carriage had risen to thirty! Being women, they not only had all the babies, but all the luggage of the men in the family; they were further up the train. There was already two layers of tin trunks and packages on the floor, bringing up its level almost to the narrow wooden seats, besides the mountains of it above our heads. Every available space was jammed with it!

As the train rolled away at last we watched fearfully the piled-up jumble on the three layers of narrow racks above swaying precariously, expecting to have to jump clear any minute from an avalanche of heavy tin trunks. Our packs made reasonable seats, but we shuddered to think of what shape they would be by the time we reached Bombay, thirty hours away.

The women sat with their feet up, crossed knees akimbo, on the narrow seats, their saris drawn closely round them. Those with babies laid them between their knees and lulled them to sleep with a rather hard tapping of the head, while their many bracelets tinkled like dull bells. It looked most unconducive to sleep to me, but the children were wonderful: not once from even the tiniest baby did we hear the slightest wail on the whole long, hot journey. Perhaps because no one ever stopped eating! Weird bundles of rags were opened as soon as we had got under way which contained boiled rice, chupatties, masses of yoghourt and many other peculiar looking concoctions, all wrapped in withering banana leaves. The children, ever curious about our white skins, contemplated us as they ate with their fingers, their enormous black eyes peeping over their bundles. The younger babies had a large, full breast plugged into their mouths at every hour, while their mothers smiled shyly when they caught our eye, unable to grasp why two of the white "rich" were travelling this way.

At every station, flies swarmed into the train and the usual array of vendors. Water sellers, with water at 1 anna a glass, "cha" (tea), very sweet and milky, at 2 annas a glass. Trays of sticky sweetmeats and fruit were pushed through the open windows for inspection. Each time we awaited the same conclusion. When the vendor eventually got around to us, the sale call gurgled and died in his throat, his jaw dropped and his eyes bulged in disbelief, then as though he had seen a ghost, he turned and on skinny legs fled up the platform, rags flapping, tray bouncing. The women enjoyed these diversions, laughing gleefully each time, and chattering away to us as though we understood every word.

It was during one of these interludes that we put a plan we had devised into operation. We heaved the tins and bundles down from the two opposite middle racks into a mountainous pile where we had been squatting, and, complete with sleeping bags, leapt up the narrow, iron steps to deposit ourselves aloft. Lying flat on our stomachs on the sleeping bags in the racks, for once in them there was no room to sit up, we had a seat in the gods to survey the mad jumble of perspiring dark humanity below. Not an inch of the floor could be seen.

It was wonderful to stretch out at last—we were much too long and tall to squat anywhere for long—and we managed to sleep fitfully through the night. Next morning the space below was even more crowded and as it looked utterly impossible to squeeze even one more body below, we stayed aloft.

"If one more gets in at the next station," Di laughed, "I'll eat my hat!"

It happened though! A woman with a baby at her breast was pushed in, followed by three cases. We gave up.

Later, with many shouts and gesticulations, we purchased "cha" and toast at every other station, and had it passed up through the window.

Buttering toast was a feat of endurance for Diana, lying flat on her stomach as she was with two inches of headroom, while I became a contortionist twisting into knots in an attempt to extract the necessary annas from my purse to hand down.

We had to climb down from our lofty perches twice. By midday nature took a hand, and much to the consternation of all below who had almost forgotten our existence, I lowered myself amidst the fug to battle over luggage, women, children, rice and banana leaves to the door of the so-called toilet, which amounted to a hole in the floor in a black cubbyhole.

After fifteen minutes of pulling and heaving at people and baggage I managed to get the door open only to discover there was no water. I had a ludicrous idea of splashing some of the train soot from my face, so, climbing out of the window, I went next door, much to the concern of its occupants who didn't seem to take very happily to the idea of odd passers-by popping in for a wash and brush up.

The other occasion we climbed down from our perches was at Poona. Diana and I confessed to each other that we had always wanted to be able to say "When I was in Poona" in that certain voice Poona always demands. The train rolled slowly into the rather dilapidated grey town. On the hills all round stood lines and lines of half forgotten khaki tanks, trucks and gun carriers. The lines of wooden barracks looked garish, grey and rotting, and over it all hung an air of dismal forgottenness. How different it must have looked when it was the British Army's pride and joy! Now the only proud and beautiful thing we could see as the train came to a shuddering halt was an ancient temple set high above the town on a distant range of mountains.

143

However, Poona had been Poona, so we hastily dived through a crack in the door, took two steps up the platform, two steps back, and scrambled back to our coffin-like positions. Diana grinned merrily from ear to ear and gloated ecstatically: "Now at last I can say it—'When I was in Poona'!"

We reached Bombay at 8.0 p.m. on a dark humid Sunday evening, waved goodbye to the round eyed children and their giggling frantic mothers, clutched our packs tightly against the horde of red frocked and turbanned porters and staggered off to find the station master and a room. We had grown smart. As porters always had a way of making out whatever tip we gave them was beneath their contempt, we clutched our packs tightly whenever they advanced, lowered our heads and charged —shouting "No!" rather than face the usual inquest at the end.

Later we dismounted from the taxi in front of the palatial Taj Mahal Hotel, standing imposingly behind the Gateway to India. With our noses in the air we stalked round the "Taj" to a dim back street giving the impression, we hoped, that we wouldn't stay at the Taj if we were paid, and in the Red Shield Salvation Army Hostel a homely faced Englishwoman, Mrs. Murray, made us welcome with good old English cups of tea, and clucked us up to a 6 anna double room, cool and clean.

The humidity in Bombay was worse than we had ever experienced, for it was now well into the monsoon period. Next morning a dull throbbing, which had begun earlier in my head, rose to a crescendo. I lay prostrate on my narrow bed almost unable to see with pain, while Di applied ice packs to my burning forehead and spoke in low whispers to Mrs. Murray about amoeabic dysentery. It turned out to be nothing more than the usual "Bombay head," which affects many white people on arriving at Bombay. You are supposed to recover in a few days, but for me the blinding, throbbing pain returned at regular intervals during our stay in Bombay.

We had thought the English rule in India had been abolished but how wrong we were!

Paddy and Ray worked in respective banks in Bombay. We met them while changing our travellers' cheques. As we pulled into the courtyard in their car below their flat that evening, a brown body came running to relieve them of the strain of putting the car away. At the door of the spacious flat two bearers appeared to help them across the room and gently lower them into the nearest armchair, where they loosened their ties and undid their shoe laces. A stiff Scotch was gently placed into their outstretched hands and, as they sipped leisurely, the bearers slid off in opposite directions and we heard the twin roar of bath water.

"Do they bath you as well?" Di asked seriously.

Silently another bearer whom we hadn't seen before deposited a tray of tea before me. I smiled, thanked him and began to pour. He looked puzzled, hovered a few steps, threw a wild glance at both boys and then wavered uncertainly away through the door.

"Did I do something wrong?" I enquired.

"Yes," Paddy said with a hint of dry humour. "Pouring is Mahmud's job. You did him out of it and he is offended. You should only have put in the sugar!"

"Oh, help! I'll apologise when he comes back," I promised.

"Oh, no," Ray said quickly. "It's done now. Don't make it worse by bringing it up again."

I was beginning to get muddled. Was there anything one was allowed to do?

Silently the first bearer slipped back to supply us regularly with sherries and rush forward with a clean ashtray before the one end just put into it had hardly spluttered out.

"Why don't they leave the ashtrays alone?" I asked.

Paddy shuddered.

"There's no more revolting sight than dead stubs disintegrating slowly before your eyes in a murky pool of water."

"Why have water in the ashtrays then?" Di asked.

"Fans," Ray exclaimed. "You'd never keep the ash in a tray without water—it would blow all over the place."

So we went on learning, gradually and with wonder, how the English live in Bombay.

"Will either of you ever have to go back to England to work?" Di asked one evening at dinner, watching the reflected candlelight flickering on the highly polished table.

"Maybe! You never really know," Paddy said, fastidiously pushing aside his half untouched plate of food. "Why?"

"Because at home you'd be cooking a can of beans on a gas ring in a poky little back room," she said wickedly.

"That's exactly it!" they said in unison. "That's why we're enjoying this—so much—while it lasts!"

"I suppose that's one way of looking at it," I laughed. "But I'd hate to be around when the change over is affected."

Somehow we understood them a little better after that!

"How about taking them to see the caves?" Paddy asked Ray as we sat at the open window of the flat, drinking coffee and liqueurs in the humid evening. Below the circle of lights around the bay, "the queen's necklace" glinted through the dusk in a brilliant half circle, outshining even those that flashed and winked on Malabar Hill, more commonly known as "snob hill."

"What are the caves?" I asked.

"I'm not sure that they exist any longer," Ray said thoughtfully. "It was a place down in the old city where women could be bought for the night for a few annas. They sat on show behind barred bamboo doorways and entrances down the length of a narrow black alleyway for about a mile: hence the name of the 'caves'."

"Anyway you should see Bombay by night," Paddy put in. "If you don't mind stepping over bodies all the while. Let's go."

In the streets of Bombay the homeless thousands slept, curled up on window ledges, in doorways, stretched out on their thin mats along the filthy pavements. When Paddy could no longer get the car through the narrow streets we literally had to pick our way over the dark forms lying in their hundreds, higgledy piggledy, all over the sidewalks.

Here were the beggars, the thieves, the hopeless, who would rise with the sun next morning from their stone couches to pull their filthy, threadbare dhotis tighter round their skinny bodies and be swallowed up into the seething mass of humanity which was Bombay, in their hopeless, never-ending quest for work and a few annas.

The caves could not be found, but in Mangaldas Market a fantastic array of saris and materials were still being displayed by dark-eyed, sleepless merchants.

Here, much to the amusement of merchants, late-night walkers and the boys, Diana and I were decked out in brilliant silk saris by the smiling, patient owner of an open fronted shop.

The six long yards of richly embroidered silk would look wonderful made into evening dresses. So rashly we bought one each for 16 rupees, which we later left with an Indian naval officer to bring by ship to England as our packs could not take the strain, which was the last we ever saw of our beautiful saris.

A little way out of Bombay, on the far side of a deep muddy river, was a beggars' camp, under the kindly supervision of a young Scots couple, Mr. and Mrs. Queen, worn thin and white after years of India's humidity. Beggars caught loitering and begging in the streets of Bombay—and there were still thousands —were sent to the camp instead of languishing in a filthy gaol only to finish their three-year sentence and again clutter the streets begging. At the camp they were taught to work.

As Diana and I stood within the wired compound of the

beggars' camp with Mr. and Mrs. Queen, perspiration dripped into our eyes. Round us the decaying remnants of twisted humanity squatted or hobbled on sticks. All were men. All had terribly twisted limbs—or none at all. It was a terrible, macabre sight which nonetheless had a fascination for us. Through their coarse cloth shirts and shorts the stumps of decayed limbs protruded grotesquely, but in their eyes there was a flicker of hope—and almost love—as they hobbled past, or dragged themselves across the dusty ground, to smile and talk in Hindu to our companions.

Mr. Queen mopped his high forehead, where the hair had started to recede long ago.

"There are three hundred crippled beggars in the camp," he explained. "Most of them were crippled at birth to be used by the mother to gain money begging. It was the usual thing up to a few years ago but now much has been done to stop this child torture. In time it is hoped to stamp out begging completely." He sighed. "Meantime we try to help the cripples and it is a formidable task. We are so short of staff in the hospital over there." He pointed to the large building we had come through. "We have seventy beds, the money is supplied by a Trust Fund but it's little enough to cope with mild sicknesses, let alone dysentery and outbreaks of cholera.

"My wife, with the help of two, untrained Indian nursing women looks after the sick, while I supervise the beggars' camp. Many nights we get to bed in the small hours of the morning to rise again before the sun."

They explained all this to us because we asked for the facts—not to free their minds of any grievances.

Diana turned to Mrs. Queen.

"You are a trained nurse, of course. Wouldn't it be possible to train more Indian women to work in the hospital?"

Mrs. Queen laughed softly.

"No, I'm not fully trained. I did a year's course of nursing in England, but there my training finished, and we were sent by the Missionary Society out here. Most of what I have learnt about nursing—tropical nursing—has been learnt by practical experience out here."

"What if a patient dies because you didn't know enough?" Di enquired, recoiling at such an admission.

Mrs. Queen shrugged her thin shoulders, "They would have died anyway," she said simply. "At least from them I learn what has to be done for the next similar case."

Between the bare wooden huts around the compound ran the

sewerage, which Mr. Queen had dug himself. Inside the huts his mobile brain had devised methods of simple work for his beggars.

An old hand loom was operated by legless beggars to make the coarsely woven cloth for their clothes. An old Indian tailor cut the material into sack-like shirts and shorts and taught the beggars how to sew the straight seams strongly together.

Inside one hut lines upon lines of different sized safety pins were strung across the length of the room and one-armed beggars were taught to bundle them for an Indian firm of pin makers. For each gross box the camp received 5 annas. It sounded paltry, but, as Mr. Queen explained, "Their mentality is such that none could concentrate on more than up to three in counting longer than a few minutes. In the bundles of pins are one large pin, two medium pins and three small pins, all hanging from one small pin."

"So I devised these long lengths of pins separated in the three different sizes. Now they can understand to three! So they know they start at the outside one and take from each line. At the end of each line of pins I built a small drop section. As the required number falls into place—you see the lines are slightly tipped—no more can be threaded on to the open pin by the threader than the number in that small device at the end, one of each of the large and medium and three of the small. Quite simple really, although I must admit,"—he smiled a little shamefacedly—"it took quite a time to think it out when so many boxes were returned because of the wrong number in the bundles."

"How much does the government allow for their keep?" I enquired as we made our way back to the hospital.

"Fourteen annas a day. Roughly 1s. 6d. a week."

We gasped. Small wonder that this gallant little man had had to make some other provision. He smiled rather shyly. " 'Necessity is the mother of invention,' don't forget!

"I built a small printing press as well," he admitted reluctantly. "With that the better class of beggar can print cards for public meetings, small name cards and even one or two notices."

"Will they be able to carry on this sort of work," I asked, "once they've finished their terms?"

"Oh yes. Many are sent back to their villages and then, instead of being an encumbrance, they can pull their weight in many ways now they realize that they really can do other things . than begging."

Inside the hospital the three wide wards were full to capacity with Indian women of all ages suffering from divers diseases.

Diana gulped in dismay. On the white covers the black flies crawled in masses. Patients who were well enough flapped a rough fan to keep the clouds of flies from their faces and arms.

Mrs. Queen sighed at Diana's horror-struck face.

"Yes, I know," she said sadly. "But we have no money for wire netting. We would need a small fortune to wire the place— and even then it would stop what little air we do get in now from circulating. Wire netting does stop air, you know," she said, as though consoling herself with the thought, but we knew she would have given her right hand to be able to wire the hospital round.

We left them standing in front of their hospital and camp, two nondescript little people with great hearts filled with a greater love for the dark skinned fellow sufferers.

How very inadequate and selfish our two wandering lives seemed against such sacrifice!

12

A Meeting with Nehru

A FEW days later we crammed ourselves again into an Indian train heading for Agra. It meant another eighteen hours in another two luggage racks, with added excitement when twice the train ran over and squashed unrecognisably the bodies of two Indians. The train only delayed long enough for the remains of the bodies to be cleared off the line, before roaring on again. It was truly said that "the cheapest thing in India was life itself!"

In the night a burglar slipped through the window of the compartment, but luckily a young Indian student woke to grab him and relieve him of his small but wicked looking knife before he could excape along the side of the fast moving train. At the next station he was handed over to the Station Master.

We reached Agra, two hundred miles east of Delhi, at 4 p.m. the next day and on alighting were immediately besieged by a crowd of Sikhs and Indians, pushing the cards of the hotels beneath our noses.

We shook our heads when we saw the prices of a night's accommodation in most of the hotels.

"We have few rupees, for we have yet to travel to England," we told them. "We stay only one night—and we'll take the cheapest offer!"

A middle-aged Indian stepped forward offering a double room for eight rupees, exclaiming proudly in perfect English, "I am a Christian! Come." No one bid lower.

So, through the flat cantonment area of Agra, we were cycled with our separate packs in two cycle rickshaws for a few annas while the guest finder for the hotel brought up the rear on his dilapidated bicycle. The Grand Hotel smelt of cockroaches, dust and ants, but our double room was cool and fairly clean. We showered thankfully beneath a dribble of water from a low tap and joined the proprietor on the worm eaten, wooden verandah for "cha." We were his only guests, for the season had finished owing to the monsoon humidity.

150

A Meeting with Nehru

"You have come to see the famous Taj Mahal," he exclaimed. "Only by moonlight can you see its full beauty but, if you go early at seven in the morning, when the mist is just rising, you may see a fraction of its beauty. I will order a boy to pick you up at 6.30 and go by cycle rickshaw. Okeedokee?"

We thanked him and set off to see the bazaars of Agra. On the flat, wide lawns of their villas groups of brilliantly turbanned Sikhs lazed, drinking and talking, their voices carrying through the quiet, hot and stinking late afternoon air. As we jigged in a tonga along the narrow open roads, dark faces, moustachioed and bearded, with long hair beneath their turbans, turned flashing eyes to regard us and then call and wave a greeting. The bazaars were tawdry and dirty with tinsel finery, bangles and fly-infested sweetmeats and fruit. So we returned to the hotel to eat and retire early to bed.

At 6.30 a.m. a cheeky, dark eyed youngster cycled us away from the hotel through the flat, dusty smelling lanes, missing swaying camels and bullocks by inches, past monkeys, squirrels, bazaars, poverty and army headquarters. With an extra rush of speed on the boy's part we topped the slight rise. Below lay the fairylike Fort of Akbar which resembled in the early morning mist a stage setting for a mediaeval play. Akbar, the great conqueror, made Agra his capital many centuries before we arrived, built the fort and ruled India from within its walls, walls seventy feet high with octagonal towers and crenellated ramparts, one and a half miles in circuit, enclosing a maze of courtyards, gateways, audience halls, mosques, private apartments and a well planned water system flowing throughout the whole fort.

I heard Diana's gasp of delight, "Look!" she said in a hushed voice, and turning I saw, like a mirage floating over the distant green trees, the fabulous beauty of the Taj Mahal. It looked as though made of cloud and completely unreal, as if it would disintegrate and vanish completely before our eyes.

Many sights are claimed to be the most beautiful in the world and prove to be completely disappointing, but to me that first morning glimpse of the Taj Mahal will always be the most breathtaking sight I have ever seen.

A dark, curly haired guide swooped on us as we stood below the walls of the Fort.

We explained that we had no money for a guide, adding as an afterthought that we were students, thinking this would stop us from being pestered.

He laughed gaily. "Students! Good. I too am student, but I

am also the best guide. Many famous people I take round. A few weeks ago I show Marshal Tito. He give many rupees, so to-day I shall take you free as there are few visitors. My name is Faisal!"

It was fun to have someone friendly and gay to answer our many questions knowledgeably.

At length we found our waiting rickshaw boy and, with Faisal hurtling along beside us on his shining cycle, came at last to the Taj Mahal.

Outside the great gateway inscribed with blue letters of the Koran our rickshaw boy curled himself up in his back seat to have a nap and we walked through the beautiful gateway into the green gardens beyond.

It was Akbar's grandson, Shah Jehan, who built the world renowned Taj Mahal as an immortal tribute to the memory of his beloved wife, Mumtaz Mahal. Built between 1630 and 1648, it took 20,000 labourers working day and night for almost twenty years to build the main part and it was completed finally in 1652. Built of pure white marble it stands on a vast marble terrace with a great dome in the centre, surrounded by four smaller domes. At the four corners of the terrace are four slender minarets.

Light passes through a double screen of pierced marble into the interior where, under the centre dome, are the sarcophagi of the Emperor and his beloved wife, decorated, as is the whole interior, with thousands and thousands of inlaid semi-precious stones, wondrous in colour and design. The tomb is set in a spacious, carefully tended garden of dark cypress trees, green turf and still waters. On the opposite bank of the Yamuna lies the foundation and remains of what was to have been Shah Jehan's own tomb, built of glistening black marble. But his tomb was never to rise higher than a few feet, before he was disposed of by his many enemies.

"You send me postcard when you reach England," Faisal asked us. Promising we would, we thanked him for showing us around and bade him farewell.

"It's a wonderful thing, isn't it," Di observed "that wherever one goes in the world people are extraordinarily friendly and ready to help. There should be no reason for war!"

I nodded. "Certainly so far we've found no reason for wars, but then of course it isn't the small people who make wars, is it? Only a few top dictators. We naturally don't expect to meet any of the Prime Ministers or Kings of these countries."

How wrong I was!

A Meeting with Nehru

The four o'clock train from Bombay to Delhi, when it reached Agra was, of course, packed to suffocation. Eventually, while the guard blew hysterical whistles at us for holding up the train, we managed to squeeze ourselves into a foot of carriage and sink on to our packs surrounded by hostile faces.

It looked as if a free fight had just taken place! Probably due to the fact that the forty Indians in a compartment meant for fourteen knew that the journey was almost over for them. Earthenware jars and copper jars rolled between tin boxes, orange peels and filth on the floor, discarded when their supply of water had run out. Tiny babies were held out by the brown arms of native women who had never heard of sanitation.

So to the city of Delhi, now capital of India, home of Jawaharlal Nehru. Surely no two cities, the new and the old, leaning side by side, could ever present such a contrast. We alighted from the train in the Old City, a network of narrow streets, greying castle walls and gateways, now crumbling with the weight of centuries. Rowdy bazaars and stinking slum suburbs have grown to hem in the walls of the Old City and forts. With a yelling gharry wallah we picked our way through the narrow streets in the blazing sunlight. Sikh taxi drivers honked and shrieked, soft drink sellers and orange sellers called as they displayed their wares, polishing the fruit across their filthy dhotied middles. The pavement teemed with stall vendors in dhotis and sandals, and scrawny beggars in nothing.

We were heading for the Y.W.C.A. in New Delhi. How different was this city with the quiet, wide green avenues stretching for miles, interlaced by large circles of green lawns, converging from Connaught Circus and spreading into a great blue printwheel of tree shaded avenues.

"We could be back in Canberra," I said to Di.

"Heaven help our feet if those visa offices are far apart," Di exclaimed, as we were shown into a small, but high roofed dormitory in the Y.W.C.A. The Indian secretary laughed as she switched on the fan.

"It is best that you see Delhi by motor cycle rickshaw," she advised. "They are slow but quicker than walking, and only cost a few annas—but remember to fix your price before you take your seat, otherwise you will pay double at the end."

We thanked her, paid her for two nights' accommodation and, borrowing a small map, set out to find a bank.

John Cross, the Manager of Lloyds Bank in Connaught Circus, eyed us approvingly as the young English bank clerk, Matthew, ushered us into his air conditioned office.

153

"Australian travellers' cheques, John. They're on their way home overland—through Afghanistan, if you ever heard such a thing. You've been to the Khyber Pass, haven't you? I thought you might make them change their minds."

"No such luck," I laughed, as we sank thankfully into the easy chairs. "We've come this far, so we're going on!"

"Well, we're going to have a try at least," Di put in cautiously. "Any idea where we can contact a lift through to Peshawar, preferably a car? We're a bit sick of third class luggage racks."

"What!" they exploded together. "Oh, my God, this is good!" John laughed uproariously. "I thought you were models for the latest thing in Australian cottons."

"Thanks. We try not to look as though we've just crawled off a luggage rack," I said.

Matthew's face grew serious.

"I think I know someone who might help you get a lift. When you've changed your money, I'll give you directions. It's not far."

"And how about coming along for dinner at The Cecil to-night?" John asked gaily. "You couldn't leave Delhi without coming to The Cecil, famous for its *cuisine* and wine. I've a few friends coming along to see my ciné films of Kashmir and I'd be delighted to have you! Matthew can bring you along. I'm sure he's dying to," he said, with a gleam in his eye. "See you around eight then. Cheerio!"

With Matthew's directions we found O.R. in a small, air conditioned office behind a great workshop. A tall, light skinned Indian, charming and well educated, he listened with appraising eyes as we drank bottles of Coca Cola through straws telling him the whole of our trip.

"So now you wish to go on. Maybe I *can* help in a few days. It would be a great pleasure for me if I can, but at the moment I know of no one going North. Wait while I 'phone the R.A.S. They would surely know of any cars going through."

After conversing into the 'phone for a few moments he replaced the receiver, shaking his head. "No, they cannot help. They will let me know if something should turn up, however."

"Anyway, we'd hate to go on right away. We'd like to see a little of Delhi while we are here. We will wait for a few days, and keep our fingers crossed," Di said.

O.R.'s eyes flashed.

"But of course. You *must* see our magnificent city. Have you seen anything yet? The Red Fort, the 'Kutb Minar?' No, of course, you have only just arrived." He paused to offer me a fine Russian cigarette.

"Thank you. We are not the usual sightseers," I explained slowly. "We both prefer to see the people and the way they live in the countries we pass through rather than do a round of dusty mausoleums and ancient tombs."

He nodded. "Good, excellent, but a few at least you must see. To make sure you do I will take you—now. Good. Let us go then. My car is ready."

"We'd also like to see Mr. Nehru," I said half-heartedly, and promptly forgot I had said it.

As he swung out into the wide street, I exclaimed to Diana, "Our luck is still holding good. Do you believe in luck, O.R.?"

"No, not luck," O.R. answered seriously. "It is meant to be. 'Kismet.' We are all in the world to help one another. We meet when one of us needs help. It is good so!"

The Red Fort dominates the city, standing still as a mute symbol of Mogul glory. It was once the Imperial Palace of Shah Jehan, who built the Taj. "He must have loved beauty," I said to Di and O.R. as we feasted our eyes on the fine pillars and beautiful inlaid walls and ceilings. On one of the walls was inscribed a Persian couplet. O.R. read it out:

If a Paradise be on the face of the earth, it is this—it is this, it is this.

"Paradise for some, hell for the rest—no in between. India is the same to-day," Di pointed out.

As we stood later beneath the shadow of the Kutb Minar, a many coloured sandstone tower dating from the 12th century, I questioned O.R.

"India is gradually changing now, though! They are being made to realize that over-population is the ruin of any country, aren't they?"

O.R. paused before he replied. Then he weighed his words carefully.

"Yes, things are changing nowadays. When an Indian visits a hospital, and many do for a thousand minor ailments, he fills in a form. If it is found that he has already five or more children, without his knowledge he is made sterile. That is the only way of gradually stopping the over-population of India." (I think it only right to say that many Indians to whom I have told this story say it is untrue.) O.R. sighed a trifle sadly. "Even seven years ago," he continued, "when I married, I was not allowed to see or choose my wife. My parents did all that. Even though I vowed not to marry unless I saw her first I was only allowed a glimpse of her, across a crowded café, where she sat with her parents for a moment and I with mine."

His dark eyes were brilliant in his finely chiselled face.

"We are fairly happy. She is a good wife, my two children are beautiful, but there comes a time when a man must have a mate who shares his changing mind, who grows as he grows in knowledge and learning. The women of India are not growing in mind as the men." He shrugged. "They are content as they are, and it is not good for a man, so I appreciate being able to talk with both of you. You have travelled and seen many things. Your views are different, yet they meet to make a good balance."

Before he dropped us in the wide gravelway of the Y.W.C.A., he said, "Come and see me tomorrow. Any time, Whenever you are thirsty. I will lay in a store of Coca Colas. Maybe tomorrow I shall have some news. And now, may the great God keep us!"

"India is not the place to race around in," Di remarked as we thankfully threw our perspiring bodies on to our narrow beds to relax and regain energy for a magnificent evening at The Cecil."

A few days later O.R. announced, "I'll have a lift for you in two days. A friend of mine is taking his car about two hundred miles North."

Our delighted thanks died on our lips and turned to amazed incredulity as he continued, his dark eyes laughing with pleasure, "If you would really like to meet Mr. Nehru, his secretary has promised that if you go to the Prime Minister's House tomorrow morning at 8.30, you will see him! Whether Mr. Nehru will stop and speak depends a lot on how busy he is. I know he has a late meeting to attend to-night after just arriving back from Russia. He is a very busy man—so be there on time," O.R. warned.

Sharp at 8.0 a.m. next morning through tree lined avenues and spacious parks, we swayed in a tonga round the great white circular Parliament House, past the imposing Central Secretariat standing at the approaches to the Prime Minister's residence and alighted by the wide gateway, where two sharp-eyed Indian sentries eyed us curiously from their sentry boxes.

"I feel a bit wobbly in the stomach," I admitted to Di. "Do we curtsy, salute, or just shake hands?"

Giving the card O.R. had given us and our names to one of the sentries, he 'phoned, presumably, through to the white residence at the end of two long avenues behind the gateway. Through the long garden where many Indian gardeners were hoeing and planting, we were escorted by a bravely arrayed guard wearing a brilliant turban.

A kindly-faced, tubby Indian woman in a dark sari and barefoot said "How do you do." She shook hands and showed us into a spacious room where a magnificent rich blue carpet covered the floor. On the walls were pictures of Gandhi and Nehru, and on low, polished, wooden shelves many miniature dolls of different countries.

Watching us intently the woman spoke softly: "I am Nehru's cousin. Please take a seat. Would you care for some orangeade?"

Without leaving us she ordered the drinks, which soon appeared, borne on a silver tray by a silent footed bearer. Behind us on the shelf the photograph of an elderly woman regarded us with piercing eyes above the inscription "To my son Jawaharlal Nehru. May the spirit of India which is you, never die."

It was strange to realize, as we talked softly to this woman and drank many glasses of orangeade, that she was checking and re-checking our every word and action, for, as far as she knew, we might fire the shot that would assassinate the one man who at the moment was the only one who could hold together the teeming millions of India's varying and widely differing religions, one of India's greatest worries.

After a while she seemed satisfied with what she had seen and announced:

"The Prime Minister is just coming." With which she slipped quietly away.

Movement at the end of a shadowy corridor announced that someone was coming, and without realizing I was still holding one of the miniature dolls we had been discussing, we rose as Mr. Nehru entered, mopping his brow with a white kerchief. There was an air of gentleness about him and he appeared younger than his photographs. He smiled rather wearily, I thought, as he crossed the room to shake hands, first with Diana, then myself. In the corridors either side of the Audience Hall, granite-faced guards stood, silently alert.

"I see you are examining my figures," the Prime Minister said. "This is a hobby of mine. I collect them from the countries I have visited. I brought one back from Russia. See, he stands up there." He pointed to a higher shelf and again mopped his forehead.

"You are feeling the heat now you are back from Europe," I remarked, for he seemed uncomfortable.

"Yes! You have grown used to it as you have travelled

through, but for me, after the coolness of Europe, it is very bad," he admitted. "How long has it taken you to travel from Australia, and how does your country compare with India?" he asked softly, regarding us each in turn with cool, gentle eyes.

"This is the seventh week," Di explained. "India is, of course, only the second country we have passed completely through since leaving Australia. We are not Australians, though we have lived there. We're now on our way home—to England."

He seemed a little disappointed that we were not Australians, admitting he had been wrongly informed.

"The two countries, India and Australia, cannot really be compared," Di continued, her eyes wide and serious, her words chosen carefully. "India is a vast teeming continent with 360 millions, Australia also is a vast continent but with a bare 10 million people."

"You are right," he nodded gravely as though pleased with what he had heard. "I am glad you do not try to compare the two," he said. "Next year I would like to visit Australia."

"It's a great country," I said. "Plenty of money for all, plenty of sun with undue humidity, and the people are casual, yet friendly. I am sure you will like it if you do go!"

We had planned to ask many questions, but in the face of his obvious weariness and apparent discomfort in the humidity —although the underlying gentle strength of this man shone from his eyes—we withheld our questions by common consent, speaking only as he led. Never before or since have I felt such quiet power radiate from anyone. At last he left us, wishing us "God speed on your journey," and his gentleness stayed with us long after we had left.

13

The Khyber Pass

FOR three days we walked or jogged around New Delhi in assorted tongas, collecting visas and spending precious annas.

"I can't give you a transit visa," exploded the Afghan Consul. "You have no Iranian visa. Get that and I'll see if it's safe for you to go to Afghanistan!"

"I can't give you a transit visa," said the Iranian official. "First get an Iraki visa, and I'll see what I can do!"

"What, no Syrian visa!" said the Iraki official. "Get that and come back to me then!"

"You are travelling to Turkey?" said the pleasant looking Syrian officer. "Good—the visas will cost you 19 rupees (30s.) each."

We were shattered. "We can't afford that. How much would it cost to have a three-day visa instead of a fourteen-day?"

The official was helpful.

"I can give you a free one each from September 1st. for the Damascus World Fair."

This was more like it.

"We'll have to delay in Baghdad," Di said, "if we get there too early. It's only two months."

So we retraced our steps. Along the broad, tree lined avenues of New Delhi, past the Red Fort, Kutb Minar and all the other forts and tombs, until three days later we had collected the lot, never wanting to see another visa again. Our passports looked wonderful with their weird markings and inscriptions.

Early one morning we were picked up at the Y.W.C.A. by a friend of O.R.'s going two hundred miles to Jullundur.

Through the wide avenues of New Delhi to the dirty backwash of the Old City, where the reek of stale garbage and dung made us quickly wind up the windows. The population was just beginning to stir from its holes in the walls, rising from charpoys, the roadway, anywhere, to wind a dirty piece of cloth round their heads and wander out in a attempt to find work. Old, gnarled women swept the cow dung and dirt to the other side of the roadway with short handled, cane brushes, a hopeless, haunted look in their eyes as we ceaselessly hooted our way through the narrow, stinking streets. Out through the flat Indian countryside, past the villages where bitter looking camels plodded in a never-ending circle round small wells to wind up the villages water supply. Mid-morning we stopped in a village to drink tea, sheltering from the scorching sun in a fly-infested hovel. Flies settled like scabs on sticky smears on the rough wooden table and fought in dozens over spilt grains of sugar. We drank the tea hurriedly, refusing the biscuits.

We reached Jullundur at 4.30 p.m., both very tired and a bit sick, the aftermath of a very hot curried meal the evening before, with O.R.

O.R.'s cousin, Mohan, to whom the car had been sent, insisted we could not travel on by bus to Amritsar that evening.

"Stay at my house. The sanitation is not as good as you are used to, but there is plenty of water to wash in. Tomorrow morning early I will see you safely on to the bus—and see you get the front seats."

He was a happy, charming Indian, his English faultless.

His small bachelor house was one of many recently built in Jullundur, a mixture of Indian and Western style under India's new building scheme.

"Yes, they look cleaner and better," Mohan said, "but most of my fellow Indians do not know how to look after these houses. They say the old mud houses are cooler. I think it's true. The thick mud keeps out the sun's rays more effectively than anything."

He introduced us to the dark, beautiful girl who appeared from the house, his girl friend, who was on holiday with him for a few days. A most unconventional thing. Flower—her Indian name to us was unpronounceable—wore the sari to perfection. Her small, graceful head was swathed in blue black shining coils of hair. As we sat on the sparse lawn in the cool of the evening and chatted, she joined in the discussions with a zest and charm that was wonderful to see, though very surprising. So far the Indian women we had met left the talking to their husbands.

"When are you getting married?" I asked.

"I am too poor to get married," Mohan said frankly. "How can I support a wife? I earn just enough to keep myself and my bearer—they are getting more expensive! Once upon a time I could give him the scraps and beat him for wanting more, but

160

not now! It's good. It had to come. But now that I have to give
him a wage I cannot support a wife."

"That's only an excuse. He does not wish to marry me,"
Flower said. But her face belied her words as she smiled at him
and us.

"Why not marry—and sack the bearer?" Di suggested, but
this evidently could not be done. Better no wife than no bearer!
Mr. Nehru could do no wrong in their eyes.

"Since he became Prime Minister, India has a place in world
affairs," Mohan said proudly. "Look how even Russia has to ask
his advice."

When they learnt that we had seen and spoken with Mr.
Nehru, their envy knew no bounds. We had to recount every
word and gesture of our visit.

"Maybe when we come to England you will arrange for me to
see Winston Churchill—he is a man I should like to talk with,"
Mohan said simply.

We were a trifle nonplussed, but promised to do all we could
if he should come.

While the bearer served a dinner of rice, curried meat and
crackling chipped potatoes, Mohan talked. He was a wonderful
speaker, his command of the English language a joy to hear.
While Di and I fumbled for words to explain ourselves, his
thoughts poured fluently from his agile brain, explaining the
Indian life and religion.

"Does it matter which religion we follow," he concluded, "as
long as it makes a better way of living for all who follow it?
There is not so much basic difference between any of them."

That night we slept outside on the verandah in the still night
air, four charpoys in line. Mohan chuckled as he fixed the fan
to blow on us all night. "Why get married when I have three
lovely women around?"

We reached Amritsar by local bus jammed between fierce
looking Sikhs, their long hair hidden beneath brilliant turbans
and the gold bangle each wore on his wrist glinting in the brilliant
sun. Long hair and a bangle denotes the Sikh religion. Tony and
Pam, whose address we had, made us welcome.

We expected the Golden Temple of Amritsar to be rather
fabulous, but actually it's shoddy. The pure gold encrusted
domes and pinnacles looked brassy and peeling as we entered
barefoot with Tony and a Sikh friend without whom it was
unsafe to enter at this time. A courtyard encircled the large lake
in the centre of which rears the Temple, like a cardboard stage
setting.

In the dim interior, however, the hand-painted Koran and brilliant murals which completely cover the walls must have taken many lifetimes of work.

In the tiny alcoves, grey-bearded old Sikhs sat reading aloud from great books, too heavy for one man to carry. At any big festival these books of the Grandh Sakeb are read unceasingly for days and nights on end, in two-hourly intervals for each reader.

Sweet-smelling incense poured from burners. The native congregation sat on the floor around the leader, chanting to the primitive music from a skin drum and silver pipe, and throwing annas on to the great pile inside a small enclosure in the middle of the temple.

We picked our way over ragged, filthy women squatting against the walls and suckling large eyed, naked babies. A few dirty pilgrims wallowed with huge fish in the Sacred Lake believing their diseases would be healed. In the stifling "Kitchen of the Poor" on one side of the courtyard, the glowing braziers lit the dim interior, while the figures who squatted in a circle on the floor took a handful of dough, rolled it into a small ball and threw it with a smack on to the side of the central oven, where it stuck, flat and round, to be scooped off later with a shovel and called chupattis when brown.

Tipped expertly by a squatting native, a sticky concoction fell from another shovel, to fall and set drop by drop in perfect button shaped sweets, hundreds a minute, all exactly the same size.

Here the pilgrims from near and far were assured of one free meal a day. For many it was the only means of living and they returned day after day, year in, year out.

We could have fried an egg on the stone tiles as we left. However, a thoughtful person had laid a narrow threadbare carpet for many hundreds of yards along the pathway round the lake, so that we reached the entrance gateway again without too badly burned feet.

That evening just before dinner, the electricity and the fans stopped!

Pam and Tony, who had kindly welcomed two unexpected guests, said this happened often. Even sitting on the dark verandah outside the house, the perspiration ran down the backs of our legs, and faces and arms looked as though a constant spray of water was playing on them. It was impossible to eat, impossible to sleep even, so Di and I took it in turns to lie in a bathful of cold water all night! The fans came on again at 8 o'clock next morning, but we decided to leave for Lahore with a Pakistani friend of Tony's before we could be caught again that evening.

As we left Amritsar he changed our travellers' cheques with a native money changer at the back of a dirty street, while we kept our heads low in the car, in case he should know it was for us. The black market exchange was almost twice as good as bank exchange, but of course it was illegal. Luckily he was well known at the Customs so we hardly realized when we had left India and were in Pakistan.

In Lahore, word soon went around that two crazy English girls had arrived en route for England from Australia.

"Bet they're two marathon-horsey types," said Clive Devereux to his wife Margaret.

He was so shaken when he saw us "done up to kill" that evening, that before he knew it he had asked us to stay and we were ensconced in the palatial mansion that he and Margaret were renting for a few months from a Punjab President.

"We certainly get some extremes." Di laughed next morning, as a bearer brought morning tea, ran the shower and took our battered sandals away to clean.

Afterwards, a tonga, pulled by the skinniest horse I had ever seen, jogged us slowly through Lahore to the narrow bazaars. We were quite used to bargaining by now. In India it had been: "Ten rupees," with a smirk from the oily owner.

"I'll give you six," Di had replied.

"Then I shall starve—my children will starve—better I slit their throats!" And here he dramatically pulled a long bladed knife from his belt. He eyed us for a moment before saying "Nine rupees."

"Ah well," I sighed. "We only have seven—too bad." Slowly we made a retreat.

"All right. Seven. I take seven," screamed the voice behind. "May Allah forgive me."

Rupees and articles changed hands in a flash. Sometimes we had been had, sometimes they had.

In Pakistan it was different! We wanted a pair of hand beaten copper vases.

"Twelve rupees," the turbanned owner said, without looking up.

"Seven! Give you seven," I said.

He fixed me with a withering look and repeated, "Twelve rupees."

"Oh, well," Di sighed, "we only have nine." This was more than we had agreed but he was a trifle fierce, and we began to retreat. We retreated out of earshot before it dawned on us that he wasn't coming after us.

"Well, I'm damned," Di exploded. "Someone should have taught him how to bargain."

We hadn't the nerve to go back to him. Eventually we found the Pakistani traders in general were all the same. On our return to our mansion, the bearer brought iced drinks and coffee as we sat listening to Grieg's Piano Concerto.

Lunch was served from many silver dishes borne by dark skinned bearers who stood to attention behind each chair as we ate. I would make to pass the salt, but a hairy brown hand got there first and took it silently to Margaret. This was a little unnerving at first but we gradually learned to relax. Then followed an afternoon nap after which tea and dainty sandwiches were brought by a bearer. So Di and I sat up in bed at five in the afternoon and wondered why we hadn't visited Lahore before. A leisurely shower and later dinner which was a repetition of lunch. Finally the sheets of our beds were turned back ready to be crawled into. A week of this was a wonderful tonic, and in the monsoon periods life would be impossible any other way.

Again we were lucky! Kurien Hayat Khan had flown from Karachi to discuss business with his brother living in Peshawar. Business arrangements meant driving to Rawalpindi and here we met him about to return to Peshawar. So, complete with chauffeur, we sped in luxury across sun scorched Pakistan, the hazy mountains, the foothills of the Himalayas, straggling along the distant eastern horizon.

Late in the afternoon, on a great modern steel bridge below an ancient fortressed and walled city where the Kabul and Indus rivers meet to continue in a wide, muddy, swirling torrent, the car was stopped. The bonnet was lifted, the tyres kicked, our packs jabbed and finally we were let through.

"What did they think they would find?" Diana wondered.

"Opium," Kurien said. "It's still smuggled from Pakistan into India via the bridge. At night it's closed; if we had arrived after sunset we would have had to wait till morning to cross."

"My brother would be honoured to have you stay as his guests," the kindly old man told us a few miles from Peshawar. "But I think you must change your mind about going through the Khyber Pass into Afghanistan. The Afghans are wild and troublesome. I wouldn't trust them an inch!" He sounded worried.

So worried was he about it indeed, that a few days later he

offered us free plane tickets to Karachi, where we could live in his mansion until we could get berths on a ship up the Persian Gulf.

We were tempted, but Afghanistan had been a challenge from the beginning. So many had said we were mad, that it was impossible for two girls to get through, we felt we just had to prove it could be done—or at least know definitely that it couldn't.

Abdul Aziz's house stood behind the shops along the main street of Peshawar. When I first saw the outside, dusty, primitive and sandy, my heart sank. But once past the cane blind over the verandah entrance, the floors were covered with rich carpets and the pale, beautifully made wooden furniture gave the interior a very Western look.

Abdul made us welcome, but he was worried lest we found the sanitation not good enough until he learnt from his brother how we had travelled through India on the luggage racks. Abdul was a tall, dark, gentle Pakistani in his late thirties. The thick black moustache he wore made his eyes appear dark and his face very fierce. He wore European clothes and was a furniture maker—hence his beautiful furniture. His wife, who was expecting her fourth baby, entered to be introduced by her brother-in-law who spoke to her in Urdu. She spoke no English. We saw very little of her during our four days' stay for she was sick all the time.

The house consisted of a living room and one bedroom at the front, another room at the back where we ate, and a small room adjoining this which seemed to be for nothing in particular. The food was cooked by a young male servant in a small mud and stone outhouse, from where it was carried across the courtyard to the house and served by the same servant. The toilet and bathroom adjoining the house and a shower was had by kneeling under a low tap from which the water slowly trickled. Sometimes it gave up completely. The toilet, a boarded-in bucket, was cleaned and emptied often—a great thing in such heat.

"It is good. You have arrived for the Id Festival," Abdul Aziz told us as we sat drinking tea round a low table and talking while the pulsating beat of Indian music came from a radiogram in the corner.

"In Pakistan there are two main religious festivals. Ramadan and the Id Festivals, for most of the people are Moslems. At the time of Ramadan all are supposed to fast between sunrise and sunset for a month, taking no water. At the Id Festival, a week-end of slaughter, a ram is killed—one for each person. A third from each household is then given to the poor.

Next morning we saw the throats slit of three large rams which were afterwards hung up while the blood flowed over the stones and away along the water gully by the side of the house. Their skins were then stripped off and the entrails followed the blood along the gully.

"One ram I shall send to a poor family I know," Abdul Aziz told us. "They will then send on a third to a poorer family, who will do the same and so on, until there is no more left. Tomorrow no family in all Pakistan will go hungry!"

Abdul had a large Chevrolet, in which next day we wound our way slowly through the narrow bazaars of Peshawar. Money changers sat amidst their pile of notes and coins, vendors sold balloons and whistles at each corner for the Festival. In the middle of cone-shaped piles of assorted marzipans and sweet-meats, the owners squatted, their dirty garments flapping over the sticky piles as they fanned themselves sleepily. Copper in a hundred different shapes and sizes filled the narrow fronts in the copper section of the bazaar. Here one could buy practically anything!

As we wound our way ever deeper, the heat grew intolerable. Gullies ran from beneath the tumbling, dirty shopways carrying refuse and human waste into the wider gullies that ran each side of the narrow lanes and under the wooden counters. Piles of sheep skins and entrails lay in the gullies, the blood drying hard and stinking in the heat. The smell was indescribable. We had breathed shallowly in many stinking spots before. In Djakarta, Singapore and India, we were used to smells, but this made my inside heave and my head ached with the glare and noise. Luckily I couldn't see my own face but I could see Diana was turning a pale green.

Abdul Aziz wound up the windows but the smell persisted. We were glad to leave.

For lunch—and for the next three days—we ate mutton: mutton in rice, mutton in ghee and just plain mutton. Normally I like it but this caught stringily between my teeth and stayed there for hours; it wasn't cooked at all for my taste and a lot of the blood was still in it. I was never very keen on rice either, but Di's appetite was good, thank goodness. It was not affected by the heat, so my small one went unnoticed.

At first I made up with fruit, dozens and dozens of mangoes. Abdul Aziz never ate less than a dozen at each meal, but when my stomach began to rumble with a good dose of dysentry, even these had to be given up, so I kept to tea and ladies' fingers, a green vegetable vaguely resembling runner beans.

The Khyber Pass

After lunch everyone retired for a sleep. Diana and I evidently occupied Abdul and his wife's bedroom. Where they slept I never found out, for it seemed the only bedroom. Kurien Hayat Khan laid himself down on the rug in the living room, a cushion beneath his head, and snored. The children must have gone with their parents.

Dinner was usually served by the young male servant between eight and nine o'clock which was usually the coolest time. So before dinner, for a couple of hours Diana and I, Kurien and Abdul, sat and talked.

Two days after our arrival news came through on the radio that the Pakistan rupee had been devalued. Abdul and Kurien were dazed and silent for a moment and we wondered what had happened until they explained. The Pakistan rupee was now worth the same as the Indian.

"I must fly back to Karachi at once." Kurien struck his hands together in despair. "Why wasn't I informed? Someone should have known this was going to happen. This will make me a poor man. My business will be ruined. I must get back to Karachi."

So next morning Abdul Aziz, Di and I saw him off at the small, airport.

Sometimes we played with the three children. The eldest was a charming, good-looking boy of twelve who spoke English well and acted as interpreter to his shy, younger brother and sister. Like any other child in the world he was interested in stamps and Red Indians, so I taught him how to make a war cry by moving his finger backwards and forwards in his mouth and whooping. The effect was colossal. They had never heard a noise like this before, and we soon had them leaping round the room, brandishing imaginary tomahawks and emitting the most terrifying howls. Abdul and his wife found us leading the war party and seemed a little shattered at the sight, but the younger children lost their shyness of us after this and we could do no wrong in their eyes.

"Don't be late," Abdul Aziz warned us, for we were to be the guests of his friend Farid Ullah, the Khyber Pass political agent, that afternoon.

"Don't worry," Di assured him. "Khyber House—we'll find it. The tonga wallah's bound to know!"

But our pronunciation must have been at fault for, by the time we had practically circled the stinking bazaars of Peshawar twice in a slow, jolting tonga and pronounced "Khyber House" in Pakistani twenty thousand times, we did arrive breathless and sticky—half an hour late.

The World at Our Feet

A bearded tribesman in a wooden sentry box outside the wide gateway presented arms sharply as we passed and I dropped my bag in alarm. Farid Ullah, in a coarse cloth uniform, the full pants caught well in at the ankles, came hurrying forward. His eyes twinkled, but his face was stern.

"You are late. The tribesmen are about to leave for they have many mountains to cross before reaching their villages."

"The tonga man did not know 'Khyber House'!"

"Absurd, he is mad. I shall see him tomorrow."

We followed him up the wide gravelway, round the brightly flowering bushes, on to the smooth green lawn where many chairs and tables were set in a half circle. Standing, sitting, eating, laughing, and drinking from the gaily coloured pots of black cha, the fierce looking tribesmen grew silent, regarding us tensely with dark eyes from beneath their flowing-tailed turbans. The coarse dark waistcoats they wore looked strange amid their other flowing garments which hung loosely on their tall figures.

Farid Ullah motioned us to sit beside him at the head of the circle and as he spoke quickly in their harsh dialect, I heard our two names amid a jumble of words. Half a dozen of the head tribesmen came forward slowly and hesitantly, touching their bowed foreheads before us, and, not knowing quite what was expected of us, we smiled and nodded in return. The rest of them backed slowly away, looking reproachfully sideways at Farid Ullah who let out a roar of laughter. "They are shy, see! They are like children. They think I am playing a trick on them. Like you—they do not know what to do!"

It was all right for him: he could speak the two languages and he was enjoying it thoroughly. But gradually their shyness died and curiosity was uppermost; they plied us with many piled plates full of sticky, coarse, homemade sweetmeats. Strange odours arose as I nibbled and hurriedly washed them down with the black sweet tea. Then Farid Ullah beckoned an old, gentle looking tribesman and, amid much laughter, made him sit between us and an interpreter. "Speak. Ask him all you want to know," Farid Ullah insisted gaily. "Make him happy. He has never spoken to white women before."

It was a strange feeling knowing we could not speak straight to him. I was lost for words.

"Do you come from far?" Di began hesitantly, and the interpreter rattled away quickly.

"His valley is across the mountains, many days' journey," came the reply.

"Could we go with him to see his valley?" I asked.

"He says you are welcome, but after three days' journey by horseback, there is another day by foot, for the village lies below steep mountains. He thinks you would not want to go to his village."

Here the gentle-eyed old man made many signs about the steepness of the mountains. Two other tribesmen began to crowd around.

Farid Ullah had never had a party like this!

"Ask him how many wives he has. Go on—ask him. He won't mind—he's probably got dozens," he exaggerated, and the old man and crowding tribesmen laughed like children as he rattled on in Afghan.

It was clear that they were very fond of him by the way they hung on his words, although they were a trifle wary of his sharp humour, not quite sure what he would do or say next.

The old man had one wife, we learnt eventually.

A pregnant silence suddenly fell. The old man spoke, bending his head sadly.

"I have asked him whether he would like two new wives!" Farid Ullah's eyes twinkled wickedly "But he says, alas, though he could give you many things, a house of your own with many carpets and rich cushions, one each of the fastest horses to carry you, he would be sad, for he is too old to take more wives, and he says you are both beautiful. You must have many sons!"

Then, in answer to my next question, Farid Ullah beckoned forward two young Afghans, their faces lined heavily with the glaring sun and endless dust.

"The guns you ask about are made in the villages where these men come from."

He took a long rifle from one tribesman and handed it to me, while the other loosened an ugly looking revolver from his belt and gave it to Di. The crowd backed hurriedly as I swung the rifle to my shoulder, aiming at the sky. Farid Ullah nearly fell off his seat.

"Careful, careful, it's loaded!"

He grabbed the rifle quickly, chiding me: "You wanted to see the mark 'Made in Sheffield,' not kill off my men."

"Eunie's a good shot," Di said indignantly.

"Maybe," he agreed grudgingly, "but I want you to get through the Pass safely; if they see you handling them too well, they may take you to guard their villages!"

Di gave me a triumphant look. So we were to be allowed through! How were we to travel though, I thought, but I pushed it away for the moment: one thing at a time.

At last, led by Farid Ullah, with our shadows lengthening on the lawn, we circled the group, shaking hands with all the chief tribesmen.

"Now I know how the Queen feels at a garden party," Di laughed softly.

As Farid Ullah handed us into a waiting tonga, he said seriously: "Thank you for coming. They will talk of the meeting for years to come. It will give them something to talk about—other than fighting." He paused. "Your permits to go through the Pass have already gone to the Fort." He brushed aside our thanks. "But how you will get through?" He shrugged his shoulders. "I cannot help you there. Since the trouble between Pakistan and Afghanistan there is no communication between the two countries. They are suffering—no provisions lorries—it's their fault. We try to help, but they are fools, the Afghans. However, I will let you know if anything turns up."

So we said farewell and jogged slowly back to Abdul Aziz's house.

At dinner next evening at the British compound with two young English officers and their wives we learnt that the Courier Mail Van from Kabul, capital of Afghanistan, was on its way down. Our hopes soared.

"Of course they may refuse to take you, or they may have no room. You'll have to talk pretty fast to get on that."

So talk we did—for three days—to Teddy Gamble, Consul Second Secretary from Kabul, and one very early morning, before the humidity could make our pores ooze, we were bouncing in the Courier Mail Van towards the towering range of mountains that rose beyond the flat Peshawar plain. Teddy sat in front with the dark Pakistani driver. Behind them, on a new padded seat, sat Diana, myself and another Pakistani passenger, Mr. Unek.

At Dakar, at the foot of the Khyber Pass, we waited beneath the sandy Fort for the police inspector to arrive and stamp our passports.

"That may mean two hours' wait," Teddy Gamble informed us genially. "He's quite likely still asleep in Peshawar."

So we watched from the cab the milling tribesmen, moving hither and thither or squatting on haunches, talking in small groups or dragging their skinny donkeys, loaded with strange fruits and vegetables, across the heat-shimmering, dusty square to sell their wares to the few stall vendors at the foot of the Fort's wall.

"I must go and see what's for sale," I said.

"I shouldn't. You'll cause too much attention," Ted warned rather worriedly.

But I was tired of sitting. So he hovered after us, like a small, round faced guardian angel as we strolled enquiringly from one stall to another.

As the tribesmen began to gather round he became more and more agitated, so, not wanting to be left behind at this point, we resumed our hot, airless seats in the cab and, when a huge melon was pushed in to us by a nearby turbanned figure, his eyes nearly popped out of his head. It was our first taste for a long while of English formality: one mustn't do this, one must do that —English you know, and all that. We didn't like it.

At 8.30 the Police Inspector came to escort Ted, Diana and me to his tiny, dark office in the wall. A gay pot of tea and the bowl was brought in and placed before him as he studied passports and papers.

Diana was staring at the pot:

"Do you think I might have some water?" she asked at length, as the minutes dragged on. The young police officer looked up.

"Of course, but wouldn't you prefer some green tea?"

Diana's face wore a triumphant look.

"What is green tea? Is it different from the usual type?" she asked.

"It's made from the young green leaves of the tea plants," he explained. "If you have never tried it before, you must now," he assured us, and at his shouting command a dark soldier appeared quickly, and was soon brewing three new pots of the tea in a corner, draining the old tea leaves on to the loose stones of which the floor was comprised. Placing the teapots and bowls before each of us, he returned to the corner and brought back a hubble bubble pipe. Unwinding the tube, he partly filled the lower part of the bulb with water. Taking a small piece of glowing coke from the fire, he placed it under the round metal top where the tobacco was pressed into place. This done, he sucked loudly through the long pipe, making the water bubble furiously and the piece of coke glow brightly as the air was forced through. It looked a very intricate process but at last it was ready to be smoked. By the officer, I thought, but to my surprise, and Diana's, she was handed the tube. After waving the tube aimlessly in the air for a moment she quickly passed it on to me:

"I don't smoke," she explained thankfully to the officer.

I had been waiting to try a hubble bubble for a long time. Now the chance was here I was a trifle apprehensive. Diana looked amused, Ted was looking worried and the officer was insisting that I should try. So, taking a gentle puff and finding the taste not too strong, I puffed merrily on for a while between mouthfuls of green leaf tea. The strength increased however.

The tea had a strange sickly taste. It was refreshing, but one small bowl was enough. I was beginning to feel a bit sick.

"Don't get too fond of that thing," Di said. "Stick to cigarettes—they're easier to carry in a pocket!"

Abruptly I felt it was time to hand it back. I was glad when we were back in the cab, watching as the barricade was raised— and we were at last in the Khyber Pass!

As we left the Fort behind, Ted chuckled merrily. Grudgingly he admitted:

"That's the first time I've ever been entertained, while detained. What it is to have women around!"

He seemed highly amused and I suddenly liked the little man a lot as he blinked from behind his dark rimmed spectacles.

Then we began the crawling, twisting journey up into the Pass; as we climbed, the smooth asphalt road sheered away below in the rear, the hairpin bends resembling a convulsed snake. On the brow of each mountain, as they overlapped into the distance, stood a sanded fort and we were never once out of sight of one of these, so cleverly were they situated.

"I never realized there would be a tarmac road through the Khyber," I said in surprise to Ted.

"It only goes for thirty three miles, the length of the Pass, then you're in Afghanistan—wait till you feel those roads," he grimaced at his own memories. "I had a new padded seat put on that rear seat specially to take the bumps."

"Just our luck!" Di laughed. "You must have known we were coming! Thanks!"

The road was a remarkable achievement through the ragged dusty mountains, but even more wonderful was the railway line!

"That goes through right to the Afghan border as well," Ted explained, pointing quickly as the line appeared for a short stretch out of a hole in the mountain to be swallowed up by another as quickly.

"You wouldn't see much of the Pass if you travelled on that," I said thoughtfully, for although it seemed continually to appear for a few minutes, most of it must have been wormed through the dark mountains, popping out sometimes on a level with the twisting road, or sometimes high above, or sheerly below us.

"There are plenty of wonderful achievements that you never

see unless you come and look for them," Ted said. "You two are very lucky."

"Anyone can do it if they want to," I said positively.

"But you don't know what fear is," he said. "Others do!"

But I did know. I had never been through jagged mountains like these before. The Pakistani driver, however, knew the road like the back of his hand.

"I could drive blindfold through the Pass," he assured us, his white teeth flashing as he looked back to laugh and point while we swung rapidly down the steep, smooth road, the end of which seemed to shoot clear over the top to a fertile valley, thousands of feet below where tall cypress trees poked up like matchsticks far beneath.

"Don't look!" Di said sympathetically, as she saw my white knuckles clutching the back of the seat in front, although she herself was enjoying it immensely. Whether it was the hubble bubble pipe, green leaf tea or just that I was sitting over the outside wheel which seemed to become poised in mid-air above a sheer drop each time we came to a twist in the hairpin road which happened every fifty yards, I don't know—but I felt sick!

Mr. Unek, the Pakistani passenger, who was going to Kabul to work for the British Embassy and who had not had much to say save this, saw my tense face and made me change seats with him, after which I soon recovered.

"You should come through the Latterban Pass in winter," he said, not unkindly. "The ice and falling snow on the unmade roads—" he paused to shrug and our imagination worked better than words. "You will see the Latterban," he continued, "before we reach Kabul to-night."

"It'll be too dark to see all of the Latterban," Teddy said "unless there's a full moon.

"Maybe it'd be better not to see it," Di laughed. "What we don't see we can't worry over!" she philosophised.

At the last Pakistan Customs our passports were stamped by an official who was quietly reading "The Taming of the Shrew" when we arrived.

"How do you like it?" I said, surprised.

"Very good. My English is getting very better," he explained.

"He'll be speaking in ye olde English when you return next," Di told Teddy. "You'd better brush up your Shakespeare." And we laughed gaily as Pakistan and the Khyber Pass were left behind.

Our passports were checked again at the bleak Afghan outpost and the smooth road ended abruptly as we bumped and rattled on, jumping on our padded seats like marionettes with an invisible giant dancing us up and down grotesquely.

Afghanistan seemed the most desolate and primitive place on earth as we drove all the morning through the sun baked earth, rock and shale between mountains rising thousands of feet above us, except where the Kabul River wound its way, bringing vivid greenness and life to the valleys. But the few villages had a primitive, forgotten look about them, as had the villagers in their dusty clothes, loose pants, long shirts and tailed turbans, the tail covering the back of the neck from the sun, as slowly they went about their work or followed skinny, loaded donkeys along the dusty track. On into Afghanistan, through lonely valleys with towering cliffs each side, sometimes the river swirling and rapid below.

We stopped in a few valley villages to drink tea from the great pots which were always ready over a fire. The Afghan men (we had seen no women as yet) were all terribly curious about us and brought melons as gifts as we sat on charpoys drinking with the three men, beneath a covering of boughs and leaves at the side of the roadway.

In one village, after taking some photos and eating our fill of melons with a dozen Afghan villagers, the young head Afghan gave Diana and I a present each, pushing it through the open window as we were about to leave. It was a small, homemade purse, wrapped in what appeared to be a small, rough, handmade table centre.

"They're all so friendly and courteous, it's hard to believe," Di exclaimed as we bounced on our way.

"They've never been quite so before," Ted said, still a little amazed about it all.

"It is your attitude to them." Mr. Unek's face broke into smiles. "Friendliness makes friendliness," he added simply.

At 4 p.m. we started up the Latterban Pass, 11,000 feet above sea level. For three hours we climbed to see the road twisting and turning away below us again to valleys hundreds of feet beneath. At length, as we reached the highest point of roadway, the full moon rose above the craggy peaks and sometimes the valleys below were quite bright while at others they appeared an inky black, bottomless pit.

Often, on a moonlit peak, we could see tribesmen standing in line like sentinels, some on horseback. There was a timeless stillness about them that might have been rather eerie and

174

frightening if we hadn't already experienced their courtesy and kindness. Fourteen miles from Kabul, we entered the Kabul Valley by great wooden doors where our passports were again inspected thoroughly. There were a few lorries standing idle but the camel enclosures either side of the gates were empty and dark.

We reached Kabul at midnight to find the Hotel Kabul full, the only place fit to stay in. Teddy Gamble was beginning to feel we might be stuck with him for ever, for that night we slept between clean white sheets in a small empty ward of the British Embassy Hospital, and woke next morning refreshed— the first time for nearly three months.

The monsoons were behind us at last!

14

Guests of the Governor

KABUL is surely the most primitive capital on the face of
the earth. Except for one sealed road boasting a single
line of two-storied brick buildings, the rest of the city
consists of flat-roofed mud-and-sand houses and shops which
spread across the Kabul Plain and crawl up the sides of the
nearest mountains. The high-walled narrow lanes are dusty and
dry, and the colourful bazaars the most primitive we had yet
seen. Every woman, and even the young girls on their way to
school, wore the all-enveloping 'bhurkha.' Their eyes gazed in
wonder at us from behind the slit of tightly-crocheted lattice-
work.

After much perseverance Diana and I managed to procure a
room next day in the Hotel Kabul for 20 afghanis (3s. 6d.) a
night each, and soon found it was the only hotel where the
waiter brings breakfast toast to you in his pocket!

Such a contrast to the high-walled city was the British
Embassy Compound with its well-trimmed lawns, shady fruit
trees and houses, reminiscent of some English garden estate.

Our mornings were spent in exploring the primitive city, and
our afternoons in the small, cold swimming pool in the Embassy
Compound.

After five days in Kabul we realized there were only two
possible ways on to Herat on the far westerly side of
Afghanistan. The first, by one of the local buses, which were no
more than gaudily-painted soap-boxes on wheels, through the
mountains, and ravines; the second, over those same mountains
and ravines by the new Ariana Afghan plane service.

"Well," Di said, thoughtfully, as we sat by the pool, "if we go
by bus it'll take five or six days to Herat—but it'll be cheap.
If we tried the Afghan plane service we'd reach Herat the same
day, but we'd each be poorer by £10."

"Let's toss for it," I said, as neither of us could decide.

We tossed an Afghan coin—and, returning to the walled city,
booked plane seats for the next day.

The author with her parents

BACK HOME

AGAIN

Diana and Eunice in Maidstone

Surprise visit from Miriam (*left*) and Audrey (*right*)

The world at our feet ! Waving to a Malayan pearl-cutter, Broome, W. Australia

That evening we were invited by the Embassy staff to a party at the International Club.

Beneath soft lights, with Western music, English voices and the sharp tinkle of glasses, it was hard to imagine the primitive city just on the doorstep. All evening I danced with a young Afghan doctor, dressed in Western style. He was the most attractive, beautiful dancer, with a keen wit and humour. Late in the evening as we circled the floor, he said again:

"But you should not leave so soon. You have yet seen little of Afghanistan. Stay a while longer. I will show you many things."

His dark eyes flashed as he looked down at me, exclaiming suddenly: "But you shall wear the bhurkha so men may not look upon you as I have."

My heart missed a beat at the very thought of wearing the coarse, airless bhurkha, and hastily reassured him that we must leave the next day.

As I joined Diana again, Ann, a secretary at the Embassy, said casually to me:

"His Highness is a charming man, isn't he?"

"His Highness?"

She laughed merrily at the expression on my face.

"The doctor—didn't you know? He's the King's nephew!"

The next morning I woke up in a cold sweat, trying to push away the heavy folds of the purdah gown that hands were drawing over me, convinced that I was enclosed forever by the rough, coarse material, looking out of the lattice of crocheted eye-pieces, never again to walk with the sun and rain on my face. I was dripping with sweat as I struggled from a drugged sleep and a twisted sheet that was partly the cause of my dream.

From across the street outside the weird, unending sound of primitive music permeated the room. Then I remembered: to-day we were leaving Kabul! The plane, God! What was the time? I sprang out of bed.

"Di—quickly—we've ten minutes before the plane goes."

And then we were weaving about the room, dashing together the last of the bits that lay strewn around, cramming them again into the over-burdened knapsacks. Outside, the many voices of men and sound of a coughing engine increased and were interrupted by the door opening a little, and the agent we had seen the day before stood watching us.

"You are ready? The bus goes."

His careful, deliberate English made him seem very formal. But suddenly smiling, he took over, and led us out of the hotel where, shouting and pushing, we clambered up to our front seats, two extra, red plush armchairs set just behind the driver, and looking incongruous amidst the tiny narrow seats that lined the interior of the bus!

A shout, a splutter from the ancient engine, the agent sprang from a group of gesticulating Afghans and, in a rush of air and dust, we were off, picking our way through the chardus and purdahed figures, who hugged the walls as they went darting like ghosts up and down the narrow, high-walled, dusty, early-morning streets. They looked like grey shuttlecocks turned upside down. Through the wider main streets we went and then we had left the town.

A couple of buildings, a stretch of wire fencing and a solitary plane sitting on the lonely earth runway greeted us as we unloaded from the bus; dumping our haversacks by the fence, we sought shelter from the burning heat under the verandah of the long, low building, inscribed with many weird writings and ciphers on the doors. No one seemed to know what was happening. The men stood in small groups watching us, the long tail of their turbans flowing out behind them as they turned and talked.

A dark young Afghan in clean overalls began industriously to unscrew what seemed, at this distance, to be the propeller blades of one engine. Lack of sleep and the heat seemed to be affecting us, for we sat silently, drowsily watching the comings and goings that seemed to no purpose. Half an hour slipped by in which the engine had been revved up many times only to splutter and choke and die away again.

"It's a wonder the thing doesn't blow up in this heat," I remarked to Diana as I watched the heat shimmering and bouncing from the smooth, shining body of the plane.

"Better it blow up now than later on," was Di's sceptic reply to that.

The agent once more appeared.

"Please forgive us," he said, fingertips touching in an attitude of prayer. "There is something not quite right with the engine, but," his face took on a look of pure pride, "these are old planes. We have done so much to them. Ariana is a very young service, and we are so proud that you will fly on this, our sixth flight, many hundreds of miles. I shall go and see how long you will wait!"

Hundreds of miles, I thought, and a flash of panic came as I remembered the Latterban Pass with its chasms and crevices and angry steeps. Had we done the wrong thing after all? Maybe the buses *were* slow and packed to suffocation but at least one might stand a chance of jumping if a bus went over a chasm.

Diana read my thoughts.

"At least there's an English pilot."

But I wasn't so optimistic.

An exultant wave from the agent hurrying back from the plane gave us to understand that all was well, but it might be best to hurry and get aboard before it stopped altogether.

A hot smell of leather and stale vomit assailed our nostrils, and, as we fastened our safety belts, I noted several jagged rips in the upholstery of the seats in front. It was like an oven: I could feel my shirt sticking to my back and sweat running down the backs of my legs. I had, however, seen a pale-skinned face in the cockpit: that helped. Then the little agent gripped our hands.

"We've given you the back seats. If anything should go wrong you will be in the safest place. Ba Muna Khuda. (May God be with you)." And he leapt happily down the steps with a wave. The young, dark flight-steward slammed the door, drew the bolts and we were bumping and jolting along the runway. Faster and faster the ground flew by beneath the wing. I heard Diana's strangled "Now for it!" And suddenly the bumping ceased and the earth slid away.

Two hours later and with only one lurching rebound from the primitive runway we had made the first half of the journey safely. The airport was about eight miles from Kandahar where the Americans, from all accounts, were making great strides in developing the country's wealth.

We stepped from the plane into a blast of hot air like an oven door opening suddenly. Great piles of shiny gallon drums of what could only have been petrol by the stench, stood ready a little way from the plane and, as we stood in the shade under the wing, in twos the Afghans carried the large tins across to the man already standing on the wing ready to receive the petrol and pour it slowly into the empty tanks.

"Phew! This is going to take all day!" Di pulled a wry face. "For heaven's sake don't dare light a cigarette."

She must have thought the sun had already touched me.

We joined a small group of passengers, the air steward and a white skinned, youngish man in his early thirties, who waved a hand indicating we were to join them all standing at the foot of a few steps leading to an open door, which we found was the waiting room.

We introduced ourselves to John Mattow, the pilot.

"Having a good trip? I heard you were coming. Sorry I didn't see you before."

"We thought you would never start the plane," I said.

"Oh! a bit of trouble." He waved it aside casually as a commonplace detail. "There'll be some 'cha' or grapes coming in a moment. Like some?"

It was reasonably cool in the shade of the building, chatting as the thin china bowls of steaming "cha" brought from another building were set down on an upturned box by the little steward. All the men passengers stood round and drank, talking quickly in the strange, harsh sounding language of the Afghans, their dark eyes sombrely watching us and occasionally smiling. It was rather like a casual "Alice in Wonderland" picnic. No rush or hurry again: we would get where we were going at some future date, whether it be two hours, two days or two weeks hence. Diana and I had learnt many things in the Australian outback, the main one being the casual attitude towards time that one finds in a hot country, anywhere. I liked it. I had time to think and talk of so many things that before had been tucked away in the back of the mind, but never allowed to surface because of the furious pace of living.

"What puzzled me is how you follow any route or way over these mountains." Di was speaking to the dark, good looking Pakistani co-pilot who had joined the group.

He smiled rather shyly, then, in beautiful, precise English, said:

"I myself wondered at first, but after one or two flights, one can easily pick out many things as landmarks. It's very easy really."

"But you use maps?" I queried.

John Mattow drifted over, the tiny Afghan bowl on the even smaller saucer, balancing precariously in one hand.

"It isn't as hard as it looks," he affirmed, "and, strange as it may seem, we don't usually bother with maps. Of course there are many sandstorms. They can blind visibility in a very few minutes, but we are usually warned when they are pending and no flying is undertaken until they clear."

A hot lazy hour slipped by.

"Ten minutes," John called as he came through the gap, holding a shining, large, empty petrol tin. "Come up to the cockpit when we're up, and I'll explain the way this system works!" He hurried on through another door.

We let ten minutes slip by after we had again unfastened our safety belts and then made our way, watched carefully by all, through the cockpit door, closing it firmly behind us, and we were in a world of dials, switches, wireless morse-code tapping out, gadgets as awe-inspiring as anything always is when one knows little about it.

Diana stood a little behind me in the narrow gangway. Down below and spreading as far as the eye could see all round, the jagged, pitted surface was barren and still.

"What are those holes like small bomb craters in such straight lines?" I shouted in John's ear above the noise of the roaring engine. From above it looked as though the earth had cracked open, in long streaks, sometimes in many different directions, and the loose sand and shale falling back into the cracks had formed the round, soft edged craters intermittently along the length of the crack.

"Those are 'kanats,' some sort of age-old water system they still use." He nodded towards a line of mountains on our left. "We follow these until a valley with only two houses, then over another range to another village. You see how simple it seems up here."

And it did. Such a wide expanse ahead and on either side made it seem as though we might have been in a glass tower. The earth moved so slowly towards and under us, ahead of us we had time to pick out and notice clearly each formation of valley and mountain.

We stayed watching and wondering until we had passed over another range of colossal mountains to an expanse as far as the eye could see of flat dusty plain, desolate and unmarked except for a fine ribbon of winding road that appeared from behind a ledge of the mountains to twist and turn away across the scorched and barren earth. We reached Herat, lying square and dusty below, a fairly large town of more flat roofed, compressed mud and straw houses, the tall minarets of a large mosque glinting sharply as we banked to land. Pitching, tossing, and lurching we finally bumped down.

At the airport we stood among the rolls of bedding, rich Afghan carpets, tin boxes and respectable suitcases.

From now on the way was by bus.

"Welcome to Herat." We both jumped in amazement.

We knew that there was only one European in Herat and so hardly thought anyone else there would speak English. An Afghan youth stood there, smiling at us, his karakula lambskin cap curling silver grey, immediately catching our eyes. After all the turbans this was something new.

We learned later that the educated Afghans wore these

"kolas" and were extremely proud of them, collecting a variety of types and colours, as a woman collects hats!

"Follow me. I will show you where you may wait until the bus is ready."

His faultless English staggered us.

He led us through the heat and dust to a large, barnlike building which was whitewashed inside and furnished with rugs and cushions like a harem. We sank gratefully on to the rugs.

"I will call you when the bus is ready to leave," said the youth gently. "You may sleep for a while."

After half an hour or so, we were awakened and shown to the front seats of an overflowing bus, our new friend joining us.

"Your luggage is on the top," he said as the bus began to move. "I am a student of Civil Aviation from Kabul helping to launch our new Air Service in Herat," he explained. "I am going to University in the U.S.A. soon and am, therefore, glad to practise my English with you. My name is Hamid. For what reason have you come to Herat?"

"We are travelling home from Australia, and thought it would be more interesting by land."

"Are you alone? Have you no escorts?" he said with the astonishment we had grown to expect.

"You must come to my uncle's home for lunch," he continued. "We would like to offer you Afghan hospitality. Where are you going to stay, anyway? We have a fine hotel in Herat—the best in all Afghanistan."

"We may stay there then," I said. "Or with a doctor—we've been given a letter of introduction to him."

I looked out at the rough, unmade road winding ahead of us through the flat desert land. As we neared the city, the intense heat was lessened a little by the tall pine trees lining the route.

"Herat is a beautiful city," said Hamid proudly as we neared the city. "We have flower gardens in the centre of the main street and all our streets are lined with trees." Then, a little later: "This is Herat. Would you please come with me to my Uncle's house?"

Our early rising and the flight had made us tired and now an overpowering weariness descended on us both. Our one thought was to crawl away from everyone and sleep; we could not offend such kindly people, however, and so, thanking Hamid for his invitation, we followed him off the bus.

Our packs were swung down from the roof by the driver's young mate and piled on to the back of a "ghardy." We climbed aboard, Di beside the driver, I on the back, and were driven through a maze of narrow, twisting lanes between high mud walls. Hamid led the way on his bicycle, and dark eyes peered at us with curiosity as we wound our way into the heart of the mud-walled town. At length we stopped in front of a narrow courtway.

"Here we are. I will send one of my uncle's boys for the luggage. Please follow me. I will take you to my cousin's house first and there you can wait whilst I inform my uncle of the great honour you are bestowing upon us by visiting us."

The courteous way in which he spoke awed us a little. We were shown into a room covered with many rather threadbare carpets and Hamid disappeared.

Two high iron beds stood at one end, and the withered old woman who came in as we were surveying the room motioned us toothily to sit and then herself sat, regarding us with unveiled curiosity from the other bed. Our jaws ached with smiling, the only language we all understood! She scuttled away when Hamid returned.

"My uncle's house is now ready," he said. "Will you please follow me?"

As we left the courtyard a young Afghan boy appeared and shouldered a rucksack. Hamid and Diana carried one between them, I picked up our string bag and we followed the boy, keeping well in the shade of the wall. Suddenly we came to a small, square trap door in the mud wall which was apparently the back door, and, struggling through, landed in a barren garden where a few fruit trees straggled.

Inside the house an old, toothless servant woman with a pitcher of water and two bowls poured water over our hands, after which we sat back gratefully on to the large, soft cushions leaning against the wall. Soon Hamid and his uncle came into the room, followed by two women, wearing wide-legged, silky trousers, covered by a loose, shapeless dress to the knees, a piece of pastel coloured chiffon draped around the hair. We had seen this type of dress before in Pakistan.

"This is my wife and her sister," Hamid's uncle introduced us in his stilted English, and quickly translated this for the women. They smiled warmly and motioned us to remain seated, asking "Cha?"

We both nodded, smiled, "Tash a ker—Choc, Tash a ker." (Thank you very much).

"My wife is a good woman," began uncle. "She cooks, bears my children, sews our clothes, but does not read or try to educate herself. We Afghan men follow world affairs and enjoy learning. You must tell us about life in your country."

A small oil stove was brought in and a large pot of water was placed on it. Next, two tiny silver trays appeared on which were minute glasses in silver holders, dainty fine china tea pots and bowls, containing sugar pieces, were laid before us.

Then the room was suddenly filled with women and children, the shy ones hanging back in the doorway, their eyes black and wondering, whilst the older ones, after we had learnt their names, and they ours, proudly showed us their national costumes. Then one woman was sent by Hamid's uncle to dress in hers and change from the longish, shapeless dress they all wore. Presently she was back, the voluminous skirt splaying wide as she moved, and shyly she pirouetted for us to see the tightly embroidered work that almost covered the coarse material. A national costume can make even a child look regal!

After two hours of sipping hot tea sweetened by the lumps of sugar held in the mouth, and talking to all through Hamid and uncle, we began to wonder if this was lunch!

Then one tall, good-looking woman commenced to prepare it. Cutting a large piece of meat into small pieces before us, she washed and placed it in the pot on the oil stove in the centre of the room.

"They are preparing everything in front of you to show you that everything is clean," Hamid told us anxiously. "For we know you have to be careful in our country."

We were very hungry, and were mesmerized by the cooking pot and the delicious odour, for we had not eaten for seven hours.

Eventually a small white cloth was spread in the centre of the carpet. Two huge bowls of glistening white rice and many small bowls of different vegetables (I recognised hard boiled eggs), all swimming in yellow ghee, were placed on the cloth. Four thick plates and several melons completed the laying of the meal.

"The women have eaten," Hamid said as we watched them smilingly retire with the children. Then, as the four of us sat cross-legged around the cloth, Hamid stated:

"You must follow an Afghan custom and eat all that is placed before you."

Was there a twinkle in his eye? We regarded the heaped dishes with dismay.

Hamid and uncle proceeded expertly to gather a heap of rice in their right hands, firmly press it into a little mound held between three fingers and a thumb, then dip it into their respective vegetable bowls, and transfer the sticky mass very tidily into their mouths.

We watched fascinated, but our fascination turned to horror when we realized that we were expected to do the same!

They sat with straight backs, eating very neatly. We tried to do the same, and Diana succeeded, but soon I was nearly bent double, getting closer and closer to the dishes on the floor in an effort to make the distance between them and my mouth less, for my rice just didn't hold together in my fingers as theirs did, but fell relentlessly in a thick layer into my lap before it could even reach my mouth. I tried an extra dip in the ghee, but this just dribbled off on to the rice in my lap. The little that reached my mouth did so unwillingly, leaving traces on my face and ruining my lipstick.

Diana looked horrified, and Hamid pointedly asked if "we" would like spoons. But I was not to be outdone. Foolishly I kept on trying to cope and ended up looking as though I had been rolled in rice.

Presently, looking over the heaps of rice still in a formidable mountain on my plate, I noticed the two men had finished theirs. Diana's looked almost untouched, although she had appeared to be eating well all the time. At last with the rice on our plates still looking almost untouched, we capitulated.

"It is an insult not to finish all the meal," Hamid said. "You eat like birds!" But we heaved sighs of relief as a child at last cleared away the rest of the rice.

Then came the melons! Four Hamid cut into about a dozen pieces and placed before Diana and me, who proceeded to select one piece each and slowly eat it. Not until we had finished our pieces did Hamid inform us, "The rice we forgive, but all these you must finish—all these!"

We both managed to struggle through another four slices, after which Hamid took pity on us and ordered the remainder to be cleared away.

We had then talked and eaten solidly for four hours, and suddenly we were mentally and physically "run out."

The whole family of aunts, uncles, cousins, children, even the old serving woman, escorted us out of the courtyard and into a waiting ghardy, then, with Hamid still as escort, we eventually reached the hotel.

It stood in trees, a great wooden building, surrounded by flowering bushes and a well laid out garden. The reception lounge reminded one of an advertisement from "Modern Homes."

Then began a tour of the hotel. Neither Diana nor I minded what the room was like as long as we could have a hot bath and a sleep, but the manager insisted that we see every room and take our pick.

"The first room is 1s. 8d. a night each—but too stuffy," he said. "The next one you would have to share the bathroom." So we were hurried on. The next seemed perfect, a little air, a separate bathroom, all Western furniture and 2s. 6d. a night each.

"This will suit us fine," we told him, and the manager, washing his hands in mid-air, apologised profusely. They kept this room for the Governor usually in case he needed it, but tonight a Russian diplomat was using it. There was a big meeting in the lounge.

Much later, having been made to see the whole hotel, we were finally given the room we had first seen, and thankfully sent Hamid on his way after he had given us instructions how to find his office in the morning. By then we were too exhausted even to go and "look" at the Russian meeting.

Early next morning Hamid appeared surprisingly as we stood in the lounge trying to make the manager and four of his "boys" understand we wanted to hire a "ghardy." These explanations always took up a good half hour, and as we seemed to be the only guests (there were no signs of any Russian diplomats), this was taking longer than usual.

"Come. First I will show you Herat, and my office," Hamid announced proudly, and we rattled in his waiting "ghardy" away from the hotel.

"Then the Governor wishes to see you both tonight. He speaks only a little English, so I, if I may, will be your interpreter."

"Oh!" I said in surprise. "But how did he hear of us?"

"I told him," Hamid said simply. "He is a friend of my father's and you will both love him very dearly, as I do, when you have spoken with him. His thoughts are only for the people of our country and he has done many things for Herat in the time that he has been the Governor. When you have spoken with him, you will see why he is such a great man!"

To us this sounded a little prejudiced, and to our inexperienced eyes a lot more could be done for Herat—one tarmac road would be a start—as we swayed on perilously across a deep rut in the baked road.

We had heard a lot of the King and Government of Afghanistan and always the same grumble. "The King and the Government are all related, they stick together, living their own luxurious lives, taking any wealth of the country for their own pockets. As for trying to help the people to a better way of life, it's a myth!" And so on, differently expressed it is true, but all saying roughly the same.

Now, here was Hamid, telling us the other side, and that he believed all he said was evident. Well, to-night we would hear a little more of the other side.

Along the tree-lined, dusty road we came suddenly to a police box, a circle of wooden boards on a small platform, with a large gay umbrella giving the necessary shade. It seemed deserted—but, as we approached, a uniformed body sprang to life from within, blew an unearthly blast on his whistle and waved us furiously on with many wild gesticulations.

As we were the only traffic on the road this seemed a little overpowering.

We turned a corner and entered a flowered square.

"Now it is summer, so the dust has covered the flowers and leaves," Hamid explained as we eyed the rather barren-looking Square.

"If it were winter the dust would not fly so much and the flowers would be bright," he said sadly.

Two Afghans with large water bags, the shape of whole sheep's carcases slung round their bodies, were languidly watering the dusty area.

On down the "main" street, now racing madly to overtake another ghardy, now picking our way slowly through the figures who leapt across the road under our skinny horse's nose. As usual we were the focus of all attention as we rumbled past the rows of garage like shops, the owner sitting cross-legged amongst his wares, past a tottering fort that stood like a centre-piece to the town.

"The Governor is having this age-old fort restored," Hamid said proudly. "It will show the people like you who come to visit Afghanistan that we are doing what we can to make it interesting for them."

Then, as we trotted on towards the bazaars at the end of the town, a distant hammering grew and grew, tapping and beating the air with a sharp, staccato, metallic sound. We had reached the Copper Market: two long, dusty streets, where a hundred copper-goods makers were at work behind their wares. Like primitive music the beating insinuated into our brains.

"How quiet it must seem to them at night," Di said, covering her ears with hands. "I'd go mad in this insidious hot row."

Hamid laughed at the expression on her face.

"They do not notice it. They are born in hammering, grow up and mostly die to the same beat." He shrugged his shoulders, and said simply, "It is their life."

We dismounted from the ghardy to get a closer look and marvel at the fine delicate work on the copper, passed down from father to son, generation after generation. And then another noise caught our ears as we turned away, nearly splitting our eardrums. In the shop next door, six tall, hefty Afghans lifted a huge hammer each in turn, high above his head, and brought it down with a resounding crash on to a piece of copper balanced on a block. Like a human machine the small group swung and worked in perfect unison: if one had delayed his stroke for an instant, the head of the next man to strike would have received the hammer and not the copper! We watched fascinated as they lifted their huge weapons almost simultaneously, the six crashes that followed splitting the air asunder.

Hamid was anxious to board the ghardy and move on, for a crowd of laughing, interested Afghans, many purdah-covered figures among them, had gathered, and we knew already that Hamid was apt to become embarrassed when too much interest was shown in us. For Herat was his home and, though his outlook was one of the most modern, he told us there would be much controversy later about his friendship with us. There were times like this when the sleeves of our shirts and length of our skirts seemed almost approaching nudity compared with the folds and coverings of the Afghans.

For they believe the hotter it is, the more one should put on!

We were hot and terribly dirty when the ghardy deposited us in the main street, and Hamid, pointing first to a large Ariana board at the top of a three-storied building, led us over a couple of smelling bodies asleep at the entrance, and up the narrow steep steps to his office. His under-manager sat at a large desk, which was the only furniture except for two large, red-plush, cosy armchairs, one either side.

"So this is where they were going to," Diana said, sinking once again into one, and we told him how we had used them before. Hamid translated to his manager amid much laughter at our thinking they had been put in the bus especially for us.

"They are yours as long as you stay in Herat," Hamid promised. "No one else shall use them."

His generosity and courteous kindness was sometimes breathtaking in its speed and directness.

The runner, an Afghan boy dressed solely in dusty rags, his

rough, boat-like shoes many times too big for him, came shyly in with the small bowls of cha, holding out sugar with trembling hands. We were probably the only women, other than his mother, sisters or wife to come, that he would ever see.

Once we had smiled like human beings, however, he lost some of his bewilderment and stood, shuffling quietly against the map of Afghanistan on the wall.

At a few minutes past eight that evening, we floated luxuriously over the bumps in a great black, ultra modern "Chev" towards the Palace.

A uniformed chauffeur, driving beside Hamid, completed the different picture of Herat. It was the only car we ever saw in the whole town.

As we reached the large brick, residential palace, Hamid greeted the bearer who appeared to show us into a large, whitewash walled room hung with many tapestries. A huge carpet covered the floor, a few chairs stood round the room like sentinels of another civilization.

A man of fifty or so, with the usual bright, gentle eyes and a slight stoop, entered the room, and took Hamid's hands gladly in greeting.

He wore a Western suit as Hamid did. A tie completed the idea of a European and not, as we had expected, a hawk nosed, loose garmented and turbanned Afghan. We felt a little cheated.

Hamid speaking quickly in their harsh language, introduced us; we shook hands, intently studying each other, and took a seat.

"His Excellency wished to say how much he admires your spirits," Hamid said. "To travel as you have done, through these countries. And he wishes that you tell him, through me, what difference to Afghanistan you found in India."

Then began another rather broken three-cornered discussion, while we all sipped glasses of "sherbaat," the sickly, watery drink peculiar to the country.

Each time, just as we had thankfully finished one each, the bearer would silently replace the empty glasses with the same concoction of another colour, and so on, and, always hopeful that the next colour would mean a new taste, we drank on—only to be disappointed!

Hamid seemed to be giving a rather lengthy discussion on the little we had said of the poverty and over-population of India as against the seeming poverty but self-supporting villages of Afghanistan.

"His Excellency is glad," Hamid interpreted, "that your eyes have not been dulled by your own way of living. That you have not compared the two is good, he says, for it is impossible to compare two such different ways of life. What might seem to be primitive and backward from your point of view, is, from an Afghan one, a life of comparative ease. He builds his own house freely, from the earth, when he is old enough and does not want for food or clothing, for as you have seen the valleys, although small, are fertile and green, with many sheep."

"This may be true," Diana said, "but there must be much that could be done to help in learning, and against diseases. This should have been done long ago, surely?"

"You must remember," Hamid interpreted, as His Excellency quietly went on, "we have had to fight many wars. There has not been time before. We have been too busy fighting one invader or another. You must know this," he went on very pointedly, and we tried hurriedly to wrack our brains and think when England was last at war with Afghanistan.

"Only in the last few years have we been able to start developing this country. There is much wealth beneath the mountains. His Excellency says this will soon be used."

"But what has he done that one can see since he has been Governor?" I said rather aggressively and to the point. I wanted some proof of all Hamid had told us of him.

Hamid explained, and they both laughed together, the Governor looking long and searchingly at Diana and me before he spoke again for Hamid to tell us, "His Excellency likes your question. He says you are very English, but with a difference. He has informed me that you may use his car while you are in Herat—he would like you to go to any village and see the work of the doctors. Each village has at least two, while there are many specially trained doctors, Europeans as well, who travel weekly to the villages to treat the people. This is a scheme started only a few years ago, His Excellency helped to begin it. Also I am to take you to the Men's Club. You will be the first women allowed in! There you will see how the Governor is educating and helping his people."

"Why can't he let women in to learn as well, if they are interested?" Di said. "Surely it is good for them to learn together."

The Governor started speaking before Hamid had interpreted, confirming my suspicions that he understood more than he would have us believe.

"His Excellency says it is too early for the women to know

these things. They have no wish for learning yet. The men must lead the way!"

So we talked on for over two hours.

"Now," Hamid said at length, "His Excellency asks if you will do him the honour of being his guests!" Diana and I glanced at each other quickly. Both had visions of moving into the dilapidated palace, but Hamid continued:

"His guests at the hotel. He says you will be more comfortable there. Stay as long as you like in Herat. It will cost you nothing. Go where you wish, see all you can. He would think it an honour if you use his car!"

In Hamid's phrasing, we again felt awed. Clearly luck was still with us. We were beginning to wonder how far luck could go.

Finally, with the usual "Ba Muna Khudas" and "Tash a kers," we took our leave, to drive quickly to the Men's Club in the large top floor of a rather dilapidated building in the town.

The Afghan in charge, recovering somewhat from his astonishment at seeing us, fed us the usual "cha" and lump sugar and showed us around thoroughly.

Round the walls were many books in different languages. Pictures of the present King and many of his predecessors took up large spaces, interspersed with embroidered, framed texts of the Koran in a hundred different sizes. Paintings, crude and good. Needlework—from the local girls' school, we were told.

Many world maps hung against the whitewashed walls, while a huge globe of the world stood invitingly for all to study on a desk.

A large table at the further end of the room turned out to be for table tennis.

"Let's have a game," I said, seizing a bat lying on the top and feeling rather tired of questions and answers. "Who plays?"

After much hesitation, Hamid and the "Secretary" took up rival positions, and the four of us began a soon perspiring game, watched laughingly by a number of Afghans who had been studying or reading, and who now closed in on us in their eagerness to see how the "fight" would go. It was a new, rather hilarious experience to be cheered on in Afghan and Di and I rose to the occasion, playing, for a change, rather well together.

But Hamid and the Secretary were brilliant players, and after three games we were limp and defeated—but still laughing.

"That was wonderful," the Secretary slapped Hamid on the back. "We must teach our women to play."

"This has been a night to remember," the Secretary said as we were saying goodnight. "You are both welcome to come any evening. Please do come. Even if Hamid cannot bring you!"

Again a jocular slap on the back. "You see! He is trying to get rid of me," Hamid told us laughingly, and then, in the way of so many Afghans, their little fingers entwined affectionately as we made for the door, Hamid to break away and follow us to the waiting car.

With many waves and shouts Hamid, Uncle and many relatives stood nearly in tears, and with Hamid's parting words: "You should stay longer, you have not had long enough to know us," ringing in our ears, the bus, swaying like a double-jointed Emmett cartoon, lurched away down the main street, packed to capacity!

We were sharing the front seat with the driver. Behind us were two men who had been in the plane, sitting with five others on a long, narrow seat, the width of the bus. Behind them peeped the turbanned faces of the other passengers and also two purdah-covered women. One held a scabby-eyed baby on her lap, brushing away with the other hand the relentless flies which never ceased to try and alight again and again on the baby's eyes, looking, when they did like large black scabs jutting from its face.

"That's trachoma," Di said, and I remembered the work being done against the same disease with the aborigines far up in North Western Australia.

What little space was left between the seats was piled with rolls of bedding, carpets, earthen jars of water and odd-looking boxes. Two great sheep made up the assorted company!

At the fringe of the town the bus stopped. We had been going for five minutes.

From an open fruit shop, armfuls of water melons were carried to the rear of the bus by the driver and his young dirty mate, and piled higgledy piggledy betwen the luggage on the roof.

Backwards and forwards they went.

"They certainly like melons," Di said. "I guess we should have brought more than one."

We only had our usual one thermos of cold water, with the melon in a string bag at our feet.

Ten minutes from the town, at the foot of another range of hills, we stopped again by a lonely house displaying a solitary petrol pump. Much haggling again transpired until the driver at

last handed over a wad of notes reluctantly, with many gesticulations and laughs.

"Everything seems a game for them," I said to Di wonderingly,
thinking of the darkness that would soon come so suddenly, and
eyeing the mountains ahead apprehensively. But the road
snaked on, not over the mountains, but away to the west
between the broad, flat plain and the foot of the hills.

Jolting and rattling, we swayed, tipped and lurched backwards
and forwards on the seat along the farmyard-like track.

"They are very wise really, tying their buses together," I
remarked. "If each piece didn't move separately as it hits a bump,
the whole thing would fall to pieces on the first journey!" We
laughed hilariously.

Then the bus stopped again!

The hazy sun was a molten half circle as it sunk beyond the
dusty plain. The driver turned as he made to clamber out, his
hands touching palms together, bent with his head towards the
last rays of the sun as an explanation.

"Good Heavens!" Di said in surprise. "A prayer meeting!"
For this was the first time we had been caught up in one.

Clambering roughly over the seats and passages, most of the
Afghans descended, except the two women who sat still and
quiet, to spread their small mats on the roadway or verge.
Taking off their shoes after rinsing their hands and faces with
water from the large earthen jars, they knelt and stood three
times in slow succession in prayer, towards Mecca.

We watched the careful rolling of the Afghan carpets at the
end of the ceremony.

As we rattled on, Di said thoughtfully, "We've come about
five kilometres in an hour and a half. At this rate we'll reach
Islam Killah tomorrow morning."

We dozed fitfully, pressing our knees uncomfortably against
the hot engine bulkhead to steady our jolting bodies. Now and
then we must have passed a village, cloaked and silent, for the
great Afghan dogs came streaking and howling from the darkness to leap and tear along beside the clattering bus, until, with
nothing to get their teeth into, they retired with sorrowful howls
back into the night, probably to wait for the wolves.

"Never run from the dogs," Hamid had told us. "If you are
ever in this predicament—if one ever comes at you from a
village, just sit or crouch where you are. They will not harm you.
They are kept to keep away the wolves that, in the winter,
finding no food in the mountains, attack the villages."

Occasionally we woke to see in the weak headlights the

flowing, dusty garments and bearded, turbanned face of another "passenger," seemingly standing miles from anywhere, waiting hopefully to cram himself and his belongings into the already overflowing bus. Somehow they always managed to stop and find room for these strays of the night.

I woke later, my mouth dry and dusty. We had stopped.

The driver's door was hanging open and in the headlights we watched as he talked to four tall, white-robed tribesmen who glanced up at the bus every now and then.

One, who seemed to be the leader, held a flickering lantern high in one hand and, with the other, he gesticulated as he talked quickly, pointing with long, thin fingers at us. All around was dark and silent, no sign of a village or camp, not even the howling of a dog.

"They've been discussing us for the last five minutes," Di spoke alertly, as one does who senses danger.

"Maybe he's trying to sell us," I laughed hollowly, trying to relieve the mounting tension. "I hope he gets a good price!"

We could do nothing but sit, cramped, hot and thirsty, and wait. But for what? Then suddenly they seemed to come to a decision. The tallest figure held the lantern even higher in the air showing a flash of white teeth in the sardonic long brown face. His eyes gleamed as he studied us!

Then all four of the motley bunch of knaves turned and stood watching as the little driver handed open our door. Beckoning us, he started to speak. Then remembering we knew only a few Afghan words, repeated again and again, "Cha, Cha, come—Cha."

"Tea! my foot," Di said wildly, looking helplessly round at the other sleeping passengers. No one stirred!

"Come," he repeated, helping her down roughly from the seat. "Cha," he said, turning his attention to me.

"No Cha, Tash a ker! Tash a ker, no Cha," we told them, as we stood in the dusty roadway. The pale headlights made two pools of light in the enfolding blackness. How friendly a place the ragged, box-like bus seemed at that moment, for we both knew with sure certainty that we would be leaving its comparative safety at any minute!

Our eyes tried to pierce the surrounding night, for if it was there, surely we would be able to see the dim lights of a "Cha Khana" or even a village somewhere at hand. But no sign of any light caught our searching eyes, only a blanketing darkness on all sides!

"My God!" Di exclaimed. "I knew everything had been too easy. I guess this is it."

"Let's make a quick dash back to our seats in the bus," I said, as we tried to smile at the Afghans through clenched teeth. We couldn't let it appear that we were scared.

"If we can clamber through to the back, they can't get us without making an awful rumpus," I said hurriedly.

We began to sidle slowly back to the door which still hung open, gesticulating and giving sickly smiles of different thanks.

Then suddenly they were all around us, covering the entrance of the bus, their loose garments flowing out like buzzards' wings as they closed in. A sinewy hand fastened on my wrist, and I heard Di give a cry as a hand clutched her arm. It was no good.

"Okay, bali bali (yes, yes). Okay. We'll have to go with them," I called, shaking off the firm grip.

Better to go quietly than be dragged!

"This is getting more like a nightmare every minute," said Diana, breathing harshly at my side.

With the driver and one tribesman lighting the way with the dim, flickering lantern, we headed between the other three away from the bus. Stumbling over rocks and sandy craters, through a spiky weed that jabbed savagely at our ankles, and over a fairly wide stream, they motioned us, on and on. It seemed ages, until, vaguely, over a sanded ridge, the dim outline of the low, flat, square buildings of a village appeared suddenly out of the darkness.

Along a narrow rough earth pathway they guided us, a high wall on one side, until we stumbled at last through a narrow wooden doorway in the wall.

Once inside by the light of the lantern which had been set down in the middle of the room, we could see the thick, rich-looking Afghan carpet that completely covered the floor. Great, dark red, silken cushions were planted around against the white-washed walls.

Then the tribesmen spread themselves out in front of us on the cushions. The central figure seemed to be a young Afghan, startlingly good looking with gentle eyes and a straight, intelligent nose beneath his huge turban, who watched us with intensity.

More Afghans brought in grapes and armfuls of different shaped melons and set them down between us and the tribesmen, who then with long sharp knives began expertly to cut them into wide pieces. Three thick plates—one for the driver, who had come along too—and common metal forks were placed before us, and the plates heaped with melon and grapes.

Then suddenly we were laughing, gesticulating and talking all at once, with a mixture of many languages, a couple of words from each. Like a United Nations meeting only they never have mouths stuffed full of melon as we did. We felt a bit sheepish when we realized what utter fools we had been to be so scared.

Gradually we learned that they had never had any white people in their village and, hearing that some were on the way, some of the villagers had been sent to fetch them to receive their hospitality. What they hadn't known was that the visitors were women, otherwise we would not have been practically carried from the bus!

In mixed English, German, French and Afghan, we talked on, mostly, however, gesticulating and smiling our thanks, while they in return made us understand that "Allah had been kind to let us visit them." As usual, they were incredulous that we travelled without escorts, their eyes showing their wonder.

Then the pots of steaming "cha," one each for all, were brought in, while the room began to fill with many more turbanned and bearded figures.

Later, glancing at our watches, we were staggered to find an hour and a half had slipped away and feeling for the people who were still waiting in the bus—not that anyone else was worried —we arose to leave and were escorted back by the whole tribe, it seemed.

"Ba Muna Khuda."

"God be with you," we wished them.

Great shouts of pleasure at this all round, and we buckled and wobbled on our way.

We reached Islam Killah at one o'clock, dead tired and aching in every bone. Then, hurried by the driver to the said "hotel," we were told there were no beds. So two Afghans were hurriedly tipped out, given a carpet each, and we went to bed!

15

At a Persian Wedding

AT 7.30 next morning we were wakened rudely by the manager pushing through the threadbare curtain at the door and shrieking, "Teleponee, Teleponee."

"That must be Afghan for 'Get Up'," I said, still half asleep. "They can't possibly have a telephone in this godforsaken spot —he's mad!"

Thankfully thus assuring ourselves, we slept again. Half an hour later he came back literally to pull us from our beds.

"Teleponee, queek, hailahoop! (Very good)," he exclaimed excitedly, his moustache waggling fiercely as he put his hands to his ears. There was no mistaking the meaning this time. Hurriedly we slipped dresses over our pyjamas, and followed him across a stretch of barren sand to a small rough building.

"Who on earth can be telephoning us in the middle of nowhere?" Di exclaimed as she lifted the old-fashioned receiver. It was Hamid. His voice came clearly, but worriedly, over the line.

"What happened to the bus? I rang twice last night. You had not arrived. I was getting very worried. Are you well?"

Diana, very amazed, explained why we had been so late, telling how we had been taken from the bus. He laughed loudly.

"Well, that is good. I ring you to wish you goodbye. You will cross the border into Persia and leave the friends you have made in Afghanistan. I can no longer help you, but do not forget me or my people," he said sincerely. "Now goodbye to you both. Ba Muna Khuda."

"Ba Muna Khuda. Goodbye," we echoed, replacing the receiver gently.

"One doesn't expect such thoughtfulness in the world," Di exclaimed, wonder in her voice.

Two hours later in the same bus in which we had travelled from Herat, with the same passengers, luggage and sheep, we at last rattled into the dusty border town for Customs checks, and to change our Afghan bus for a Persian one to continue on to

197

Meshed. Having checked and re-checked our passports thoroughly, the official regarded us not unkindly with bloodshot eyes, explaining in a mixture of languages that the bus to Meshed "u go-char heure, to travel now by day il est too hot—la nuit cold!"

"Four o'clock? It's now 11 a.m. Can we rest somewhere?" we asked. "Somewhere out of the sun!"

He called loudly for a pock-faced youth, who shouldered our packs quickly and, with a flash of yellow teeth, led the way up the dusty street and through a large wooden gateway into what looked at first sight to be a stable. There was a pile of hay in one corner and chickens in another: a few threadbare mats covered half the stone floor. An old woman appeared to chase the chickens out into the courtyard then, directed by the boy, she brought cushions and laid new carpets on the floor. After bringing glasses of tea and many sugar lumps, they left us to look through barred, glassless windows into the hot, dusty roadway outside. Then we lay on the mats and slept until the old crone woke us bringing more tea, and water, and a messy mixture of eggs and tomatoes.

All during the afternoon one or other of the Afghan passengers from the bus, who were also waiting to travel on to Meshed, popped into our "stable" to offer their grey cigarettes and enquire with gesticulations whether we were comfortable. Later in the afternoon, with the help of one passenger, we were buying our seats for the Persian bus when an unshaven soldier in drab uniform burst in and intimated that we were to go with him. Wondering what was wrong we followed him. We entered at last a square, shady courtyard, encircled by a thick mud wall. Two dark-eyed children splashed gleefully in a dirty pool and, watching them, clad in a brightly coloured pyjama suit, sat the officer who had checked our passports. We saw many officials wearing these loose-fitting, cool pyjama suits even when they were on duty. Our escort saluted several times, bowed himself to the ground and retired.

The officer rose, smiling and greeted us in French.

"Excuse me. I do not speak English very well. French is the language diplomatique. I sent my man to find you an hour ago. I wish you to take tea with my wife and I. I am sorry they did not find you before. Were you comfortable? Is there anything I can do for you?"

Wet as they were the children drew near to hang on to their father's trousers, and smile shyly. I laughed at them.

"I'd like a swim in that pool to get rid of some dust."

"But, of course, you would like a wash. My wife shall show you, then we can have tea."

A tall, dark woman with lank, greasy hair came quietly from the house when he called. She also greeted us in French, and when he had explained our need, she led us to the bend of the garden in the rear of the house where crystal clear water ran from beneath the high wall into a small round well and then on down the garden. This was the water they drank from, washed in and which kept the garden reasonably green. She brought soap and a clean large towel from the house and, although a young gardener was watching fascinated from a little distance, intimidated that we should undress and get right into the deep pool. Seeing us hesitate she laughed and bade us take no notice of the boy and, perching herself on a nearby stone, she chatted merrily as we gladly took our unusual shower. How cold the crystal water felt in the burning afternoon! Unfortunately, the exhilarating coolness barely lasted until we had finished our afternoon tea party with the family.

"Two of my men will take you back to the bus," the official told us. "We would like you to have stayed here for a while, for we get few white travellers through this desert post, and never before two mademoiselles. Give my love to Teheran: would that we return there soon!"

So, with many salutes all round, his men escorted us to the bus, where our packs were already roped high on the roof with a mountain of other luggage.

Below a sandy hill, above which stood a large, embattled fort of mud and sand, the bus stopped. Down from the fort rushed a number of soldiers and Persian officers. While the officers kissed cheeks in many farewells, the soldiers hurried backwards and forwards from fort to bus with yards of forms, and several boxes, which were heaved on to the roof, while we sat, and sat. The Afghan buses had been empty compared with this one with great rams in the back and not an inch to spare anywhere. However, officers being what they were, four villagers were at length pushed out on to the front mudguards while the two young, good looking Persian officers and their batmen blithely took over their seats. Di grimaced wonderingly and voiced my puzzled thoughts as we bumped on.

"Are they supposed to balance on the mudguards for the next twelve hours? They'll fall off in the night."

With luck we would reach Meshed some time the following morning.

The officer sitting opposite us turned dark, rather shy eyes our way. He spoke a little English, and had heard Diana's remark.

"To-night they dormer—sleep, yes—on roof," he explained. "Hialahoop—they like, good air!"

His friend spoke no English, but Namat and he were a charming pair. As night fell we came to a square mud village. By a dim chia khana the bus stopped and the load of turbanned Afghans and Persians spilled into the rough eating place. Namat and his friend led us in and we sat cross-legged and shoeless on the flea bitten, threadbare carpets set on long, stone seats.

"You must eat well, for the night is long. I shall order for you!" Namat said kindly, as his friend offered us long, thin Persian cigarettes, and we sipped scalding, black tea from small glasses. Each of us was served with a separate tray on which was a large flap of *nour* and a plate heaped with rice, tomatoes and a long many-seeded vegetable which looked like green corn cobs. As we ate, a face peered through the dusty window and a moment later the dusty village policeman in drab uniform entered, demanding to see passports.

"They are curious about you: otherwise they would not have bothered the others," Namat said laughingly to us as they eyed our passports and dusty figures, arguing lightheartedly about us to the room at large. Eventually Namat and Sadnie grew annoyed and, picking up the two amazed policemen by their scruffy collars, tossed them out of the door into the dusty gutter. The squatting men around shouted uproariously, enjoying the interlude. The driver of the bus doubled up with mirth in a corner, called something and Namat explained.

"He says we go soon—before they bring their friends back!"

So hurriedly we finished our food, squeezed ourselves back into the bus and, with the surplus passengers atop the baggage on the roof, we swayed merrily away into the night. One of the soldiers from the Fort produced two large bottles of vodka, and proceeded to get more and more drunk insisting that Namat, Sadnie, the driver and ourselves share his second bottle.

"Have you ever drunk vodka?" Namat asked as a flat lidful was passed shakily over by the soldier to us.

"No," we admitted, "but we'd like to try."

"Be careful. It is very strong," Namat warned.

It was harsh and burning. Di and I had a bare mouthful each, to the soldier's disgust. He was trying hard to get the driver drunk, tipping the fiery liquid down his protesting throat as he drove. Luckily the driver seemed to have enough sense to realize that he couldn't drink too much vodka and drive a loaded bus at sixty miles an hour through the night, although, like all these drivers, he gave as little attention as possible to driving. Eventually a tribesman, slightly fed up with the swaying soldier, threw his lidful of vodka into the soldier's face and a wild skirmish began around the half buried driver, who still hurtled the bus on through the blackness.

I began to wonder if I was having a nightmare. The driver pulled the bus to a stop and the drunken soldier was deposited at the side of the road to find his own way to the nearest village. We rattled on again, but not before the soldier had pushed another bottle of vodka through the window to us. Thoughtfully Di and I had pushed it beneath our seat thinking to keep it as a souvenir, but evidently someone had other ideas for it had disappeared by the time we reached Meshed. We had just begun to doze fitfully, cramped and aching in our narrow seats, when a terrifying wail came from the rear of the bus. Di nearly jumped through the window in fright. Namat stirred and laughed. "He prays," he said, but after half an hour of crude shrieking everyone was awake and feeling murderous.

Suddenly Namat and Sadnie started singing loudly to drown the wails; from the roars of appreciation, they seemed to be dirty army songs, but they sounded better than the awful wailing and so alternately on through the night they sang until the wailing one gave up.

At 2.30 the driver decided he must have a nap, so in another cha khana, we drank tea—then Namat showed us into a lantern-lit cubbyhole and left us to sink exhausted on to carpet-covered, stone couches. Dawn was breaking when he shook us and we stumbled out to drink more and more tea, filthy, aching and flea bitten, and to breakfast on huge water melons, *nour* and cheese. As usual Namat waved our money aside. "Our guests do not pay," he said proudly, adding, "One day I come to England maybe, and you do same for me."

Long before we reached Meshed, we spied the huge, bright blue dome and golden minarets of its famous mosque, gleaming in the brilliant sunlight.

Meshed looked very modern after primitive Afghanistan, with its paved, tree-lined streets, fairly modern shops, the women in their not so enveloping "chardus". Meshed is the second centre of Mohammedanism, the first being Mecca. To Meshed, thousands of pilgrims flock each year to pay their respects to the Prophet. Namat's home was in Meshed so, after booking us into a small hotel, he left us to fill in police forms, saying: "If I may, I will return at 5 o'clock and take you to see town. We eat Persian food—very good. Maybe see American film. Goodbye."

Tired, dusty and full of aches we looked a sorry pair. Then after a tepid shower, we hung our clean, wet clothes around our small room, and threw ourselves gratefully on to the soft beds and remembered no more till Namat knocked on our door at 5 o'clock, resplendent in a well pressed uniform. Proudly we strolled through the evening crowds with our handsome escort. This was the hour when all the town filled the pavements and colourful gardens of Meshed. Everyone seemed in holiday mood.

In a small Persian hotel we ate a delicious meal of various meats and strange vegetables, washing it down with sherbaat apple water.

In a Persian Open Air Cinema, we ate ice cream and watched an American film, punctuated every two minutes by Persian script. Later, in a café, with a windowful of a hundred different cakes and sweetmeats, we drank many glasses of sherbaat. In one day we had come from a primitive civilization into a fairly modern one. It was difficult to believe that two countries as close together as Afghanistan and Iran could be so very different.

As Namat presented us with a huge box of gaily adorned chocolates and escorted us to our hotel, he said sadly:

"Tomorrow I return to Fort. Ten days I come back. Maybe you still here—I hope."

We nodded, not having the heart to confess that we would surely be in Teheran by then. When eventually we did reach England we found a letter from him.

"I wish you will both be happy. I think you are in your country now. I hope you have pleasant memories during your stay in Iran as our country people are generally kind and hospitality and they are fond of friendly relations between all the nations, and as you have decided to make a travel 'too' to many countries of the world for the proud and glory of your country you did your travel successfully. I shall congratulate your journey sincerely. But I am sad I could not be longer with you in Meshed (where there was a dome golden). My dear friends I cannot think of another think. Here is hopeing you write soon, with my love, Namat."

Despite what Namat said in his letter, due to unhappy relations at that time between England and Iran about oil, the British Consulates had all been closed except the Embassy. But behind a high walled compound at the side of the city next morning we found the American Consulate. As we made our way across a large brick courtyard, shaded from the burning sun by tall, green willows, a great, white Afghan hound, the size of a small donkey, with a thick mane like a lion, rose from one side and stalked towards us. He growled ominously, as we stood our ground looking round fearfully for help. At his bark a tanned, dark haired woman appeared suddenly from a door across the courtyard, dressed in minute shorts and sun top. She hurried across, waved the still growling hound away and in a slow, lazy, American drawl, said: "Gee, I'm sorry about that dawg. I just don't know what's gotten in to him these days," she said with a frown. She eyed us appraisingly. "Excuse my get-up. I've just been having a dip in the pool. You're Americans?" It was more a statement than a question.

"No, English," we told her. "We're sorry to barge in on you on a Sunday, but we heard there might be a point-four truck going from your Consulate to Teheran soon. If so, we rather hoped there might be room in it for us. We're on our way home to England overland from Colombo."

She whistled softly.

"You'd better come on in—you must be tired. I'll call my husband—he's having a swim with the kids. He'll know more about transport. We get up late on Sunday morning," she explained. "I was just gonna cook some bacon for breakfast— you must stay and join us."

Di and I sniffed the air.

"Well, as you mention bacon, we'd love to. We can't remember when we last had bacon."

Barbara Jesperson and her tall fair husband, Jess, were a charming pair of Americans. Stuck in the wilds of Persia they were glad to see new faces. As we ate canned, sizzling American bacon, Jess explained thoughtfully, "I don't know of any point-four truck going at the moment. True, they do bring provisions from Teheran, but not very often. There'd be plenty of room on one going back. I'll check up and let you know. Where are you staying?"

Thanking him, we explained.

"I have an idea," Barbara drawled. "We've a great spare empty compartment on the side here. They use it when 'higher ups' come. How about moving in here? We'd love to have the company, eh, Jess? We've a small swimming pool," she went on enticingly. "You can stay till a truck comes along. What about that?"

We needed no second invitation. A swimming pool and good company! The gods were kind.

"How about coming to a Persian wedding?" Barbara asked next day. "I have to go along to represent the Consulate, being the only wife on the Staff."

"Of course you don't see all the ceremony," Barbara explained. "That's a three-day affair. Yesterday the men had their day of celebrations and to-day is the women's day and no men are allowed in. Tomorrow they are officially married, and the bride goes to her mother-in-law's house."

As we stepped from the Consulate car that evening outside a high wall where many other cars were already parked, the music from a gay string band greeted us from over the wall. It was a Persian version of "Anna."

Inside the large square garden the brick floor was completely covered with beautiful Persian carpets: there must have been a hundred. Over the long benches and loaded tables, where many gay and beautiful women sat talking and eating, brilliant, many-coloured fairy lights swayed, casting a reflection in the large, still pool in the centre of the courtyard.

"I've brought two English friends along—they've never been to a Persian wedding," Barbara drawled as she introduced us to the bride's handsome mother.

"You are very welcome," the mother exclaimed in beautiful English.

Through the smiling rows of women she showed us to our seats, and soon we were plied with glasses of tea, sherbaat and wine. Our plates were loaded with delicacies from the groaning tables. Barbara made it her business to give us a running commentary.

"In a while the bride and her new husband will come out of the house and mingle with the guests. It's the bride's privilege to ask any one of the guests to do something—dance, or sing, anything. Then the selected person can, in her turn, ask whoever she likes to carry on—it's great fun!" Barbara laughed darkly. "As long as we don't get asked! We'd never be forgiven if we refused." Luckily we weren't asked.

After the beautiful Persian bride in her sparkling tiara and flowing bridal gown with her rather tubby husband had walked smilingly but rather nervously through the avenue of women to take their seats by the pool, a sinewy, dark eyed beauty was pulled from her seat. Slowly and beautifully she began to dance to the strange Persian music, a perfect picture of rhythm and poise in her shimmering tight gown.

"This is the Dance of Desires," Barbara said softly.

And it looked it; no wonder only the bridegroom was allowed in! The girl the dancer chose next was not Persian.

"Oh good. It's Marie," Barbara laughed. "She's one of the American girls married to an Iranian. She's always asked to perform."

With the bridegroom, Marie danced for the bride a complicated tango. The bride loved it and so did the appreciative audience.

Marie joined us after the dance, her eyes sparkling as she exclaimed effusively: "Gee, aren't Persian weddings something? I had one like this after we got here from the States."

"I think I'd get a little tired after three days of meeting people," I laughed. "It's a bit unnerving, isn't it?"

"Well yes," she admitted. "I guess I slept for a week after." But it was a wonderful sight.

Much later, led by Barbara, we filed by the bride and groom to take their hands for a moment and, copying Barbara, wished them in Persian "A long life and many children after tomorrow." For they had still a night and a day of feasting to get through before the ceremony was over.

It was good to relax by the pool each morning after an early swim with Barbara, Jess and their two young children, where breakfast and even lunch was often eaten, brought by the fierce eyed servant.

The Afghan hound, however, became no friendlier, much to Barbara's concern for she and the children could do what they liked with him. But Jess explained that he was now old enough to revert to the ferocity of any Afghan village hound, so Di and I always kept well out of his way, and he was no longer allowed to roam the compound when strangers were about.

The bazaars of Meshed were hot and gaudy. Turquoise is dug in abundance from the soil of Persia, and it finds its way in a million different forms to the bazaars. There are rings, earrings, necklets, bracelets, all forms of adornment made from various stones, good, bad and indifferent. By the time Di and I had walked the length of the crowded bazaar, we felt we should now know the difference between good and bad stones. For about 15 shillings we purchased three pairs of earrings and two beautifully marked stones for rings.

"Gee, they're beautiful," Barbara exclaimed, when later we displayed the earrings. "I've been meaning to get some turquoise earrings for ages—but you know how it is when you live in a place—one leaves things, and leaves things."

"Oh good," we said happily. "We bought a pair for you." Her delight was pleasant to see.

"We have to go to the Pakistan Independence Day celebrations tomorrow evening," Jess informed us. "Shouldn't wonder if you gals get a special invitation."

Sure enough next morning it came by special courier. Inside a large courtyard we were all greeted charmingly by the Minister for Pakistan and his wife. The garden was decked out in much the same style as the wedding garden had been, and we had a strenuous hour of meeting ministers and diplomats of various Eastern countries and magnificently dressed Eastern Princes and Princesses.

A week after our arrival in Meshed we rather reluctantly donned our faded travelling skirts and blouses, jammed our things once again into our packs, bade a sad farewell to Jess, Barbara and their children and roared away at mid-morning into the silted looking horizon in a point-four truck. The back was piled high with furniture and carpets. The American owner who had been transferred to Teheran had flown on. The Iranian driver spoke very little English and looked on us suspiciously. By late afternoon our sandy, desolate road was only five kilometres from the distant, silted mountains of Russia.

"Russ! Russ!" The little driver shouted excitedly, and by the time we had all shouted and gesticulated, waving imaginary guns at the distant hills, we were all the best of friends. Through a desolate looking world we bumped and bounced, stopping occasionally for food and cha in dun-coloured, forgotten villages. Sometimes the black tents of roaming nomads were huddled in the sandy wastes by small springs of water. Their leathery faced women filled earthen pots and gazed wonderingly at us as we refilled our water bags.

At 2 a.m. even the sturdy little driver could not see out of his dust-rimmed eyes. Thankfully we all piled on to the hard furniture in the back of the lorry and slept the sleep of exhaustion. At 4.30 we were on our bumping way again, and when dawn broke we washed in a rippling stream by a lonely cha khana where a few buses and great oil trucks were pulled up. The buses were carrying pilgrims from Saudi Arabia to Meshed. As we ate a scanty breakfast some of the pilgrims joined us, their long, flowing robes amazingly white in a dusty, sunbaked world. In beautiful English they questioned us and we them. As we left, a noble faced Arab of high birth told us:

" In a few weeks we shall return to our country. I shall give you my address and maybe you will come to my country on your way home. My people will be honoured to have you as their guests. Do not forget. May God be with you," he said gently.

So on again all day through more desolate scenery—nothing but dry, flat arid ground. Jagged lines of mountains advanced and retreated. The sparse villages with their square, mud-domed houses were fertile and green, an occasional flash of vivid brightness in an otherwise dim horizon.

By nightfall we had bounced and bumped nearly 300 miles in twenty-six hours, only two of which we had managed to sleep through. Taking it in turns to rest on the other's padded shoulder we tried vainly to sleep. But as the shoulder heaved with each bump, it was rather like trying to sleep on the kick of a mule. The night wore on in an agony of bumping and jolting. Our Iranian driver drove in a quiet sort of desperation, his bloodshot eyes nearly popping from their sockets. When at long last, lights appeared dimly in the far horizon he grinned suddenly and, with a sigh, breathed "Teheran," but it was to be another three hours before he at last pulled up in the deserted main road in the city and motioned that this was as far as he was taking us. There were no signs of any hotels or *pensions:* indeed we had seen none as we entered the dimly lit, sleeping city.

"He can't just dump us here at midnight in a strange city," Di exclaimed. "Jess said he'd take us to a cheap hotel. Heavens, I know he's tired but so are we! We might walk the streets all night!"

The driver was so exhausted he didn't give a damn what happened to us, but after a loud argument in the dark, deserted street he decided it might be simpler to follow his previously given instructions and get it over with. Even with his help we had a hard job to find a hotel open after midnight, but eventually, in a wide avenue below the British Embassy compound, we found a room in a small, cheap looking hotel.

The night was hot. Outside our open windows on the verandah stood a line of small beds filled with sleeping Persians. In the courtyard below they slept in the open beneath the stars. We even fell over them outside our door, but we were too tired to care, and thankfully we sank on to our beds and slept like the dead till late the next day.

16

Feast of Mourning

AFTER two days in Teheran we booked seats on a bus to
Kermanshah for 18s. each, the only two that were left—
in the back! And at 6 a.m. one morning we bumped and
rattled out of Teheran. Hanging wildly on to the seat in front,
we jumped in the air over each bump with the other three
Iranian young men who shared our springing back seat, which
caused much mirth to the loaded bus. Peering back in the long,
narrow mirror above the driver's seat, which he shared with
four passengers, the speed merchant of a driver hurtled the bus
along at 90 kilometres glancing back with sparkling eyes and
quivering moustache, laughing gaily as we cracked our skulls
again and again on the sloping roof as we hit each bump in the
unmade road. At first it was fun. Along the flat, dusty road we
came at last to Kazerun. One road led west to Tabriz, ours
led south to Kermanshah, ten hours' away, and thence to
Baghdad.

With roads that are ever flat and unendingly straight there is
nothing better loved by a Persian bus driver and his colourful
passengers than a race with anything that moves—but preferably with another bus load, and in the 600 miles from Teheran
to Baghdad we saw many, many buses all loaded to capacity,
for this is the only means of travel for most people. There is no
railway line across this barren country and buses are cheap.

Hurtling through a blinding cloud of dust, our bus gradually
drew up to another bus in front. We pulled level and with a
blare of horns and shouts from the passengers we were racing
neck and neck. The shrieking passengers shouted encouragement to their separate drivers and hurled insults and abuse
through the open windows at the other passengers. We hurtled
on, with a bare two inches between the buses and deep crumbling
ditches on either side of the narrow roads as neck and neck still,
we raced on for almost a kilometre. God help anything appearing
on the horizon towards us, I thought, cursing the driver for his
madness, yet nevertheless admiring his skill.

Races like this helped to break the monotony of the long journey.

After two hours we stopped for breakfast at a dirty solitary dwelling, the only habitable place in a dusty, desolate plain. In the baked mud garden stood homemade wooden tables, on the rough benches flea infested carpets were laid. As we thankfully alighted from the bus with the other passengers, a young dark haired and moustached police officer, who had boarded the bus on the outskirts of Teheran and for whom the best seat next to the driver had been saved, detached himself from a group to introduce himself and shout for cha and food for us. Khalid Fisuni spoke a little English. We gathered he was on his way home on leave from Teheran to Kermanshah, and a more helpful and pleasant companion we could not have wished for. At each stop from there on he took complete charge of us.

Each two hours' drive between cha houses began to take on a macabre pattern. Both Diana and I had "Teheran Tummy"—not a pleasant thing at any time, but in the back seat of a Persian bus it is a slow sort of torture. This was the pattern; cha, followed by half an hour of laughter as we soared towards the roof, then the aches began, bumping became an agony, now we were hitting our heads regularly on the roof, our rumbling stomachs began changing gears more often, cramp set in. Still the driver grinned back in his mirror and hurtled us on, making ribald comments, Khalid grinned cheerfully back in the mirror, unable to help until we stopped. One and a half hours later we were suffering sheer agony and feeling we couldn't endure much more.

"I shall scream if this bus doesn't stop," I moaned to Di through clenched teeth. We looked at each other's agonized faces and wanted to laugh but couldn't—it hurt too much.

At the top of a mountain pass some old greybeard wailed a prophet's prayer for safety and everyone answered him: "Salaam Alikan Salaam ah Mohamed."

They all laughed until we felt we had to as well. At the bottom of the pass there was another prayer chant, another laughing answer, and this time we were made to join in amidst roars of encouragement and appreciation.

Picking up speed the driver hurtled along again at 95 kilometres an hour, by which time we were past caring whether we arrived or not. A little over two hours from the last stop, a village came into view, thank heavens—"All out for cha!" It was music to our ears. Refreshed, the pattern started again, and so on for ten hours!

Crossing the hottest most desolate part of the earth, at its hottest time (the temperature often reaches 140 degrees), it was small wonder that, when we opened a window the burning wind peeled the skin from our noses and lips. Yet when we shut it again, we nearly suffocated.

Twisting herself into knots beside me, her long legs and back cramped beyond belief in the narrow seat, Diana eyed me wryly:

"Whose idea was it to come across Asia?" she asked.

"I'm beginning to feel sorry I ever dragged you along," I admitted. "Why didn't you hit me over the head with an axe? It's your fault for not putting your foot down and making us go the easy comfortable way—by ship."

"Well, I guess it can't be helped if we're both mad!"

"We'll have a drink on that," I said, handing her our battered Thermos water flask.

"At least when we get home we can make our fortunes from the manufacturers," I chuckled, holding the flask aloft. "Think of it: they can say 'Only our flasks can travel across three continents, 26,000 miles round Australia, Asia and Europe'."

But at that moment as we took another mighty leap into the air, our much travelled flask slipped from my hands and crashed to pieces at our feet. Almost in tears we threw it from the window and watched it glinting behind for many kilometres, mute symbol of water in a barren desert land.

At six that evening, 15 kilometres from Kermanshah, a whole contingent of cars and taxis bearing relatives and friends of those in the bus came out to meet them. Good humouredly the driver stopped and all aboard heaved themselves out to hug and kiss all round. Watching the performance outside, Di chuckled as the driver's hand was nearly pumped off by the waiting relatives.

"They realize it's all up to the driver whether their friends ever do arrive," she said sagely.

All sprang aboard again and another race was on to see who could first reach Kermanshah.

It lay below at last, a green fingered, shallow, valley town amidst acres of yellow corn stretching on into waste and barrenness.

Almost as thick with dust as the outside of the bus, we all alighted and Khalid supervised the handing down of our packs from the mountain of baggage and carpets on the roof. A taxi appeared magically.

"I will take you first to hotel," Khalid explained, and after shaking hands and saying goodbyes all round, for we felt by now we had known our friendly passengers and driver a lifetime, we headed out of the bus yard. The streets and pavements were teeming with Kurds, hawk-eyed tribesmen from the surrounding hills and villages. On foot and mounted on wild looking horses they swarmed everywhere, as we honked our way slowly through the sun-baked, jostling crowds. The streets were alive with vendors, dark-eyed children scampered dangerously beneath the horses' hooves, and black eyes peered curiously into the taxi as we passed.

Something was afoot; there was a restless feeling of excitement everywhere.

"It looks like a Persian August Bank Holiday," I remarked facetiously to Di. Khalid had not understood what I said, but his eyes twinkled gaily as he watched our darting, inquisitive eyes.

"Feast of Mourning," he said slowly, "Muharram tomorrow —great procession! Many tribesmen come!"

Both the hotels in Kermanshah were full to capacity with great six foot tribesmen! They thronged the pathways and corridors watching us with eagle eye's as we followed Khalid to make enquiries from the owner of the hotel.

Suddenly a Persian, dressed finely in white European clothes, pushed his way commandingly through to doff his straw hat before us. His English was perfect.

"So!" he laughed. "You have picked a bad time to visit Kermanshah—but do not look so worried. You cannot get a room here—I know—but I have a spare room. With my wife and me you shall stay, so now you can smile. Ah! that is better!" he exclaimed. We were thanking him as Khalid came back shaking his head. The other man spoke quickly to him in Persian, but Khalid shook his head again and smiled. "Tash a ker, the hotels are full—they stay with me." So saying, he motioned us to follow him into the street. The other smiled sadly.

"A thousands regrets are mine," he said. "My wife would love to have met you. Maybe we shall see you tomorrow. Goodbye."

Leaving the taxi at last with Khalid we picked our way through rubbled, narrow streets overshadowed by high, stone walls and came at last to a great wooden doorway which led into a cool bricked courtyard; in the centre was a round pool in which two white ducks sat serenely. A tall tree gave cool shade. At the head of the courtyard five steps led to a fine stone house, heavy curtains of fine embroidered material hung over the windows to stay the glaring sun-rays. Khalid's family came bursting from the house to greet him. A beautiful young dark-haired girl, a baby in her arms led the way, to be caught up excitedly in Khalid's arms, swung into the air, baby and all, and kissed many times. This was Mahany, his wife, who smiled her welcome delightedly tasting our unfamiliar names and repeating them again and again to the cooing baby. Then came her attractive young looking mother, followed by her sister and brother, who all greeted us warmly—bringing water in long spouted jugs to wash the dust and grime from our hands and faces as we stood by the pool. Then the usual tiny glasses of black tea were brought from the dark cookhouse on one side of the courtyard by an old serving woman.

As dusk fell a flaring lantern was placed in the centre of the wooden table and with much laughter and chatter we played rummy and drank endless glasses of tea, merrily exchanging English and Persian words.

After an hour with the dust falling in layers from us, we asked Khalid:

"Is it possible to shower—you know, wash all over?"

At last he understood.

"Yes, but you must go to public baths."

So, collecting a dress, our towels and soap, with Khalid and his young sister-in-law leading, we made our way deep into the backwash of the town, through narrow alleyways down steep steps with towering walls either side and under small dark archways; miserable looking dogs sniffed and howled at our heels until Khalid beat them off. At length we descended into a dimly lit passageway where wreaths of steam rose eerily from below. For a few rials, which Khalid would not allow us to pay, we were ushered into what was a near approach to a Turkish bath.

"Jahsrine will wait to bring you to house." Khalid explained. "I will return now."

While Jahsrine watched our clothes, Di and I stripped and gradually eased the dust and sweat from our stiff limbs.

After a merry supper of rice, salad, meats and fruit in the lantern lit courtyard, we donned night attire in turns in a carpeted room inside the house, then all came out to the cool courtyard to sleep. Two extra beds had been placed near the others for us. Mother, daughter and son slept in one large mosquito-netted bed. Khalid's and Mahany's bed, where the baby slept also, was a little way along the terrace, and Di's and mine were by the pond.

Next morning early we breakfasted in the courtyard. They were a happy family. They all helped to lay meals and clear away for there was no servant to wait at table, although the food was cooked by one old serving woman, while another looked entirely after the baby.

Later in the morning we strolled through the main street of

Kermanshah, even more full with vendors and tribesmen than the evening before, and once again dark eyes turned suspiciously at us. I was glad that Khalid and his young brother-in-law were with us, remembering what Barbara and Jess had told us of Meshed during the Feast of Mourning. Being the religious centre, the worshippers of the Prophet walk the streets bleeding as they beat and slash themselves fanatically with chains and knives. Many heads are cut open by a heavy sword being beaten sharp side down in mistake for the flat side on to their heads by the mourner's own two hands. Any Christian was likely to be murdered on the spot as an infidel.

This practice was kept up in Baghdad until only recently, when it was forbidden by the powers-that-be. The Kurds in Kermanshah certainly didn't appear to be over friendly; to Khalid's dismay we furtively managed to take two photographs of splendidly attired tribesmen. The heat soon became intolerable, so we gladly returned to the house to eat lunch inside and rest before going to the "28th Muharram."

At 3 p.m., when the broiling heat outside the courtyard had abated a little, we made our way with Khalid, Mahany and her young brother and sister, all dressed in their Sunday best for the great occasion, to the main street of Kermanshah to watch the procession. With some difficulty we managed to make our way through the great crowds of Persians lining the streets to take up positions in seats in an enclosed rostrum by the side of the saluting dais, where stood American officers and Chiefs of the Persian Army.

"The Americans are in our country to teach the Army," Khalid explained.

Above the crowds in the street every window and roof was packed with spectators, houses were decked with pictures of the Shah. Suddenly a band, the men in gay colours and wearing peculiar hats, started up a jangling march on many weird instruments. The crowd stirred restlessly in the blazing sun, sweat dripped from our bodies as we waited.

"Does this procession take place every year?" Di enquired of Khalid.

Khalid looked a wonderful figure, dark, handsome and resplendent in his best uniform.

"Yes. It is the '28th Muharram' proclaiming Mosadec's downfall, and the Shah's return to power. Much blood was shed then. This is to remind the people that it must not happen again.

"Ah! here are the mountain Kurds on foot," he exclaimed excitedly. "Stand on seats—you see better!"

213

Down the street came the Army on foot, clad in dusty clothes and even dustier boots. They made a fantastic array. As they neared the rostrum the quick march turned to a slow goose stepping as they turned eyes right. It was the first time Di and I had seen real goose-stepping and it gave me a strange feeling.

"Mord Kurds," Khalid explained as after the Army on foot came the mounted tribesmen.

All looked terribly dusty and dirty. The tribesmen's nervous, highly strung horses reared and snorted as they trotted by, four deep. This was certainly the strangest procession I had ever seen. With their layers of dusty baggy trousers, waistcoats, huge filthy turbans and rather evil looking faces, they made a ragged, cunning and motley crew. For almost two hours they rode by until the street was thick with manure and many horses slipped, throwing their riders, to their furious embarrassment.

"Here come the tanks," Khalid cried, as a dull roar shook the air and they rattled and crashed by the dias. Lastly came lines and lines of dust-covered lorries and buses, crammed to capacity with Persians, young, old and indifferent, shouting slogans and singing raucous, patriotic songs.

On each side of the vehicles, much-used Persian carpets were draped, while on bonnets and roofs were balanced precariously large pictures of the Shah.

"What a primitive, fantastic—yet frightening—display," Di exclaimed slowly, as the last lorry load roared past, and Khalid helped us down from our seats.

Khalid booked our bus seats on to Baghdad, insisting on paying for them as well and early next morning we were presented with a parting gift from the family—a brooch of a miniature Persian dagger for Diana, and for me an engraved Persian cigarette case. Once more we were bumping and jolting for the next seven hours on to the border of Iraq.

At the desert border control as we left Iran we waited two hours while luggage and passports were examined.

Ten minutes later at the desolate looking border post of Iraq the search started all over again. As we waited in a small, dark cubbyhole for our passports to be checked a grubby looking official suddenly entered, bearing an ugly looking hypodermic syringe.

"You must have! All must have! Smallpox!" he grinned, advancing as we backed hurriedly out of reach.

"But we *are* innoculated," we exclaimed waving our certificates at him.

214

"That does not matter. You cannot enter Iraq without this—here!"

Diana, watching his grubby fingers on the needle, winced.

"If we're innoculated with that, we'll certainly never enter Iraq," she croaked. "Where's the officer in charge?"

Luckily he entered at that moment, and perusing our Innoculation Certificates he reluctantly waved the hovering "doctor" away and we hurriedly escaped before they could change their minds.

After another two hours we discovered that the hold-up was due to an Iranian not having an entry visa for Iraq.

By now we were thoroughly dazed and tired with heat and ravenously hungry.

"At this rate, we'll get to Baghdad tomorrow morning, instead of this evening," I said thoughtfully, as the voices still wailed and argued from the building.

We opened a large tin of pears which we had carried from Amritsar and the waiting bus load pronged into the can with assorted weapons, laughing gleefully as pear juice dripped all over them.

Suddenly a car appeared out of the blue and drew up before the bus. Its two occupants looked like Arabs, but were dressed as Europeans. One made his way into the building.

"They're going towards Baghdad," I stated, seizing a thought.

Diana looked as though she was past caring. I pushed her quickly out of the bus and we greeted the surprised Arab.

"Do you speak English?" I asked.

"Yes," He still looked a little bewildered.

"Are you going to Baghdad? If so, could you possibly take two passengers—we've been stuck in this godforsaken spot for nearly five hours."

He laughed suddenly.

"We can take you into the next town, but we do not go to Baghdad. Come, of course! You could have a meal there until the bus arrives—and then go on."

It was a good idea. Our packs were soon bundled from the bus into the car. Quickly the Arabs told the driver to pick us up at the next small town, the other Arab appeared and away we sped. It was sheer delight to sail over the bumps instead of being jarred to pieces. The two Arabs were friendly; they laughed in astonishment as we talked.

"You must love to travel, if you come all the way by bus. If you can travel by Iranian buses you can travel on anything in the world," they said seriously.

"I'll never travel through Persia by bus again," Diana vowed.

"Nor I," I agreed, "But it *was* an experience."

They hooted with derision as we sped on over the desert road. An hour later we reached the small Iraqi town. Our driver dropped his friend, and then took us to a small open café, where we chose many platefuls of delicious meats, and the owner scurried off to find some milk for tea.

As we ate, our friend suggested thoughtfully:

"If you do not wish to continue to Baghdad by bus, you should go by taxi—it is only one hundred and fifty kilometres!"

Di nearly choked in alarm, while I laughed inanely.

Taxi! Ye Gods! Was the man mad! We had about £2 in Iraqi money. He saw our faces.

"But for ten dinars each, is it not worth it?" he asked.

At first we wondered where the catch was. Ten shillings for a hundred miles? It seemed ridiculous—although even ten shillings was too much for our meagre purses.

"You forget that this is a land where petrol is cheap," he reminded us. "Many Iraqis own large American cars which they use to take five or six people from here to Baghdad. Many people travel so. From here you must cross the desert to Baghdad. There is no particular roadway from 50 kilometres this side of Baghdad."

He saw our waning morale and added darkly: "The bus is very bumpy over the desert."

Diana was the keeper of the purse for Iraq. The thought of the next seven or eight hours jolting by bus was too much. Our friend grinned happily as she exclaimed: "O.K. Let's go by taxi; we'll have to cut our stay in Baghdad by a day to make up for it!"

'I will let the driver of the bus know you have gone on," our friend told us, as a little later he paid our money to the Iraqi owner of a luxurious taxi and soon, with three other Iraqi passengers, we were speeding in luxury over the desert, to reach Baghdad at 10 p.m. At a small hotel, low down in Rashid Street, we climbed the narrow stone steps and shook the sleepy owner.

"We would like a cheap room and clean!"

He looked perplexed.

"You go Hotel Sindabad, Hotel Semeramis," he said, mentioning the two most expensive hotels in Baghdad.

But eventually, after studying our passport for a long while, he stuffed them into a drawer, made us fill in police forms and only then did he smile amiably and escort us to a clean double room overlooking Rashid Street. All night the honking of taxis and cars filled the air with clatter, but we were too tired to care.

17

Birthday in Baghdad

BAGHDAD, city of dark-eyed sheiks and veiled beauties, legendary city of the Arabian Nights, a city also of skinny beggars and date-fed humanity, where amazing wealth and appalling poverty walk side by side.

After a meagre breakfast next morning we made our way below into Rashid Street, where the pulse of the city can be felt. We jostled with the crowd towards King Feisal Bridge, hoping to find a bank and change a small cheque. Here were the sheiks in flowing robes, the Turks, Arabs, Armenians, the sweet sellers, trinket sellers and vendors by the thousand. It was a hot, dusty, gaudy street: expensive large American cars, bigger than any we had yet seen, honked their way up and down.

"The sheiks don't ride wild galloping steeds any more," I observed sadly to Diana as two silk-clad sheiks sailed by in a taxi.

At a large bank below the Sindabad Hotel we changed a lowly £4 travellers' cheque, and watched covetously with wide eyes as a sheik merchant counted from beneath the change window a mere two thousand pounds, stuffing the wads of notes into his belt.

"If only a one thousand dinar note would fall out and float across here," I said dreamily. "Think of all those lovely things we could buy!"

Di laughed softly.

"Come on—we can't stand here dreaming. We must find the Embassy and Mr. Stenn."

But our contact had flown home to England two days before. As we crossed the wide Tigris on our way back to Rashid Street we sat in the bus checking the strange new Iraqi money when a hand from behind grasped each shoulder and we turned to see the smiling face of a middle-aged European.

"I'm Major Tomsett—Tommy to most—" he said. "Heard you discussing the dinars so thought I'd see if I could help you to sort it out. It's a bit tricky, new money, eh?"

217

Tommy's second name was surely Aladdin and quickly he rubbed his magic lamp, for after we explained how we came to be in Baghdad, he gasped in astonishment.

"Well, strike me pink!" he exclaimed excitedly. "I've lived in Baghdad for thirty years and you're the first two English girls I've met doing this marathon. I can help you too," he went on as we all alighted by Rashid Street.

"You see, I work for an Iraqi Transport Company and our trucks often go to Damascus. Come along to the office and have a drink. You can meet the boss."

As we sat in the office with Tommy's Iraqi boss and sipped glasses of delicious mint tea, Tommy told his boss all about us, looking in his excitement as though the whole idea of our trek had been thought up by him.

"Now don't tell me the English spirit's dead," he exclaimed delightedly to the boss, who regarded us admiringly, a thoughtful expression on his swarthy face.

"Two girls—girls, mark you!—still have the old spirit. Why, your men wouldn't go where they've been," he added scornfully. "We've just gotta get them to Damascus!"

I had the feeling that as an Englishman working for an Iraqi, Tommy was suddenly very glad that this Iraqi should know that most English people, even the women, had more sense and initiative than he had. His boss was impressed, though he tried not to show it.

"In ten days I am driving to Jerusalem," he said, his eyes bright, "through Damascus and Amman; you are welcome to go with me, either just to Damascus or on to Jerusalem. I do not think you would like a hot, thirsty drive for three days across six hundred miles of barren desert in one of our transport trucks."

"Your suggestion is very kind," Di thanked him, "but we couldn't stay for another ten days in Baghdad—we thought just two or three days since our money is getting alarmingly low."

We laughed in unison for by now these words had an all too familiar ring.

"Might there be a truck going tomorrow?" I asked, but Tommy waved the words away.

"You can't cross the desert by truck," he declared. "I won't let you. I insist that you be my guests. My hotel is air conditioned —thank God." He laughed as he mopped his face. "No arguments—it's settled. Come on, let's go and get your packs."

He bustled us by taxi back to our hotel and waited below while we hurried up to pack our bags.

"I think the boss may have queer ideas about this sudden trip to Jerusalem," I said slowly to Di. "Do you think we're wise to wait?"

She paused. "Well, Tommy's O.K. As there's no other way of going on yet, let's wait and see what transpires, huh?"

The hotel where Tommy stayed was cool and clean and our small, air conditioned room felt like an ice-box after the heat of the streets.

"Well, I must get back and do some work," Tommy said ruefully. "You can explore Baghdad. Meet me on the lawn of the Sindabad about six, and we'll have a drink—that is, if you like," he added tentatively.

The Sindabad—we were stepping up! He brushed aside our thanks with a brusque "Glad to help. Don't think you owe me anything—I just like to talk to people with spirit. Cheerio for now, and mind those sheiks!" With a quick wink he was gone.

One morning a few days later we strolled on the flat roof of the hotel, high up and level with domes and minarets all round. Below lay the wide Tigris along which honked small boats and tugs. On the far side tall date palms lined the water front. A brilliant motley throng teemed across King Feisal Bridge, a little up river. Occasionally small canvas-covered boats carrying passengers were rowed to the far side of the Tigris by dark-skinned, long gowned ferrymen. The temperature was easily 130° The river looked very inviting in such heat. We quickly donned bathing costumes and wearing our dresses over them and carrying towels beneath our arms we wandered from the hotel, over the sandy ridge and down to the water front.

The dark and shining naked bodies of small boys wallowed and dived in the mud at the water's edge. Upstream, below the luxurious garden of the Sindabad Hotel, a group of washer-women beat the stones with their washing to exorcise the devil dirt. We approached an old grey-beard and skull cap. "How much to cross?"

He almost bowed double, his face crinkled and puckered.

"Fifty fils, laties."

"One shilling, good. How much to hire for an hour?"

He thought hard, sizing us up. "Five hundred fils."

We hooted in derision.

"We're not Americans, old man." He looked a trifle discon-certed at that. "We don't want to buy your boat—we want to swim." I executed breaststrokes in the air.

He looked amazed. Clearly we were mad, but our money was as good as any other, so, our price fixed, his skinny arm extended for the 150 fils, and we wobbled across the stepping stones into his tiny craft. In mid-stream he leant on his oars, his lined old face cracked into a grin. "Okeedokee!"

The slight mid-stream current made the water here cool and clear—or fairly clear. "Okeedokee Tesekkur," we thanked him and, quickly slipping off our dresses, we lowered ourselves over the side of the boat. The water was heaven after the scorching air! For almost an hour we swam lazily up and down river, while old greybeard in the boat rowed gently to stop the boat being carried downstream. Calling to us in Arabic, laughing and chattering away as though we all understood each word, he was thoroughly enjoying the madness of the "whites." He was a merry old boy and in a deaf and dumb sort of way we did understand what he said.

"Okay to swim for Arab boys, you not swallow water, bad germs, bad ill. Keep head up," he called. "You good swim," he cackled as he pulled on the oars to catch up with us.

At length we heaved ourselves back into the small craft. Our suits were almost dry by the time we reached the bank again. and, as we donned our dresses, he exclaimed: "Tomorra you come swim, 100 fils, good, huh, okeedokee!"

"Good. At this rate in four days we'll be swimming for nothing," I laughed to Di as we waved goodbye and made our way to join Tommy in the bar of the Sindabad for a lunchtime drink.

Tommy nearly fell off his stool when we told him what we had been doing all the morning.

"Strike me pink!" he said in a low voice. "I know you're used to germs, but the Tigris is the city's washing trough—and sewers. You'll be lucky if you don't get cholera!"

He paused as a dark skinned Iraqi friend of his drew up a stool. Luckily Di and I didn't look as though we had just been swimming.

"You'd never believe this," the Iraqi exclaimed. "What's Baghdad coming to? Did you hear? Two white women swimming in the Tigris all the morning. Should think they're dead by now. I know the Arab boys swim in it but they don't expect to live long anyway. I always heard that the English were mad. Well, Tommy, now I know."

He flashed a row of white teeth at Di and I as we wriggled lower in our seats.

"I wonder who they were," he mused. "I don't suppose we'll ever know now. They won't do it again—because they'll probably be dead by the morning."

I gulped. Tommy winked from behind his glass at us, and said earnestly:

"No, I don't think they'll do it again, but let's hope they won't be dead by morning."

When the Iraqi had left, still wondering at the madness of the English, Tommy laughed.

"You see what I mean. Most Iraqis wouldn't run the risk of putting a big toe in the Tigris. They'll all be waiting to see if you do it again."

"Well, we only swam in the middle where the current made the water clear," we explained. "We couldn't get into one of the swimming pools. You have to own a Cadillac or a thousand dinars—or anyway wait fourteen days before you're sponsored, so we may swim again tomorrow if it's as hot as to-day—and we're still alive."

Tommy laughed good humouredly.

"Well if you want to swim that badly," he said "it looks as though I'll have to get you special permission to swim in the European pool."

His eyes twinkled affectionately as he spoke, and he was as good as his word. From then on, we left the wide, muddy Tigris to the small naked Arab boys.

A few days later, as we were trying to make a 'phone call on the Arabic-numbered dial of the telephone in the passageway outside our room, a clattering of feet up the stairs announced some new arrivals. They were two white men in slacks and open-necked shirts, heavily tanned and covered in dust. Both had curling "Flying Officer Kite" moustaches. We were surprised and delighted to see them.

"Have you just walked in across the desert?" I asked, eyeing their dusty figures. The taller of the two laughed lazily. It was strange to hear an Oxford accent.

"Hullo. Well, we've not exactly walked, but it's just as dusty driving."

They eyed us mischieviously. The shorter, stockily built one curled his finger and thumb round the end of a long moustache and grinned.

"Actually we heard that a couple of girls had walked to Baghdad from Australia so we hightailed in from the desert to congratulate them!"

Di and I glanced wonderingly at each other, taken in for a

moment, but suddenly the pieces fell into place as I saw the amusement on their faces.

"You've seen Tommy of course. He told you about us, didn't he?" I demanded.

The tall fair Englishman draped himself over the stone stair rail. "Right first go." He turned to his friend with merry sarcasm. "They're bright as well," he quipped. "You see," he went on seriously, "we've been buried in the desert for the last year building roads for the Iraqi Government; about every three months we get cheesed off with eating sand so we high-tail into Baghdad for a decent meal—and to see a few fresh faces—never dreaming this time we'd see two such charming, beautiful explorers that—"

"Think we'd better introduce ourselves," his friend laughingly cut in. "This is Nick Carter and I'm Joe J. Davies."

"He's always like this. Take no notice—in time you'll get used to it. Actually we came in to round up some lazy equipment, but as Tommy informed us that it was someone's birthday tomorrow we've ordered champagne and turkey at the Sindabad to-night. That is, of course, if you both like champagne and turkey," he said with an engaging grin. He looked like a little boy who thought he might be disappointed.

"We thought you might take pity on two lonely, forgotten men who've been practically buried alive in sand for years."

Good old Tommy! We thanked them excitedly. "I always thought a birthday in Baghdad would be wonderful," I exclaimed.

"Well, that's settled. I've half the sand of the desert in my tonsils," Nick laughed. "How about ordering some tea? We'll have a shower and then join you. We want to hear how you arrived here." And in high spirits they ambled off to find their room.

That evening with Nick and Joe we wandered through the bright crowds in Rashid Street into the Sindabad Hotel and out on to the cool lawn overlooking the Tigris. Tommy rose to greet us from a table at the end of the lawn. Reflected lights winked and gleamed from the opposite bank in the water below, the evening air was cool and smelt of honeysuckle and palms. Groups of dark-eyed Iraqis talked softly in strange dialects at the groups of tables and chairs set out on the large lawn. A subtle air of luxury pervaded the atmosphere. Later, relaxed by a first class dinner and champagne, we all sat talking softly in the tropical evening. Tommy was looking very pleased with himself. Both boys were wonderful storytellers and, with an appreciative audience, they sparkled with humour. Di and I were enjoying it to the full. It was the English subtle humour that we had missed for a long time, and after the strain of living conditions for the past few months forever meeting different races of people, their humour was doubly appreciated.

"They're going to sleep," Nick quipped during a momentary lull. "Quick! Tell 'em that one about beuka bolom bhind."

Joe lit my cigarette, eased his own into a slim holder and curled his finger and thumb round the end of his moustache in a now familiar gesture, and began slowly:

"Well now, there was a fellow who wanted to get married; he was getting on—about Nick's age." He chuckled. "At last he became engaged. The night before the wedding he confessed to his bride-to-be that he was colour blind. She called off the wedding, and said goodbye. This happened three times; each time he managed to get engaged, the bride-to-be called off the wedding at his confession that he was colour blind. The fourth time he became engaged he decided to wait until after the wedding to make his confession—and hope for the best. Eventually they got married. Everything went fine on the great day and they drove away on their honeymoon. That evening his conscience smote him and in their moonlit room he slowly broke the news to his new wife. She took his hands and kissed him softly. He was delightedly amazed.

'You don't mind, you really don't mind?' he asked.

'Who me, honey? Of course not,' she said in a lazy, Southern drawl. 'Hush thy mouth, white chile—and go to sleep'!"

And so they slipped easily from one joke to another.

"I think they've been making these up in the desert for the last few months," Tommy exclaimed, holding his aching sides.

At length the crescent of the new moon rose in the purple night sky and the jar of strange noises of the city reached our sleepy ears. Down below us, a few feet from the water's edge, an Arab spread his mat and bent to kiss the earth with his forehead. It seemed unreal and a little too wonderful for we two ordinary, lucky people, a mixture of the magic of the East with that blend of Western humour that we knew and enjoyed so much.

"Baghdad is the place to celebrate a birthday," I said sincerely. "I'll never forget to-night."

Di sighed dreamily.

"Last year we both had them in Australia. This year, yours in Iraq. We'll be in England for mine in October. I wonder where we'll celebrate them next year?"

Tommy laughed, "Timbuctoo I bet!"

Joe and Nick stayed in Baghdad for three hilarious days and nights.

18

The World's Oldest City

THE 'Nairn' buses are almost a household word in the Middle East. In 1923 two New Zealand brothers decided it was time to link the two great Eastern cities, Baghdad and Damascus separated by six hundred miles of trackless, barren Syrian desert. This was a land of unmapped sand and rock where bands of meandering Bedouins killed and looted those who dared to venture forth without sufficient guard, and thirst killed those who took insufficient water.

So in 1923 a small British reconnaissance party set out to explore the wastes with compasses, water and food for many days. From that first crossing, which took five days, the desert buses now make the trip in fifteen hours across the Nairn track, aptly named.

In the early 1930s the large cars used for the crossing became inadequate and the desert saw the first of the large buses to be used. But the roughness and speed of the crossing demanded more flexibility in the long bodies and trailers were hooked on to the heavy touring cars as they seemed to withstand better the corrugated surface of the sand. The first of the long silver Diesel trucks with their pullman-like trailers soon took over for they were capable of a speed of fifty miles an hour for fifteen hours, and they weighed sixteen tons.

Tommy's boss was unable to make his trip to Jerusalem at the last minute so he booked Di and I first class seats on a Nairn bus. At five in the evening, we slipped out of Baghdad in the silver monster, leaving behind the mosques and minarets glinting in the sun, the loaded camels swaying along the side of the road, while loose robed Arabs led the way on skinny donkeys.

With a blare of the horn, such as one hears from Diesel trains in the Gare du Nord, the driver changed gear, eased the shining bus down a rough slope off the road, and headed into the desert.

Di and I reclined on the airliner type of cushioned seats in air conditioned comfort. The interior of the bus was insulated against noise and dust and we had the sensation of a never-ending plane take-off. It felt as if we were completely cut off, onlookers in a glass turret. We were no longer a part of the heat, dust and rabble that was Iraq. The bus was half empty. Besides passengers the bus also carried mail to Damascus. In the rear end of the coach there was a toilet and wash basin.

Late that evening, a small, square picnic-box of sandwiches and fruit was handed to each person by the steward, and reasonably priced drinks could be bought from him. For those who needed them, there were blankets, for the air conditioning made the interior slightly chilly. We settled back in our tipped seats and slept, waking once only for our passports to be checked at a dark desert outpost. When we woke again the sun was high and we were well into Syria. Through the now dust-covered window we watched the scores of camels walking in line, mile after mile, across the desert. Then came the vineyards and fruit orchards and at 8.30 a.m., $15\frac{1}{2}$ hours after leaving Baghdad, the now white dust-coated monster drew into Damascus Bus Station with a hiss of air brakes.

In one night we had journeyed through half of Northern Arabia.

Damascus is reputed to be the world's oldest existing city. Built at the foot of Mount Qasyun, a ramification of the Anti-Lebanon chain of mountains, it is situated in the midst of a fertile plain called the Ghutah and is connected to Beirut, the capital and chief sea port of Lebanon, by railway and road.

From the River Barada (or River of Gold) seven streams branch off before entering Damascus; the main river passes into the middle of the city and all the branches go to irrigate the fertile El-Ghutah Plain and its gardens after they pass through the streets and houses of Damascus.

Arabs, coming from the desert and beholding such abundance of water and vegetation considered Damascus the earthly paradise and they called it "El Sham," beauty spot of the earth.

The city to-day has extended from beyond its old walls and gates, whose remnants are still standing. To the south lies the expanding "Meidan" quarter, but its modern quarters Salhuje, Abou-Rummane are in the north west. In the old walled part of the city we wandered through a labyrinth of bazaars, through streets with many monuments and eventually through the Souk Hamidujeh, the richest bazaar in Damascus, and came at length to the Umayyad Mosque. Inside this monument of Islamic art stands the fabulous tomb reputed to contain the remains of John the Baptist. The niches or "Mehrabs" indicating the direction of Mecca to where the Moslems pray, are wondrously decorated in coloured marble inlaid with mother-of-pearl, carved white marble and beautiful coloured mosaics, while on the floor are rich carpets.

Back through the Souks jostled by Bedouins from the desert, peasants from the neighbouring villages of the Ghutah and city dwellers in the latest European dress. On all sides we were accosted by screaming leather, copper, trinket, spice, mosaic jewellery, silk brocade makers and fig sellers.

"White ladies, you look—you no buy—you look!"

We squeezed our way through Bedouin women decked in bangles, earrings, necklets and rings of gold, lifting their veils to examine cloth in avenues of gaudy silk and bright prints, though the noisy rabble of men and women, whining children scrabbling for a tossed coin. And from the high curved domes of glass and iron roofing, shafts of dusty yellow sunlight burst through gaping holes and patched the dull interior of the bazaars with pools of quicksilver.

"You like buy leather bag—verra cheap, verra good—verra gaudy! Verra nice, white ladies—you look!"

Whining, arguing, cringing and angry, the voices mingled with the smell and odours of spices and humans. The bazaars were merry places indeed: we could have stood for days and watched wide-eyed, but we had to depart in search of a clean, cheap room.

In the cool of the evening with a swarthy Arab from the Exchange Bureau, Azim Kujeh, we drove along the Pass of Rabweh through the Valley of Barada; all along the valley are the open, fairy lit garden cafés where the Damascenes wine and dine in palaces built long ago for kings. At the foot of a creepered summer palace Azim drew in the car and we climbed the mellowed steep steps to the mountainside verandah and sat in a vine-covered alcove overlooking the narrow valley and river, in the same place concubines and queens had awaited their masters' summons.

I shivered in the cool air and Azim flung his wide cloak around me and tried to hold my hand beneath the folds.

"It is not yet cold in Damascus," he chided me. "But of course you have come from Baghdad. I am sorry I do not have two cloaks." He smiled gallantly at Diana. "But when you have drunk the Damascus Arak you will no longer be cold.

He called loudly to the waiter to hurry. We looked at each other and winked.

With the milky-looking Arak which tasted highly of aniseed

came many small platters, fourteen in all, of hors d'oeuvre, olives, sardines, cucumbers the size of a finger, tomatoes, figs, crackling slivers of potatoes, skewered meats, ladies' fingers and yoghourt, and other weird and tasty morsels.

"It is very kind of you to bring us here," I said formally. "Everywhere we have travelled the people have been kind and courteous."

His hand dropped from my shoulder but his eyes gleamed as he swallowed a neat thimble of Arak.

"I am honoured," he said. "My wife is away on holiday. Without your company I might have spent a lonely evening. Of course—there are the night clubs!" he paused archly. "I do not frequent them, unless I must. It is not often I meet two blonde English girls even in my work." Diana's hair at the front was a little sun bleached.

In the garden below the many coloured lights twinkled in the growing dusk. In our tiny arbour the smell of aniseed overcame the odour of lemons and figs and grapes that hung on branches above our heads. The Syrian beer which the waiter brought next was dark and cold.

"You have good appetites," Azim laughed.

His arm slipped along the back of my chair again. Little did he know that this was our dinner. Most of the small, pear shaped platters were empty. At a shout from Azim the waiter brought bowls of fruit, and what fruit! Grapes as big as tangerines, bananas sweet and golden, piled into great mounds before us.

Later, as we sipped black sweet Turkish coffee in tiny china thimbles, Azim expanded: "You must not go to Jerusalem," he said. "It is an unholy place. My family fled many years ago from there. One day I returned to collect their jewels and money which was owed to them."

He fingered a large scar at the side of his eye, then drew my fingers across it.

"Feel! It is very deep. I was caught and tortured because I took what was rightfully mine. Then imprisoned. A friend of my father's helped me to escape. Since then I have become Syrian. But you should not go to Palestine—that is an unhappy country and always there is trouble."

"If there is a bus going tomorrow we shall go, if we can get visas," Di said. "Our money will not allow us to wait long here. If there is no bus, then we must go on to Beirut; there are still many countries to pass through before we reach England. Maybe it is better to go on anyway!"

Azim spoke quickly. "Your visas will take three days—it is my business to know these things. Beirut!"

His eyes gleamed as he imprisoned my hand.

"Beirut is a city of cities. Beautiful Americans and French daughters, princess summer palaces and the design of the buildings are a feast for my eyes. Wait in Damascus until the week-end. I will drive you to Beirut and show you what a wonderful place it can be!"

"Your wife is in Beirut! What if she should see you?" I said cheekily.

He winced and sighed. "My wife—she no longer understands me. Already she is having a good time there. And so shall we. She will not see me."

"Tomorrow afternoon I will take you, if you wish, to see the street which is called Straight, and the window where St. Paul was let down to freedom. It is in the old city wall: you would not find it alone. Everything I will show you," he promised.

"You are too kind. We do appreciate your courtesy. And I hope we can repay you if ever you come to England."

He chose to ignore the reserve in my words and, as the evening breeze was now wafted on cold fingers from the mountains beyond, we descended the many carved stone steps from the vine-covered verandah and were soon again in Damascus.

At our tiny *pension* he leaned back to open the door for Diana and wished her goodnight. His meaning was obvious: I was to go on with him. Before he could speak again I slipped out to stand with Diana in the road.

"Your friend is tired," he pleaded. "Come with me. The night is yet young! I will show you the million lights of Damascus from the mountains."

"I too, am tired," I begged off. "Maybe tomorrow we can all go?"

His black eyes gleamed. "If you do not come I shall go on to the night club. There are many women there—but I do not want to go if you come with me. Are we not friends?" he pleaded.

"Of course—let us keep it that way!"

19

Beautiful Beirut

LATE one evening in a large American, Arab-driven taxi with four natives of no distinctive nationality, we dropped down from the high chain of Lebanon Mountains into the cobbled, tram-cluttered streets of Beriut. In a vine-covered *pension* in a narrow cobbled street behind the waterfront owned by a German and his mother we found a clean, cheap, double room.

Beirut was all we had heard and more. Here the women were mostly unveiled, in European dress with lavish hair styles, the men dark and lecherous.

We were heading for the "Bain Française," recommended by the son at the *pension*.

"There are no open beaches, until quite a few miles each side out of Beirut—only private baths all along the waterfront. Tell the "Bain Française" I sent you," he had told us that morning.

At the clear blue watered "Bain Française" we met Lebanon's champion swimmer, so he said, and could well have been. Bedrose, a Christian Armenian, spoke eight languages fluently, and his tanned sleek body swept through the clear water like a fish. He loved all women—on sight.

"You swim here every day?" I asked. "No work?"

"*Certainement, toujours.* I am on holiday for three weeks. I come every day—all day—I live in the water. My mother sends my lunch down with my young brother. When it comes you shall join me." He paused. "You have tried Armenian cooking? My mother is the best cook," he boasted, "but I am her best son!"

He jumped up and executed a lithe pirouette before us.

"Come. I will fetch the goggles and we shall dive beneath the sea and watch the fishes. Great fish, many beautiful colours. Come! Is it not good to be alive in Lebanon?"

So we dived with him into the depths of the blue Mediterranean to discover and explore a new world, coming to the surface only for air. When we were tired he paddled us along in front of him: when we made weird finds he dived deeply to retrieve them from the ocean bed and bring them to the surface. He never tired and always he flirted outrageously with us both.

"Ah!" he shouted as he came up for air, tossing the water from his glossy brown mane. "You must stay long in Lebanon. I have an eye for the mommies." I rocked with laughter.

"I will teach you to speak in eight languages. Diana, she speaks French *très excellent*—but you! Poof." He puffed his cheeks and did a wonderful imitation of an English Colonel learning French.

"I must go back," I laughed helplessly, "or I shall drown. I cannot swim and laugh."

"No one drowns while Bedrose is near," he boasted, "but we will go back and sample my mother's cooking with frozen yoghourt." He sighed ecstatically to the sky and raced ahead to the side of the "Bain Française" where the small, shaded café was situated.

From then on, each day his mother sent larger bowls of many delicious and varied dishes. "For I told her you ate with me and she was glad," Bedrose informed us.

We sat beneath coloured umbrellas and watched the sparkling blue sea and acquired an even greater taste for frozen yoghourt, while the tubby Lebanese owner of the baths put "Blue Tango" for the hundredth time on to the recorder and joined us as we lazed. Bedrose knew all the girls, and most who came to the baths in the day worked in the night clubs of Beirut which were many and fabulous. We laughed and enjoyed his antics as he jumped up blithely to join dark-eyed beauties.

One morning, as I lay with him on the swaying raft a little from the shore and squinted across to the "Bain Française" where Diana lay sunbathing, Bedrose stirred and rolled on to his back.

"Soon I must send for my daughter," he said slowly.

"Your daughter?" He had not spoken of a wife.

"When I was twenty I married an Italian girl—she was on holiday in Beirut. We were wondrously happy—and so young."

"You speak as though you were forty," I chided him: we had thought him only twenty-seven.

"That was twelve years ago," he continued. "We had a daughter, then I went to fight with your Desert Rats in North Africa. My wife died of pneumonia before I even knew she had a chill. We only had four years together." He turned on one elbow, his eyes piercing and sad.

"That is why I like all the girls. I am not bad, although you

230

you may think it of me. If I could marry again I would never look at another woman; when there is one always waiting with gentle words and slippers to put on tired feet—who would care for other pretty faces? His sober face was tense. "You understand?"

"Where is your daughter, Bedrose?" I asked. Words of sympathy had obviously been said years ago.

"She is in Italy with her grandparents. I have not seen her for three years, but my job is poorly paid at the airport. I could not afford to have her live at my mother's house."

"With your knowledge of languages, surely you could get a good position anywhere?" I asked.

"Poof!" he laughed derisively. "All in Lebanon are bi-linguists. That is nothing here. Well paid jobs are not easy to catch."

"Well, marry again. Find someone to love you and she will not mind that you have little money. Then you can bring your daughter back to live with you."

I sat up to dangle my feet over the raft into the cool water, while Bedrose followed and laid his hand on my lap gazing up mischievously.

"But no one will marry a man who can only swim like a fish and has no money. Would you?" His words were serious but his eyes laughed.

"I would never marry a man who flirts with all Beirut, and couldn't be trusted out of sight," I teased, then shrieked as he lifted me bodily and jumped from the raft still holding me. As I came up for air he was there first.

"If you have more children, they will probably be fish," I spluttered and raced for the shore. For the rest of the day, much to Diana's amusement, he flirted madly with her alone.

As we left the baths that evening he pirouetted towards us.

"You will come tomorrow—early?" he asked Diana: he took her hand speaking wickedly to her, but he looked at me.

"Bring your friend. She is not beautiful—but—" he paused, searching for words, his eyes no longer laughing, "but—her face —it has something for me!"

By local bus early one morning we left beautiful Beirut. Through leafy, narrow lanes boarded by hanging vines and bright flowers the bus roamed its way along the foot of the Lebanon Mountains, to follow the twisting road through villages and drop down through ancient tiny ports, the sparkling

Mediterranean serenely lapping to the back doorways of the grey stoned, two storied houses round the bays.

"Surely from Tripoli we can start to hitch again," I said to Diana. "The Lebanon is so civilized after what we have come through."

"In Turkey they know the meaning of hitching, but I think not in the Lebanon, but if you are determined to try—good. Our money is low."

In a horse-drawn tonga for a few piastres we were set down outside the town. In the shade of a fig tree we sat on our packs and waited while a few inhabitants from a nearby line of stone houses drew near to question us in Arabic and then French.

The first few cars, thinking a family were with us hitching, pressed their foot harder on the accelerator and roared on without a backward glance. Most of the cars were taxis, crammed with Arabs and luggage. We knew the taxis and didn't wave—they had red number plates. Our onlookers retired to watch the game we were playing from a distance. After two hours the only response we received as we waved our thumbs were answering waves from the drivers as they shot by, white teeth flashing as they grinned back over their shoulders.

So we gave up and went back to the town, cursing. At the bus station a bus was loading up ready to depart for Latakia, the last Lebanon town before the border of Syria. So paying our money—about 7s. 6d. for 130 miles to a fat overseer of the buses—we bought figs and apples and were shown our seats by a roguish looking driver. Soon we were hurtling along the coast of the blue Mediterranean again. As usual the driver who was multi-lingual, speaking English, French and Arabic, put on a special performance for our benefit. Screaming round corners and sending the dawdling occupants of tiny ports flying as we hurtled down through them from the mountains he cracked jokes with all and sundry over his shoulder, catching our eyes and winking. He lit cigarettes, holding the huge wheel with his knees and flung toffees over his head to the merry passengers. Then he jumped from his seat, leaving the young mate to grab the wheel and carry on as best he could, while he bounced down to our seat and, with elaborate gestures, offered Diana and I the much thumbed bag.

Back to his seat to drive another hundred yards and up he bounced again to bring me a strong brown cigarette, shouting to his mate for matches so that he could light it for me.

Drinks of varied tastes and colours were poured from the earthenware vases and pressed on us by the passengers, while the old women cackled and berated him with their long tongues, and the dark-eyed men, young and old, wished that they, too, were drivers. And so we came to Latakia where old and dirty ships lay side by side with proud, white hulled vessels in the wide blue harbour.

With the driver, Achmed, we found a clean restaurant where spicy flavoured odours assailed our nostrils and a bottle of drinking water cost two piastres.

"I shall order for you," Achmed said, flashing a grin all round, happy at the curious looks we received from all sides. Soon the small plates were placed before us. Yellow beans in oil and spice, green beans in oil with a flavour of tomatoes and chiles. Delicious shredded meats with onions and spices boiled into them, so that the meat fell from one's spoon with tenderness. Potatoes that tasted of anything but.

"You will go to Antioch by bus?" he asked between mouthfuls, for we were all ravenous. "It is better that you wait for the morning. To-night I will show you Latakia; there is much to do. We will buy from the bazaars. I know a better café. There we will eat like kings and to-night, when the moon is up, I will bring a friend and we shall walk on the shore and see the lights of a sleeping town in the water."

But we had other ideas. "By bus we will not go on. But by taxi—for a few Syrian pounds we can reach Antioch by nightfall."

"No, stay," he shouted gaily. "Between Latakia and Antioch is the border; they will keep you waiting, those devils. They like a pretty face, as I do." He kissed his finger tips and blew the kiss lightheartedly away. "It is better that you wait!"

"It is now only 3.30 p.m.," I said. "By taxi we can reach Antioch by nightfall however long they may keep us at the border."

He realized sadly we had made up our minds to go on.

But he was a helpful, if disappointed, rogue. So we ambled to the Street of Taxis and, with four young Syrian farmer's sons, paid the last of our Lebanese money for two seats to the border.

"There is bound to be a bus on from there. If not to-night, to-morrow!" Achmed said lightheartedly. "Those at the Customs will be only too glad to give you a bed—or you can 'phone to Antioch for a taxi!"

High up through the tree covered hills and dales we at last wound our way down to a sparse valley. A grass bound stone building stood square and lonely at one end. One road led East. Ours led on through the barred-up roadway a little on from the building. The taxi and its occupants turned left to a distant mountain village while we humped our packs to the stone verandah and entered a bare whitewashed room.

"Where have you come from?" asked the surprised young Syrian officer as he flicked our passports. "Ah, Lebanon! You go to England. There is no bus to-night. Have a cigarette. I will go and get your passports stamped."

I helped myself from his pack of thin white cigarettes, and we leaned back to wait. He returned later as Di and I were scanning a large scale map of Syria that hung on the wall.

"Forgive me for keeping you waiting. My officer in charge is busy; it is he who must stamp the passports."

"Can't you do them?" I asked.

He shrugged. "At my last post—yes, but here everything must be done by Captain Dinsha. He is a difficult man. This is his first head post," he explained, and he left us again to the map.

Half an hour later he returned with a bristling, sharp-eyed, handsome figure. About him there was an air of "I am King here." It stuck out a mile.

He glared. "You realize if I stamp these now you must go over the border to-night. There is no bus before the morning, and no taxi."

Be nice to him, I thought.

"We thought you might be good enough to 'phone to Antioch to see if a taxi is coming out to the border—if not maybe we could walk to the next village and find shelter till morning. We'll pay for the call," I added.

He snorted. "It will soon be dark."

English, American, rich or poor, he was enjoying lording it over us. He made no move to 'phone. Indeed I couldn't see a telephone in the room.

"Would you mind phoning?" Di asked cautiously. "You have a 'phone, have you?"

He eyed her sarcastically. His authoritative manner was jarring to say the least.

Belligerently he spat out the words. "A 'phone, of course!"

He thumbed through the passports again—no order to 'phone was issued—no move was made.

In the quiet room Di's level words cut through like a thunderbolt.

"There's no 'of course' about it. If I'd known you had one I wouldn't have bothered to ask. There are many ways of saying 'of course,' and you have the wrong intonation for my question."

Her eyes sparkled, her cheeks were flushed and she sat back

quietly in her chair. I waited for the explosion. The young lieutenant stepped back quickly expecting it as well.

Cold fury swept the handsome older face, his eyes were black as Di and he weighed each other across the room. Then, in an electrically wordless silence, he pounded the passports together and blazed out of the room.

"Phew! That's torn it!" I muttered. "We *will* be here all night."

Diana let out her breath:

"Offensive ill mannered pig. Just because he's head of this fly-blown forgotten post, he'd have us licking his boots. O.K., we'll be here all night, but he'll remember not to say 'of course' in that tone again!"

Not ten minutes later the young lieutenant brought back our stamped passports. This was too good to be true. He grinned at Di:

"I've 'phoned. No taxis are coming out but they say a bus may come in a few hours."

"Thank you very much. I'm sorry if I put him in a bad mood."

"Don't worry," he told us. "That is nothing unusual. You can wait for the bus at the top of the first rise beyond the barricade; it turns there."

But as he helped us on with our packs, his superior thumped out from a room at the other end of the verandah. Here was the catch. His voice dripped with sarcasm as he planted himself before us.

"Do you usually walk off without having your luggage inspected? This is a Customs Post." His eyes were beginning to bulge. "When you leave Syria we want to see what you've got. I'm here to see it. Bring your things in here, tip them out—all of them. If other countries want to see what you're thieving, so does Syria. Do you think I'm here for fun?"

He was a nasty piece of work.

"You're the first one who's ever demanded we open up—the others take our word when we say we've nothing to declare," I said sarcastically.

The damage was done, we had nothing much to lose, except time.

"What do you think we've got in these packs—Damascus?"

The young lieutenant laughed. His superior's face took on a mottled, purple look.

"Don't answer me back!" he thundered. "I'm here to do a job and I'll do it. So open your packs. I'll come back when I'm ready and see to you."

He roared something at the lieutenant who sprang after him as he disappeared through a door.

Di and I contemplated the barricade at the top of the rise. On the other side lay Turkey. As we were about to sprint for it, a taxi appeared from the direction we had come and soon pulled up in a cloud of dust at the post. A young man in shirt sleeves and trousers hurried up the pathway. Two gold teeth flashed as he nearly cannoned into us.

"American?"

"English."

"Hullo. I'm David Abdo, once Syrian—now Turkish. Going to Turkey?"

"Yes—if we ever get away from here."

He glanced towards the open door and laughed:

"Playing up again, is he? Wily old bird—he wants some "baksheesh." You haven't given him any, have you? I'll see to him."

So saying, he disappeared through the door. The next minute loud voices proclaimed that he might be thrown out at any minute. But he emerged laughing.

"After I've been to a village over the hill I shall be going on to my father's house in Turkey by bus when it comes later. Leave your packs here and come with me to the village. Afterwards we'll catch the bus together. My taxi will be going back to Latakia from here."

Up in the Syrian mountains we wound through shaded lanes to a sprawling village set amidst grape vines and fruit trees. The ancient walls of the scattered cottages were creepered and mellowed with age. At one David left a huge basket of ripe tomatoes. On the side of the mountain overlooking the shaded fruit gardens we sat beneath fig trees, drank Syrian wine and forgot that there were such things as officious men in a world mellowed with sun and wine.

"You say you are Syrian. You look like a Syrian," I told David, "but you live in Turkey?"

His wide brown eyes crinkled at the corners through much laughing as he lent over the rough, wooden table.

"The village where my father's house is—was—before the War in Syria. The Ottoman Turks ruled for four centuries—1516-1918. At the end of the first World War we became independent under the short rule of King Feisal, father of Iraq's boy king now. The French ruled from 1920 as mandatory over Syria. Their rule lasted twenty-five years and ended with complete evacuation in April 1946. But before the French left they signed over the Northern portion of Syria to Turkey for their own gain. So now, though I was born Syrian, I and my people will in time be Turkish, as will all the inhabitants of the villages in that area."

The sun shone. The wine was beginning to caste a glow and life was good.

"You should all have refused to recognise the change," I said, magnanimously raising my glass. "We'll drink to your getting your country back."

Our glasses clinked and we drank. David pushed a hand through his thick curls.

"It is done. There is nothing my family or neighbours can do now—Syria has just begun to rule itself and we are not part of it. But let us not be morbid," he said. "I am wining with the daughters of England: we must be merry. To-night you shall sleep in my father's house! My mother shall serve her rare cheeses and yoghourt as we sit on cushions around the low table. Later you shall tell my sisters and the women of the village as they enter in their black, shapeless dresses how the women dress in England and Australia, and make their eyes glow. Maybe they, too, will wish to travel the world and see the things you have seen—maybe not, for they are Syrian!"

20

Trouble in Turkey

EARLY next morning in the dusty main street of David's village, we changed our travellers' cheques, then sat beneath a vine covered arbour with David, his father and the heads of the village, drinking tiny glasses of black aromatic coffee and answering their many questions. When the bus for Adana finally arrived we were shown gallantly into the best seats and they waved us on our way. They continued waving, until the rickety bus topped the nearest mountain that rose all round the green valley, and we could see the villagers no more.

From Adana we travelled on by bus. In many of the mountains and valleys of beautiful Southern Turkey, we stopped and with the bus driver and other passengers, drank from huge bowls of strange tasting soups served to us for a few kurus beneath vine covered open gardens.

Then for ten hours the bus jolted on through a flat, barren, but ploughed land, and late that evening we reached Ankara, a sprawling city.

Our bus finally pulled into a large, open station between a wierd assortment of other buses and passengers, and we unloaded our aching bodies.

"As we want to travel on in the morning, we'd better try and book our seats to Istanbul now," Diana said wisely. "If we can find where to book among this noise and rubble."

Humping our packs on to our shoulders, we battled our way eventually to what appeared to be the booking hut and proceeded to shout our requirements above the noise of the many revving, coughing engines and shouts.

"We don't want back seat—back seat," we tried to explain to the uncomprehending Turk in charge.

There were only two seats left on the bus leaving next day we eventually understood.

"Good. Two seats—not back ones, please."

"Not back no—not back, these good seats," the wily Turk explained indignantly drawing on the back of one of the profferred tickets a plan showing where the seats were situated.

"By the numbering of them I'd say they're a lot further back than he's trying to make out," I said wearily.

We eyed the Turk as fiercely as we could while Diana shouted:

"O.K., we'll take them—but if they're back seats we'll have a few words to say to you in the morning."

After paying our liri to the grinning Turk, we gathered up the tickets and made our way thankfully to a clean, cheap *pension* in the city.

Very early next morning we presented ourselves again at the bus station, which was now even more noisier and crowded than the evening before, and battling our way at last to the right bus, found to our furious indignation that indeed we had booked the back seats. With murder in our hearts and thoughts of twelve hour's jolting journey to Istanbul on a back seat, we made swiftly for the booking hut, but the Turk saw us coming and, as we pushed through the front door, he was hastily disappearing out of the back one. After him we charged through the hut, brandishing our tickets and causing the startled subordinates to scatter in all directions. By the time we reached the back door, however, he had disappeared completely into the noisy rabble outside.

Our fury abated somewhat at the thought of the fleeing Turk. Laughing we made our way back to the bus to make the best of a bad job, for although we could have waited a few days for decent seats, the thoughts of reaching Europe at last, that evening, after all this time, helped us to forget somewhat our jolting discomfort.

Istanbul, the only city astride two continents, Asia on the East and Europe on the West, is situated at the entrance of the Bosphorus, linking the Sea of Marlmara to the Black Sea. She is one of the main gateways to Turkey although no longer the capital.

We unloaded our packs in the late afternoon from the bus— at last on the banks of the Bosphorus. We were still in Asia. Across the water the afternoon sun glinted on mosques and minarets that pierced the skyline of the golden hour. There lay Europe at last. But we had an address on the Asiatic side where we now stood. First we must find the house in Kadikeni.

"Kadikeni Ah Evet!" exclaimed Dorhas, the young Turkish officer we had met on the bus. "I take."

His English was only a little better than our ten words of

Turkish. He took the scrap of paper on which the address was written, hoisted one pack over his arm and Diana and I following with the other, led the way from the waterfront. Through narrow, cobbled streets and alleyways, the sunlight dazzling the uneven roadways, we came at last to Frau Arslan's house.

There was no answer to our persistent ringing: she was out.

"Now what?" Di said slowly.

Dorhas' handsome face looked perplexed, then he brightened. "Leave," he indicated the packs. "I take Stanbul."

It was a good idea. We were hungry: therefore why not cross to Europe to eat, and return to Kadikeni that night?

Frau Arslan would know our packs when she arrived, and they seemed safe enough in an alcove outside her flat door, high up the narrow steps on the third floor of the building.

While Dorhas waited on the steps below we hurriedly changed into our cotton dresses, stuffed our rumpled travelling skirts and blouses into the packs and were soon at the waterfront again where Dorhas bought tickets for 25 kurus each at the ferry gateway and on the streamlined steamer we sat excitedly watching the approaching shores of Europe.

Europe spelt home for both Diana and me. It was almost two years since I had left England and over three years for Diana. Through the Eastern countries we had said, "When we reach Istanbul we will be in Europe and—home." It had seemed the last hurdle of many, and we were here at last.

As we stepped excitedly from the boat below the Galata Bridge, the city rose above on three sides, for it is said that Istanbul is a city built on seven hills, and from each height rises the fluted minarets of many mosques. Santa Sophia or the Blue Mosque, The Mosque of Suleiman, Yemi Cami, the new mosque, the Mosque of Fatih, the Conqueror, and many more Dorhas pointed out as we stood atop the Galata Bridge amid the jostling, laughing populace.

Looking back over the Marmara we could see the sun drenched houses of Kadikeni. Further up stood the great building of Haidar Pasha, terminus of the Anatolian railways and, further, where the Marmara Sea flowed on into the Bosphorus, lay Uskudar.

"Eartha Kitt," I exclaimed, humming the old Turkish lullaby which we knew so well through her strange voice.

"Evet, Yes!" Dorhas laughed, pulled his cap to a rakish angle, tucked an arm through each of ours and, humming the weird, pulsating melody together, we danced merrily across the Galata Bridge and through the cobbled streets of old Istanbul and on into Beyoglu.

At the top of a cobbled laneway with a hundred steps we stopped before a fragrant café—from the open doorway came mouth-watering odours. Many white capped chefs bent lovingly over their tempting *cuisine*.

As we entered the vine-covered garden of the café a chef hurried out to greet Dorhas with a shout of "Giriniz" (Come in) and a bearlike hug, for Dorhas, who was stationed in Ankara, was home on leave after many months.

"Cok, cok, Evat! Evat!" The chef's huge cap bobbed precariously as he took the orders for food.

"Asure, Ayran, Biber Dolmasi—Evet Ic peelaha, Imanr Bayildi—cok."

He clasped his hands across his belly with satisfaction, winked wickedly and hurried into the café.

From a great vertical spit we could see him slicing thin layers of meat with a long, villainous knife. He hurried out to place them on the brightly clothed table, shouting all the while in Turkish or whistling blithely. Next came a kind of pudding with boiled corn, sultanas, dry figs, hazelnuts, walnuts and beans; whipped yoghourt; a huge plateful of big stuffed green peppers —these were not hot; rice, with spices raisins and pine nuts; eggplants mixed with onions and tomatoes and cooked in olive oil. Last to the lurching table came sour red wine.

"Cok tesekkier Ederim," Dorhas thanked the chef.

"Cok tesekkier Ederim," we copied laughingly, and the chef delightedly threw his cap into the air, slapping Dorhas loudly on the back.

"He say 'Good—speak Turkish'," Dorhas told us. He say, 'Good eat. Turkish food good, huh'?"

"Evet, cok," we agreed as we devoured hungrily.

The chef's face grew serious as his voice dropped to almost a whisper in Dorhas' ear. Now what conspiracy was in the making!

Diana pronged a large green pepper to her plate.

"I bet he wants to join the party," she prophesied. "It's a good thing to know a cook in a strange city."

She was right. Dorhas explained that his friend would join us as soon as we had drunk our black thimbles of coffee.

"Your friend looked very serious." I pulled my mouth down at the corners to imitate the chef as he had talked to Dorhas.

"Jok, Jok," he shook his head. "He say trouble soon—No! Stanbul no trouble. Turk not like Greeks, cok Greeks in Istanbul. No trouble!"

Dorhas laughed away our offer of kurus, tipped his cap to a jaunty angle and, with the chef, we made our way down the hundred steps as the dusk drew in.

In the chef's flat overlooking the main shopping thoroughfare in Beyoglu we talked in nouns and drank cognac and tea. As Eartha Kitt's husky voice pulsated from the much worn gramophone about Uskudar, the sounds from the street below drifted up.

Suddenly there came a mighty crash, followed by an unending tinkle of falling glass. Many voices called and heavy feet clattered over the cobbles. The chef and Dorhas leapt to the window pushing us behind the curtain as we made to follow. They exclaimed in undertones as they looked below and then backed from the window, peeping from between the folds of the thin curtains again into the street. Crash after crash shook the night air, the sound of raining glass went on and on. Below in the street there was turmoil and riot, down the street a crowd of Turks came along smashing the glass windows methodically with great canes and throwing the contents of the shelves into the gutters and across the cobbles. Some shops they passed to continue at the next in another frenzy of splintering glass, wrenched doors and flying debris. The crowd that followed threw the rolls of beautiful materials purposefully to each other, silks and cottons alike, dashing it across the gutters and cutting the great lengths to shreds with huge scissors and knives. The quick methodical way they worked denoted much planning. In heaven's name what was going on? Dorhas and the chef urged us to be silent as they gesticulated and talked in horror stricken undertones, not daring to move the curtains.

We gasped as the window below the flat was torn out, the glass splaying far out into the road. The sound of shelves being torn from their brackets crashed in our ears. Any moment the frenzied mob might rush up the stairs. The voices below were harsh and quick. We waited with baited breath. Here indeed was something to write home about, if we were still around to write at all. Why the rioting? Because of the Christians, the Greeks or the English? Surely not only the English for it seemed that their own shops were being wrecked and the contents flung far and wide. Gradually the voices faded down the streets and more crashing glass followed as they carried on their destructive onslaught; the crowd smashing and trampling underfoot the contents of the shops, crunching the glass-spattered cobbles with heavy boots.

From a few streets away came the dull sound of an explosion and flames leapt into the dark night.

Barely fifteen minutes after the first crash the street was empty. The shopkeepers who lived above their shops crept down into the street to gesticulate wildly, then stand pathetically amidst the chaos of glass, smashed wood and littered belongings, knee deep in slashed and torn material and clothes.

"God! It looks like an air raid," Di gasped as we leant from the window, the better to see. Dorhas drew us back into the room: "Greeks!" he said, pointing below. "They Christians, not Moslem. Bad—not go Kadikeni."

His dark eyes were troubled and anxious.

"Frau Arslan will be worried—we go," I exclaimed. "Rioters gone?" I enquired hopefully.

"Jok, Jok," he said urgently. "No gone. You go," he pulled his hand across his throat to indicate the danger if we tried to return to Kadikeni. He spoke quickly to the chef, then turned to us.

"To-night stay! My friend give room. Tomorrow go Kadikeni," he insisted.

"We could 'phone, maybe," Di said quickly. "Frau Arslan would know we were O.K." She gesticulated. "Telephone!" Taking the address and telephone number in Kadikeni from her purse she handed it to the Turks.

"Evat. I tell her," Dorhas said quickly, copying down the number.

"My friend good, stay! Tomorrow!" he pointed to eleven by his watch, "I come, fetch, Kadikeni."

He clattered away down the steps. In Turkish Army Officer's uniform he would stand a good chance of getting through the wrecked streets. The chef brought more stuffed green peppers and tea. When we had all eaten he brought blankets, indicated by signs that he was going into the streets to see what was going on and with a flash of gold teeth left us to sleep.

Frau Arslan had married a Turk in Germany and returned with him to Istanbul. Her two beautiful daughters, one now married, had been born in a tiny port on the Black Sea which later had claimed the ship and all its crew in which her Turkish husband had been an officer. Hating the Black Sea and Turks in general, she had tried to return to Germany to no avail and had finally brought up her two young daughters in Istanbul. She found it hard to understand them at times for they were completely Turkish while she would always remain basically German. This much we knew from two Australian friends of hers and ours, through whom we had received the invitation to stay with her on reaching Istanbul.

She looked younger than we had expected when she opened the door to us after Dorhas had returned safely to Kadikeni next morning. But there was a sadness about her eyes that lingered even as she smiled a greeting.

"It is good you are safe. The boy rang me," she said.

In the homely but beautifully furnished flat looking out on to the Marmara Sea she and her lovely daughter Lémon listened intently as we told them all that had happened of the night's rioting.

"They will never learn," she said as we finished. "The Turks, they fight always."

"But why did they wreck Istanbul? It's their own city."

She spread her long beautiful hands in resignation.

"The trouble was against the Greeks who are Christian," she explained. "They are good workers. All hours of the day and night they work. They are getting rich. Maybe they deserve their riches. But the Turks think not—they hate the Greeks.

"The Turks are afraid that one day there will be more Greeks in Istanbul than Turks, so they organize a riot, killing and looting as you have seen, to scare them back to their own country. But they are fools," she said bitterly. "They cause more hate, as if there is not enough, and the only thing that happens is a curfew for a few weeks. The Greeks stay on with a greater hate in their hearts. Lémon is engaged to a Turkish boy." She threw a wan smile at her lovely daughter who understood only a little of the English conversation, but who nodded and smiled as her mother interpreted in fluent Turkish.

"I would like now to return to Germany and take her back, but," she sighed, "now she is grown, she does as she wishes. My other daughter is married to a Turk. She is bitterly unhappy, for now he goes with other woman and leaves her. I cannot tell her, I told you so! My husband was the same. So will Lémon's be."

She smiled charmingly.

"However, now you are here. We have expected you many days. As soon as they raise the curfew we will show you Istanbul, but till then you will be safer to stay in the flat."

For the next few days we rose leisurely, showered and ate breakfast after Frau Arslan and Lémon had left for their respective jobs in Istanbul. From our window the minarets and mosques could be seen across the Marmara, needling the sky over the golden horn, the ferrys cutting through the quiet waters of the harbour to Galata Bridge, while the many small, oddly fashioned kiaks went swiftly about their work in the harbour and on up the Bosphorus.

As we pottered about the flat, thankful for a chance to catch up on writing and mending, the sound of heavy boots clattered up from the cobbles below through the days and into the nights as the Army patrolled up and down the streets, demanding identification papers from Turk and foreigner alike. At 8 p.m. the city was deserted except for small bands of meandering troops in drab khaki uniforms; any civilian who ventured forth after curfew was clapped into gaol.

In the evenings when Frau Arslan and Lémon returned Diana and I learnt strange Turkish recipes as Frau Arslan cooked the evening meal. After the meal they taught us to play the game of Tavla which men all through the East sit at all day in open cafés, drinking coffee and clicking the markers round the board. When Frau Arslan and Lémon played, their hands flew above the board moving the markers almost quicker than the eye could see. It took Di and I many hours to learn.

A week later we ventured forth to make our way to the British Embassy and exchange travellers' cheques. In Istanbul the effects of the night's rioting were slowly being erased. In many streets the gaping window fronts were being patched up and work went on as usual behind in the open shops. The legal exchange was not good, so we changed only one small cheque. Later Frau Arslan contrived a much more satisfactory exchange with a friend, although, of course, this was illegal.

The next Sunday, with Frau Arslan and Lémon, we boarded a ferry and were sped over the smooth waters of the harbour towards the islands at the mouth of the Bosphorus, but actually in the Marmara Sea.

"Lémon comes often to the Island with Kassie, her fiancé, and their friends," Frau Arslan explained as we neared the pine-fringed shores of the Third Island and made ready to land.

"Here they swim, dance, eat—and make love," she finished with a quick wink to us, and a quicker glance at Lémon. Lémon laughed delightedly as though she understood and spoke quickly to her mother.

"Kassie and his friends are coming later," Frau Arslan interpreted. "He will bring his accordion and we will all dance."

All day we swam and dived from the rocks in a deep clear bay below a pine-fringed café and shore. Frau Arslan seemed happier than we had ever seen her. She swam faster and dived better than we three. After we had swum we lazed beneath the tall pine trees and feasted on many small fish, caught straight out of the sea, tipped into a great pan and served, still sizzling, with bottles of Turkish beer.

Afterwards I dozed. When I woke Kassie, his brother and friends had arrived complete with accordion. Beneath a bough covered arbour on the side of a smooth square they set up the band. Kassie played the accordion, two handsome young Turks beat wildly on the tops of upturned boxes with pine sticks and spoons to give the impression of drums. The café owners soon produced a thin pipe and every one danced, clapping in time to the music. Here were no organized amusements: they played or danced as the mood took them, exchanging partners for instruments, and vice versa.

The darkening sea lapped sleepily below the impromptu musicians and dancers. Lights began to twinkle on the surrounding pineclad hillsides and with merry words and laughter Diana and I were swept by dark, bright eyed Turks into the midst of the merry throng.

At length the moon rose. The laughing, tired but contented party wound down the uneven hillside to board the last fairylit ferry to Istanbul.

One morning the 'phone rang and a strange voice announced: "I am Dorhas' friend. You like to go Black Sea. Evet?"

"Evet—tasherkin Ediriun," I exclaimed, surprised.

"We come—half hour," said the voice.

"We're going to the Black Sea with a mysterious voice and Dorhas," I announced to Diana.

"Good! I wonder how his wife is?" she said thoughtfully hemming up a torn dress seam. I pondered for a moment.

"Perhaps it wasn't his wife after all. He wouldn't keep ringing if he was married."

Dorhas greeted us gaily below, still smartly dressed in uniform. He doffed his cap and introduced his English-speaking friend, Johas. Tall and dark, his friend could have been mistaken for an Englishman, except for his accent.

As we walked to the queue, Di asked innocently of Dorhas: "How is your wife?"

He glanced to Johas who spoke rapidly to him.

"Tok no!" Dorhas exclaimed. "Brother's wife."

His eyes laughingly reproached us, while Johas explained:

"The girl on the bus was his dead brother's wife."

They exchanged quick looks.

246

I laughed: "He seemed extra fond of his sister-in-law. Of course, she is very pretty."

Johas explained as we boarded a larger ferry, "We must catch this boat up the Bosphorus and Dorhas says there we take a sailing ship—small one—into the Black Sea."

He paused in his stride and gazed quizzically at us.

"You can sail a boat?"

We shook our heads.

"Nor I," he exclaimed, "but Dorhas suggested it—he can sail."

But after procuring a small craft at a tiny mellowed port at the mouth of the Black Sea for four Turkish lire (about ten shillings) and pushing off, it was obvious no one could sail it. So the oars went into action.

Dorhas tentatively unfurled the sail and it flapped slackly in the faint breeze, then the boom swung back sharply, hit Johas as he bent and over the side he sprawled amid gales of laughter. Clambering aboard be stripped to his bathing trunks and hung his clothes to dry at the top of the sail. Laughing, he said:

"Maybe people on shore think this a new distress signal!"

Along the shoreline we zigzagged like a distressed snake. It didn't matter: we were making for nowhere in particular, the sun was hot, the smell of the sea in our nostrils, a strange language in our ears, our companions were gay and charming and full of make believe.

"This is Kara Deniz—Black Sea," Dorhas exclaimed.

"We sail to Russia—good! We'll drink vodka and kill all Russians," Johas continued, his eyes flashing as his forefathers must have done as they raided with Mustafa Kemal.

"O.K! let's go," I shouted. "How long does it take to get to Russia?"

Johas took Di's hand.

"We get there for lunch tomorrow," he cried enthusiastically.

"I'm hungry now," Di said, bringing us back to reality.

We sighed, turned the boat with difficulty and headed back for the shore of Turkey.

In the late afternoon we returned to Istanbul to explore the old Byzantium and Mosques. At the Mosque of Sultan Ahmed, the only mosque in the world to boast six minarets and better known in the West under the name "Blue Mosque," great soft slippers were pushed over our shoes by the doorkeeper, for which he received ten kurus from Dorhas. Inside the vast interior we realized suddenly why this was called the Blue Mosque. The high walls and massive dome were adorned with magnificent pale blue tiles and the effect was completely blue. A thousand small candles in an iron framework overhead lit the tiles to perfection, the dome rose hundreds of feet above the vast, carpet covered floor. To encircle completely the huge pillars supporting the roof would take ten men or more with arms outstretched. At the further end of the Mosque a few Moslems squatted on the beautiful carpets, dwarfed beneath the vastness of the dome. A Mullah chanted. Indicating to the squatting lines of men, Joe said softly, "We pray."

"Can we, too?" They nodded.

"Follow what we do—but you must go into an alcove."

They led us to a blue tiled alcove, then joined those before the Mullah. At a louder chant all stood to their feet, hands clasped simply before them. He called again and all dropped forward on to the palms of their hands, foreheads touching the carpet. Up they came to a kneeling position in perfect unison, hands on knees, to stand again at last. Three times they made obeisance like this. Then, as the Mullah began a strange haunting chant, they squatted again and there was perfect stillness. How small and ineffectual man seemed beneath this vast dome, and yet there was a feeling of oneness with a greater power.

Late one evening we crossed again to Kadikeni and our two handsome Turks bade us a sad farewell, for the next day we were to leave by train for the border of Greece.

Frau Arslan looked sad.

"I think it not good that you go," she said sincerely. "Life will be very dull. I shall miss you, and my English is good since you both are here."

Next evening we boarded the night train to Greece. With tears in her eyes, Frau Arslan waved until the darkness swallowed her. The lights of Istanbul receded and we were journeying on our way into Europe. Two young Germans shared our carriage, and we tossed as to who should spend the night in the two racks. Fairly we won one each. So Di climbed aloft to change with my softer couch at midnight and we settled down to sleep fitfully as the train sped through the night towards Greece.

21

Back Home Through Europe

DANGLING our feet precariously from the back of a creeping bullock cart next morning, we wound our leisurely way on into Greece, while the old driver of the plodding wagon sprang blithely from his seat to bring us the choicest, dewy, purple grapes from the many vineyards along the white, dusty roadway. The sun was hot, the air smelt of grape wine and the world smiled upon us. We had breakfasted on new bread, ripe tomatoes and cucumbers in a sunny Greek village just over the border.

After a few kilometres a large truck pulled up and we gladly exchanged our slow transport for the fast lorry. The kindly Greek bullock driver loaded us with many bunches of grapes, and thanking him we travelled quickly on. The dark rogue of a driver spoke no English but intimated, to our pleasure, that he was travelling to Salonika—"Selonikey." He pointed to three by his watch to indicate when we should arrive.

"That must be 3 o'clock tomorrow morning—another fifteen hours," Di explained. "A lift right through! That's luck."

All day we travelled through the pleasant vineyards and farms of Northern Greece, through orchards and winding laneways. At nightfall we came to a gaily lit village beneath a cluster of dark mountains and in a tiny drivers' tavern we sat with the lusty crowd of Greek drivers, eating platefuls of varied food, brought from great cauldrons set on a high, open, brick oven. Our rogue of a driver, gallantly showing off to the others, bought large bottles of milky wine and quickly proceeded to get merry, urging us to drink and hoping, no doubt, that one of us would become fuddled and reciprocate his many meaningful glances. Later he drove on, swinging the swaying lorry precariously through the dark night, while with one arm he tried gleefully to embrace whichever one of us was near him. At length, grumbling to himself, he gave up, drew the great lorry into the side of the mountain road and soon fell asleep, snoring loudly.

As the sun rose we drove down from the mountains into

Salonika through narrow cobbled streets set on the side of the steep hills. Mellowed, whitewashed houses shaded the roadways and, below the honeycombed hills, many small craft, fishing vessels and cargo boats dipped serenely in the blue bay. We alighted thankfully but in a dismal part of the town, by a large railway station where, in a small enquiry office, we found the Greek in charge.

"Yes," he explained, "there are trains from Salonika, across the border of Yugoslavia and right through to Belgrade. A third class ticket will cost you each £3."

It seemed a lot even with a third reduction for we had thoughtfully acquired students' visas for Yugoslavia.

"We'd better try to hitch," Di said.

"Ah, you are hitch-hiking," he beamed suddenly. "In Greece many people hitch-hike, but," he spread his hands in an attitude of resignation, "in Yugoslavia I think you must travel by train for none of the people have cars, and there are few lorries. However I wish you luck!"

Following his instructions, we found our way to a public bath to clean up before going on. An old building, set with wondrous mosaics inside and outside. It was a Turkish bath. For a few drachma an attractive Greek girl, clad only in minute briefs, pummelled and rubbed our naked bodies until the tiredness left us and we felt fit to resume our travels. But Perrprini and Moirosi had other ideas! As we tried to order breakfast in a tiny eating place, two handsome Greek twins helped our fumbling orders and joined us as we ate.

"But you come thousands of miles and do not stay one day in Salonika. This is an insult to all Greeks. Ah, Moirosi," Perrprini exclaimed as he eyed us delightedly. They waved aside our explanations. "No, we shall not listen. To-night you shall stay with a friend of ours who owns a small hotel on the waterfront; then tomorrow we will drive you to the border of Yugoslavia. You might wait all day for a lift to-day. Please stay," they begged. "And to-night we watch the fishermen calling in the fish. Yes! Good!"

After taking our packs to the small, cheap hotel, we walked along the crowded waterfront with them. Then they left us saying they would pick us up at the hotel at seven that evening.

By eight o'clock they still had not come so, feeling very hungry, we counted out our few drachmas as we waited at the desk in the hotel corridor with a few loitering Greeks.

"Well, we haven't enough for one meal. We can just afford a coffee each—maybe." Di sighed. "It's a pity we changed all the rest into Yugoslavian dinars. It looks as though we'll have to go hungry until we reach Yugoslavia tomorrow."

Suddenly a smartly dressed Greek, complete with bow tie and white silk scarf, turned to us: "Excuse me, I couldn't help but hear. It is strange that my countrymen have let you down," he said, regarding us intensely. "I have been many times to England. Always people are so kind!"

He paused for a moment hesitating as to which words to use, then charmingly he continued:

"I would deem it a great honour for me if you would accept my help and let me give you this small sum." He drew quickly from his vest pocket a crisp note. "Alas for me, I would have taken you to a wonderful place I know, but I cannot do so to-night. I have a previous engagement. Please do not be offended, but take this small gift and have a good meal on me!"

"You are very kind," we exclaimed, still a little astonished. "If you would give us your address," Di said, "we can return the loan later."

"Please!" he exclaimed in horror. "It is the least I can do. If your friends come, I shall tell them where you are."

We thanked him graciously and following his directions to a wide street, we found his highly praised restaurant. Tables were set out on the wide pavement and, with the help of a merry-eyed waiter, we ordered a lavish meal and one bottle of Greek beer.

"At least we must drink our host's health," Di exclaimed. "God bless him! I'm starving!"

We had nearly finished the sumptuous meal when, with a shrieking of brakes, the rickety old car belonging to the Greek twins pulled up and they hurried across, both immaculate in striped waistcoats, bow ties and narrow trousered suits. Moirosi explained: "We beg forgiveness. Our poor, battered friend broke down so we had to push it home—five kilometres—but now she goes again—we hope!"

They called for more beer and our lonely evening was the merrier for for its earlier threat.

On the East side of the twinkling bay stood a tiny wooden tavern, set crazily at the water's edge, at the rear of which was a small wooden dance floor. There were only a few couples there for it was some way out of town. We sat overlooking the darkened waters of the bay and drank many small glasses of rich, sweet Cherry Brandy as we talked and laughed. Later, from the distant shore, many of the small fishing boats put out into the now moonlit bay. Perrprini slipped an arm around my waist, and pointed with the other. "Now! See, they come to fish. They will spread their nets across the bay. Then they call the fish into the nets by beating loudly on a gong as they sail back over the lines of nets."

He grinned and kissed my cheek, while Moirosi, not to be outdone, whispered softly into Diana's ear.

"Ah! all fish have to be caught—eh! my brother!"

Perrprini laughed and winked at Di.

"Hear him, he calls you his fish! He has no manners, my young brother."

Across the quiet waters came suddenly the sound of a hollow beat of a gong, then another beat and on and on it boomed repeatedly every few seconds.

"Now the fish come hurrying in from the sea to be caught," Perrprini said excitedly, leaning forward as a silent boat slipped by beneath us, a lighted lantern in the stern. The dull boom sounded again.

"All night they will fish and beat the gong. By morning they have many fish to sell on the waterfront—they hope."

"Ah! I should like to fish like that," I sighed.

Perrprini and Moirosi exchanged quick glances. Quite seriously Perrprini said: "Well stay in Salonika. If you both marry us, we will buy a small caique and we will fish every night when the moon is full. We are not poor, for our father died and left us his orchards and houses. Marry us, and we will take you to see our beautiful Athens. We would swim in the blue Aegean Sea and watch the fishers bring up soft sponges from the depths."

It was a pretty proposal and both were very serious. We could not mock them, so sought quickly for an excuse.

"It sounds a wonderful idea, but you are alike as peas in a pod. We cannot tell which is which until you tell us. I would not know whether I had married Perrprini or Moirosi, and that would never do."

They thought hard for a long moment, then Moirosi laughed loudly:

"I have it!" he exclaimed. "It is easy." The matter was evidently settled. "I will shave off my moustache. Then Diana knows who she marries, and Eunice can safely marry Perrprini."

Diana was enjoying herself. "Ah, but maybe one day for a joke he, too, shaves off his moustache. Then what happens? No—that will not do. You will have to think of something else!"

Next day they drove us sadly to the border. They were still trying to think of a solution.

"Soon we shall think of a solution," Perrprini promised as we boarded the train which would carry us to Belgrade. "Then, if

you think it well, you will return to us in Salonika. Goodbye.
Maybe we meet again." And with only slightly dented hearts
they waved gaily until the train lumbered away across the border
into Yugoslavia.

All day we travelled in the fast, loaded train through
mountainous, green and misty country, over great swirling
rivers, muddy with recent rains, which tumbled savagely through
deep valleys. A hundred thousand leaves of tobacco hung in
thick lines to dry on the sunniest side of every farmhouse and
building. "At least cigarettes should be cheap in Yugoslavia,"
I said hopefully to Di.

"They'd better be! Otherwise you'll have to give up smoking,"
she said for the hundredth time and without rancour.

By evening the train was packed. Our carriage was jammed
with farmers and soldiers. From the vendor who walked the
train with loaded baskets, they purchased many small bottles of
Cherry Brandy and the famous but bitter Yugoslavia plum
brandy, Slivovitz. They plied us with the tiny bottles insisting
that we drink with them, and sang patriotic songs well into the
next morning. They seemed a happy, though drabbly dressed
lot. The farmers wore black caps and shirts of coarse cloth, the
soldiers warm, grey uniforms. They appeared to be on holiday
and insisted next day that we join them for an expensive dinner
in the dining car, after which they again sang and drank much
Slivovitz until we reached Belgrade, late that evening.

At 10.30 that night, Belgrade was a dreary, wet and dark city.
As we alighted from the train and made our way through the
main street at the front of the large station, we shivered with cold
for the night was freezing to our heat accustomed bodies. The
city looked dead save for a few dark hurrying figures. Everywhere was shuttered and silent and there was not more than a
dozen cars in the whole city.

A skinny porter, unshaven, in a uniform of grey rags,
scampered swiftly over to us and, at Diana's tentative "Hotel,"
swung our two heavy packs on to his thin shoulders smiling
shyly, as he nodded and beckoned us to follow. For an hour we
trudged the wet, dark streets in search of a cheap room at the
large hotels and on down to the wide Danube where small
crafts were turned into floating hotels. Many were full and those
with sparse accommodation asked 1300 dinars, over 15s. each,
for the room alone. It seemed crazy to waste so much on the
few hours that were left till morning.

At midnight we stood marooned on a traffic island outside

the station again. Our little porter, still kind and helpful, pointed up yet another street. I smiled wanly and shook my head.

"I'm not going any further Di. Let's slip into the railway waiting room. There must be one! Surely they wouldn't mind us sleeping there until morning."

Di nodded.

"We'd probably get a cheap room somewhere early tomorrow. But we haven't any dinars for this fellow until we change a travellers' cheque. We can't just send him away with no tip after he's been so helpful."

"We'll make him understand that we'll pay him tomorrow," I said. "He'll have to trust us, that's all."

I was weary and cold, and to judge by the sag of her shoulders so, obviously, was Di. We turned to the patient porter but, as we started to explain, a voice from behind asked clearly: "Can I help you? You look lost. I am from Putnik-Information."

We turned to behold a tall, fair Yugoslav. He wore a light tailored mackintosh and a dark beret was pulled well down over his eyes.

"I suggest you let me take you to the Studenski Hostel. It is cheap and you have students' visas. You have travellers' cheques?" he enquired.

"Yes, but no dinars to pay this man. He has been very helpful."

"No matter. I will lend you three hundred for him," he said without hesitation. "For that he will carry your packs to the hostel. Come! I will take you now. It is a good way."

As we walked, he explained: "As I told you, I work with Putnik, the Yugoslav Information Offices. Tomorrow you can return the money. This is my name and address."

Diana took the proffered card.

"It's very good of you," we thanked him.

"It is my job," he said coolly. "We do all we can to encourage tourists."

He meant to be friendly, he was doing all he could to help, but there was an underlying aloofness which almost amounted to suspicion in his words and gesture. At the great modern Students' Hostel on Marshal Tito Avenue he led us into a cold bare hall, and watched as we filled in small cards. Our passports were taken by a Yugoslav seated at a bare desk. A few students, mostly men, sauntered up and down the wide stone steps at the end of the hallway.

"They will hold your passports until you change a travellers' cheque. You pay tomorrow, and can stay as long as a fortnight here." The man from Putnik counted three hundred dinars into the porter's hand.

"This you pay me tomorrow at my office," he said to us, and with a swift "Goodnight," and another cool smile, he was gone.

"We'll go to the British Embassy and see that friend of Frau Arslan's, Mr. Carr," Diana said as we stood in the cold hall next morning, surveying a large map of the city.

"O.K.," I agreed, "but we'd better first change a travellers' cheque at the bank and pay the Putnik man."

As we tried to make out the map, a tall, quite well dressed Yugoslav joined us and in perfect English explained that he was a teacher on holiday.

"My name is Vladiv Slovity. Please allow me to escort you to the bank—and round the city if you wish," he added after we had explained what we were doing in Belgrade.

His voice was friendly, but his eyes above the high cheek-bones and neatly clipped moustache darted nervously from side to side.

We thanked him, glad of his offer, and he led the way out of the building into the sunny, tree-lined avenue. The lack of cars was even more noticeable by day, although many trams swung up and down the wide avenues.

I felt suddenly as though I was once again in wartime England. There was such a lack of colour and prettiness about the clothes; the women wore square, boxy looking jackets, short skirts, thick woollen stockings and low heeled, thick soled shoes; the men, rather coarse black and brown suits.

"What a difference here from Australia," I said to Di. "It hardly seems fair—Australia, land of sun and plenty and Belgrade, the drab city! Admittedly no one looks miserable. But why should one have so much, the other so little?"

"But things are good here for most now," Vladiv said. "Each year they get better. Yes, I know the clothes are drab, but my people have small wages—perhaps 10 to 15,000 dinars a month."

"£15 to £20 a month!" Di said quickly. "That's awful!"

"Yes. Now you see why we have to wear strong, sturdy clothes. They have to last and keep us warm for a long time."

At the end of Marshal Tito Avenue, in the city, Vladiv ushered us at last into a high domed bank. There were a good number of people there and, as we waited, Vladiv's eyes again darted nervously from face to face. What was he afraid of? I wondered. After filling in a few forms and our cheques, we handed them to the quite attractive girl behind the iron grill, and stepped back with Vladiv to wait again.

"How long are you on holiday?" Diana asked Vladiv.

Again the quick, darting look and when he spoke his voice was very low.

"I have not had work for three months," he said.

"Oh! you're on a forced sort of holiday. But surely there are plenty of jobs teaching," I said in surprise.

He shrugged, licking his thin lips.

"There are—but I would not join the Partisan Party—so I cannot get a job."

"Wouldn't it be better to join and work?" Di asked. "Is the Party so bad?"

Our voices had risen a little.

"It is a good Party," he said loudly. "It has done a lot for the people." Then his voice dropped to an urgent whisper. "Please keep your voices down—I will not join the Party because the things they do are against my principles."

His eyes still darted hither and thither, the apparent distrust with which he viewed all about him was beginning to give us a creepy feeling.

"You don't like Tito's régime," Di said softly. "We understood that all Yugoslavs think he's doing a good job."

Vladiv shrugged.

"Yes—he is good. He is doing the best he can. My quarrel is with the Party. I will not join. I would rather starve."

Suddenly he drew in a sharp breath and furtively looked away from the glass door of the bank as a thickset man in a blue mac entered and, after an intent look round, made his way slowly to a counter. At that moment our names were called, and having collected our dinars we were hurried swiftly by Vladiv out into the street and away from the bank.

"Who was the man who entered the bank?" I asked, now feeling we were getting mixed up in something we knew little about.

"That man!" Vladiv said fiercely. He is a member of the Party; he always follows me. Because I will not join the Party, I must have an ulterior motive, so they keep a check on me," he said bitterly.

"I'll bet they want to know who we are." Di sounded uneasy.

"They know by now, of course," Vladiv stated flatly. "They know everything. That is why I cannot leave Yugoslavia. It is my country and I love it, but if I cannot get work because of the Party, I must leave. That is, if I can get away."

"Now I understand," I said. "You offer your services as a guide to foreigners, hoping they may suggest some means for you to get away."

There was no need for him to answer, and we walked on in silence to the Putnik offices.

Later in the People's Restaurant (one of the best things we saw in Belgrade), we ate an inexpensive lunch and paid for Vladiv's also as he appeared to have no money. Since he had offered to show us Belgrade, we decided to make our visit to the Embassy that evening. But everywhere, all day, by the flowering gardens along the Danube, on the trams and in the city, we were followed surreptitiously by the man in the blue mac. Each time he appeared, Vladiv would hurry us on. All day he questioned us about possibilities of an escape until we, too, began to jump at shadows, and looked as nervously over our shoulders as he did. By late afternoon Vladiv came to the conclusion that we knew nothing which could assist him in any way and, after giving us terse instructions how to find the British Embassy, he turned on his heels and walked swiftly away.

Half an hour later we were lost in the maze of avenues. After two more lots of helpful instructions, however, we found our way eventually to an Embassy, but not the British Embassy. This was the Canadian Embassy.

"At least they might give us the proper directions," Diana said. "We'll get someone to write them down for us this time."

The building at first sight seemed to be empty of staff. We peered stealthily into a number of rooms before we found anyone. In the last room a tall, red-headed man was busily packing papers into a large brief case. When he noticed us, he grinned cheerfully and, eyeing our small Union Jacks, asked in a strong Canadian accent: " Have you got lost, or are we taking in overflows from the British Embassy now?"

"We managed to get lost," we told him. "Please can you help us with written instructions how we get to our own Embassy?"

He laughed.

"Gee, nobody ever finds that place first go—tell you what. Wait five minutes till I clear up this pile and I'll run you over there. My car's outside—Oh, I'm Sergeant Johnson, by the way, Canadian Embassy."

We were half way to the Embassy by the time he learnt our reason for wanting it—to see if there was any transport going West.

Suddenly he gave a loud guffaw and asked with a twinkle in

his eyes: "Was our meeting by any chance a put-up job?"

Then, seeing our blank faces, he grew serious. "No, I guess it couldn't be—only two people know I'm going."

"Going? Going where?"

"To Trieste—tomorrow."

"Trieste—Italy?" we exclaimed.

"Yep. Going on holiday with my wife. She's English, too— guess she'd never forgive me if you didn't come along with us!"

It was a good ten minutes before we could believe our luck.

"Well, God bless all those who give wrong directions to strangers," I exclaimed happily.

Very early next morning with Ray Johnson and his wife, Joy, we speeded in their small car out of the spacious city of Belgrade along the road to Zagreb. All the morning the road lay straight to the horizon, through flat, uninteresting farm country where corn cobs, pumpkins, and sunflowers (for fat) grew predominantly. There was very little traffic and what there was bore for the main part foreign number plates.

Suddenly, from a long way in the rear, a shrill, wailing siren came faintly to our ears and grew steadily nearer as two darkly uniformed figures on separate motor cycles raced over the horizon and gradually closed the distance between us.

"Politzei—Police. Something's up," Ray exclaimed as he peered through the rear mirror with troubled eyes.

"Vladiv," I thought in instant panic.

"The man in the blue mac—he's had us followed," Di exclaimed.

We had quite gaily told Ray and Joy about our day with Vladiv but suddenly it didn't seem funny.

In silence we watched as the shrill whining motor cycles at last drew abreast with the car and the uniformed riders signalled urgently to Ray to stop. We listened anxiously, not understanding a word, however, as they spoke rapidly in Yugoslavian, gesticulating excitedly to Ray for the next few minutes.

Our imaginations ran riot. Were we to be taken back to Belgrade? Maybe the Party wanted to question us about Vladiv! If only we could understand what they were saying! Then suddenly, with a stiff salute, sirens howling again, cycles and riders raced on and away. Ray let out a long breath which ended in a dry chuckle.

"Talk about the 'Country of the Cloak and Dagger.' I'll be glad when our term here is up. They've even got me jumping at shadows—our friends merely came to say there's a famous

Marathon Cycle Race on from Belgrave to Zagreb. If we see them,—we're to stop and let them go by—that's all!"

All that night in a tiny *pension* high up in a misty chain of mountains, we froze in bed, while a loud speaker at the front of the building blared out an incessant medley of Yugoslav folk tunes. When we left early next morning it was still blaring.

On by mid-day to Rijceka on the beautiful mountainous Adriatic Coast, then to Suzana through the orchards and valleys, the trees loaded with ripe red apples, delicious and cool to the taste.

Then, after a three-hour trip by a slow rackety train deep into the famous, icy cold stalagmite and stalagtite caves nearby, we crossed the border of Yugoslavia into Italy. In Trieste we wished Joy and Ray a happy holiday, thanked them for a wonderful trip, and, after buying them a coffee, (the most they would let us do to show our appreciation), we set off for Venice.

Alberto Chicario, an Italian car racer, was also on his way to Venice, and although his trip was for the purpose of testing the speed of his new Alfa Romeo sports car, he was not averse to taking us with him. We didn't know his purpose until, at 140 kilometres an hour, he roared the car expertly through the mountains and valleys, while Di and I clung to our seats in alarm wondering how we had ever got round each bend safely.

"Is she not bee-utiful?" Alberto screamed over his shoulder, his eyes gleaming in exultation.

Presently we reached a long flat stretch of roadway.

"Now I show you just how good she is," he exclaimed, pressing his foot down hard on to the accelerator.

The car leapt forward and when the speedometer needle reached 170, I closed my eyes and sat back, while Diana sat forward and egged him on! With this sort of driving, however, we reached the outskirts of Venice in record time, and as we saw the islands and buildings of the distant city, Diana exclaimed:

"Ah! Venice. There's nowhere quite like it!"

Venice, the island city of a thousand wonders, with its hundreds of tiny bridges and waterways, its intricate alleyways and narrow, cobbled lanes, its high, proud gondolas and its high powered gondoliers, its thousand pigeons in San Marco Square and its thieves and pilferers who are everywhere.

For four and a half months our thick slacks and sweaters had reposed, unneeded, at the bottom of our packs. It was now the beginning of October and in Venice and Europe the days were getting cooler.

"We'll be needing thicker things in a couple of days," Di said, as we sorted through our packs in our small, cheap room next morning.

"Well, these slacks and sweaters will need hanging for a week to get the creases out," I said eyeing them ruefully.

So we left them hanging on the end of the bed while we went off to explore again.

That was the last we ever saw of them—perhaps someone was expecting a chilly winter in Venice that year, for on our return all our other stuff was intact. Only the two pairs of slacks and two jumpers had vanished, leaving us to contemplate a very cold end to our journey.

Next morning we left Venice to make our way on hurriedly, just two more hitch-hikers and no longer unique. A few days later we breathed a sigh of relief as we crossed the border into France.

In Marseilles we bought long new bread, tomatoes and butter, and at the sea end of the busy harbour, sat, our legs dangling over the stone wharf, eating ravenously. Many trim sailing craft bobbed serenely in the harbour while barges and pleasure boats chugged merrily backwards and forwards across the bright water. A little way out of the mouth of the harbour lay Monte Cristo's prison, the 'Chateau d'If,' looking dark and craggy against the brilliant blue water all round. From a tiny open café facing the harbour and just behind where we sat, a small, jolly faced man made his way over to us.

"Mon Dieu! I know you're English—the English are all mad. Would you not like a table to eat at? See, I have many—with gay umbrellas to keep out the sun."

"Merci, but we like to sit in the sun while we can," we told him, "for in two days we shall be in England."

"Ah! then I sit here with you—permit me? I am Jacques and this is my café," he said with a wave at the empty café.

"I am not busy, so we shall talk—you don't mind my talking? Good—I know many English," he told us confidentially. "I worked with them in the War, so it is good to talk, huh!"

So talk we did for the next hour, Jacques of his exploits with the British in the War and how unexciting his life was now by comparison; we of our trip, while his eyes gleamed with admiration. Every now and then he rushed over to the café to supply us with steaming cups of coffee as we talked.

"Mais oui!" he exclaimed softly at length. "So! You have seen the world and what it offers—Bon! Bon!—but Marseilles has many things also," he exclaimed brightly. "You do not go on to-day—so? It is good. To-night you come my café for dinner. My brother come also. I will show you how a Frenchman cook —I have fish from the harbour which make your mouth water— si bon. You come at eight o'clock? Au revoir."

Promptly at eight o'clock we presented ourselves at the café to be greeted expansively by Jacques almost enveloped in a large, brightly coloured apron.

"Ah, mes amies! Bon! All is ready. I tell my customers no business to-night," he laughed, "for I cook special for you. See, this is my brother Jules," he said, leading us to a small bar in one corner, behind which a large man sat smoking a small cigar. His brother nodded, greeting us merrily in French.

Behind him on the shelves stood an array of wines and liqueurs, to make a connoisseur's eyes sparkle with delight.

"My brother speaks—in English—six words!" Jacques told us gaily. "But he is the best wine chooser in Marseilles! Now you choose what you like! Jules will show you the best. I get the food —good." So saying, he bounced off happily, to reappear some minutes later bearing a huge silver tray on which was the most wonderful display of different foods we had seen for a long time.

As we began to eat a shy-eyed little man entered the café bearing a large guitar. Jacques sprang to greet him.

"This is Henri—see—I tell him to come play while we eat. He sing too—any song. Which do you like? Henri is Spanish— do you like the Spanish dance, yes?"

So, in the warm evening with the lights of busy Marseilles twinkling beyond the harbour lights, the Spanish guitarist danced and played on as we ate and talked, marvelling again at the friendliness of the world.

Late in the evening the guitarist left. Jacques shut the café and we all squeezed into Jules' tiny car, thinking the evening was at an end. As we tried to thank them, Jacques exclaimed:

"But this is only half the evening. Now we go to the 'One Eyed Pirate.' It is my brother's nightclub," he explained. "You like to see a real French nightclub, yes!"

Jules spoke quickly to him in French as he swung the small car through the night traffic of Marseilles.

"My brother say you cannot leave Marseilles without seeing the 'One Eyed Pirate'," Jacques explained promptly.

Leaving the car at last, we climbed a flight of cobbled steps and at the top turned down a narrow street to halt finally outside a dimly lit entrance. The two Frenchmen were greeted inside by a scantily dressed girl who eyed us intently as she took our jackets. Then Jules led the way down a flight of dimly lit stairs into a long brick cellar. As my eyes grew accustomed to the dimness, I could make out a small three-piece band playing on a dais. Small tables were set in alcoves, rusty cutlasses and fishing nets covered with cobwebs adorned the walls, while tiny green and red lamps, flickering on the tables, gave an eerie effect. Following Jules and Jacques, we made our way carefully to a table at the edge of the minute dance floor. The cleverly concealed cellar smelt just as a pirate's cave should—dank and smoky with an elusive musky perfume. The shadowy couples who danced before us to the soft music on the tiny floor clung as though moulded together.

Some while later, to a soft roll of the drum, lights blazed on to the dance floor as a beautiful girl stepped forward.

Against the other girls' tightly swathed dresses, her dress appeared almost prim. Suddenly the place was very quiet. Placing a chair in the centre of the dance floor, she pivoted slowly around it as Jacques explained softly:

"You have seen a strip-tease, No? Now you see a good one."

Garment by garment the French girl gradually shed her clothing in a clever and complicated routine until, wearing nothing but a tiny spangle, her white body gleaming in the concealed lighting, she snaked gracefully round the floor.

This was the real thing all right. It was a clever and artistic act. Then, coming to a halt before Jules, she helped herself to a cigarette from his pack, waited as he lit it for her and, with a flash of white skin, disappeared between the dimly lit tables.

As the dancers returned to the floor once more I turned to Jacques and asked, "How much does she get for doing that?"

He spoke rapidly to his brother.

"Cinq milles. £5 a night," Jacques told us at length. "Now she go—two more night clubs, c'est bon money, huh? You like to do strip-tease act?"

We laughed, shaking our heads quickly, but Jules leant forward to take my hand, speaking rapidly.

"My brother say," Jacques said seriously, "the girl, she go in two days—finish, huh! He says he give you the act, he teach you and pay you £5 10s. 0d. a night—it is good. You like—yes?"

"I like—no," I exclaimed quickly as Diana chuckled softly. Jacques turned to her.

"Then you—you like do the strip-tease?"

With a Frenchman's logic they just couldn't understand how we could turn down such an offer.

The friendly Jacques promised later as they dropped us

outside our small *pension:* "It you want change your minds later—O.K. Let us know—Good money—Goodnight!"

In the large warm cab of an enormous French trailer, we left Marseilles next evening for Paris, and thirty hours later wished adieu to our tired driver and set off to find a room and a bath. But Paris was in the throes of a great Car Festival: every cheap *pension* and even the more expensive hotels were full to capacity with visitors to the exhibition.

All the afternoon we trudged the streets, then, in a tiny café on a wide boulevard, we ordered coffee and sat counting out our last few hundred francs.

"We've £4 over our boat tickets," Di said ruefully. "It'll be just our luck to walk the city for hours, find no room at all in the end, and finish up in the most expensive hotel Paris has to offer —they always have plenty of rooms, and we'll arrive at Folkestone with ten cents between us!"

She meant it as a joke, but two hours later we found ourselves outside the fabulous Anglo-American Hotel and we still had no room for the night. We were getting desperate. In our crumpled clothes with two huge, dusty packs and only £2 each to spend in our pockets, we eyed the hotel, then each other.

"We can but get thrown out if we enquire," I said with a grimace.

Di nodded, then chuckled softly, remembering her earlier words.

So hitching our packs higher on to our shoulders with a nonchalant bravado which we certainly weren't feeling, we stalked past the magnificent doorman who regarded us in astonishment, and made our way across the richly piled carpet to the hotel desk. Ten minutes later, in a large, luxuriously appointed room of the hotel, we noted merrily the many service buttons and telephones at each bedside. Di sank thankfully on to one of the soft beds.

"Well, we've a room but we've now barely enough money for one meal before we reach England—and I am starving!"

"Never mind," I said cheerfully, opening the door into our private bathroom. "Look! Just think of all the baths we can have in the next twelve hours."

All next morning we drove slowly northward through a thick white mist with a friendly Spaniard, while we tried to make him understand why, after all our journeying, we didn't want to travel on through Belgium and Holland with him, but simply get home to England as quickly as possible. This explanation took all the morning for, although our French could be understood by a Frenchman, to a Spaniard it was a different language altogether.

With many mixed feelings Diana and I stood that afternoon on the deck of the cross-Channel steamer as it ploughed out of Boulogne Harbour into the misty sea.

"Well, at last we have crossed the last country—for a while," I said slowly. "It's been wonderful. Au revoir, all the friends of so many nationalities who've helped us.

Di nodded, tightening her thick scarf round her neck, and solemnly we waved together in the direction that we had come, thinking silently of the many friends we had encountered on our long journey. Then Diana turned to me brightly:

"We're not going to see much of England until we're actually standing on it, if this fog keeps up."

But there it was at last: brilliant green fields, grey looking cliffs against the white patches of mist—and my parents' faces anxiously peering through it all. We were back in England. At last.